The Data Elephant in the Board Room

Driving Data Integration from the Enterprise-wide Data Town Plan

John Giles

Technics Publications

SEDONA, ARIZONA

115 Linda Vista, Sedona, AZ 86336 USA

https://www.TechnicsPub.com

Cover design by Lorena Molinari

First Printing 2025

Copyright © 2025 by John Giles

ISBN, print ed.   9781634626972
ISBN, Kindle ed.   9781634626989
ISBN, PDF ed.   9781634626996

Library of Congress Control Number: 2025932329

Endorsements

In *The Data Elephant in the Board Room*, John presents us with a simple, practical, and human-centric way of understanding an organization's data assets in the form of a Data Town Plan. Many organizations today are distracted by an overtly technological focus on data and AI development. John's approach allows everyone, not just the technical experts, to focus on what really matters: how data reflects the actual reality of the business and how we can and should capture that reflection to give our initiatives a solid blueprint, while still avoiding getting tangled in never-ending enterprise-scale documentation efforts. The real-life examples and anecdotes from John's long career not only offer further proof that this can really be done and it works, but also help us remember that it all comes down to understanding and learning from our fellow human beings. Few data books can make you smile while you learn like John's does!

<u>Juha Korpela</u>: Independent consultant

John Giles has consistently been an inspirational and trusted voice in the world of data modeling, with his prior books, *The Nimble Elephant* and *The Elephant in the Fridge*, serving as cornerstones in my own career. These works have been profoundly influential, shaping my approach to data modeling and solidifying my appreciation for John's unique ability to bridge the gap between business needs and technical execution. His contributions to the data modeling space have brought clarity, practicality, and a much-needed focus on the business perspective.

This new book is a compelling continuation of that legacy, masterfully building on the foundations he has laid. By introducing the concept of "Data Town Planning," John positions data as a vital bridge between IT and business, advocating for collaborative workshops, pattern-based planning, and iterative refinement to align organizational goals with technological execution.

Through clear themes of strategic vision, the power of patterns, practical integration, and future-proofing organizational data strategies, John offers both inspiration and actionable insights. His work continues to remind us that, at its core, effective data modeling is about enabling businesses to articulate their vision and empowering IT to deliver on it. This book is a must read for anyone seeking to elevate their understanding of how to turn data into a truly strategic asset.

<u>Keith Belanger</u>: Data strategist

Data modeling is a complex and, unfortunately often time-consuming activity. That's why it is often left out. Nevertheless, in recent years, every technical advance in corporate IT ended with the demand that the data models had to be clean first.

In his book, John Giles shows how a future-oriented enterprise-wide conceptual data model can potentially be created in just four weeks in collaboration with the relevant departments. This is achieved with a so-called data town plan, a clever combination of proven methods. At its core, his approach consists of a strong categorization with nine basic concepts, their relationships to each other and the use of sample data models for these nine concepts. The taxonomy allows competing definitions to be listed side by side in a conciliatory manner. The patterns at the individual concept level allow for quick customization based on proven concepts. In addition, there is a clear roadmap of workshops for creating and maintaining the data models.

The methods are clearly explained and illustrated with an impressive number of examples from practical applications. All of these factors make the book extremely readable, easy to understand, and entertaining.

A much-needed explanation of how to quickly develop an enterprise-wide data model and maintain it in the future.

Michael Muller: Independent consultant

Organisations need data models supportive of the way they do business. How to achieve this interoperability *without* de-railing the way they work is challenging. John's book clearly communicates how to develop high-level data models that work for the business and will support ontology models necessary for future operational interoperability.

Professor Melinda Hodkiewicz and Dr. Caitlin Woods: The University of Western Australia

Contents at a Glance

Contents

Figures

Tables

Acknowledgments

There are so many wonderful people who have enriched my life, both personally and professionally, so I must limit this list to some standout folk who have directly contributed to this book.

You've got David Hay and Len Silverston, whose publications on data model patterns have been applied by data practitioners for decades. Before them was Christopher Alexander, who some see as the father of the "patterns" movement.

There are those quiet, behind-the-scenes individuals who have influenced my career and provided solid, long-term friendships. Rob Barnard generously gave of his time to help shape this book, and for that, and his continued friendship, I am indebted. Another person who I need to mention is Larry Burns. A number of entries in this book reference his contributions.

In the world of data modeling that is intended to reflect how the business people see their world, I highly recommend Juha Korpela, Joe Reis, and Keith Belanger as respected voices who keep on contributing to the profession. And then there's Bill Inmon. He has spoken boldly and with insight on so many topics for so many decades, but here, I wish to acknowledge his contributions to discussions on the need for data models that reflect the business view.

More recently, I have had the privilege of interacting with Melinda Hodkiewicz and Caitlin Woods in the area of "ontologies." They represent a rare breed of people with solid academic credentials who also engage fully with industry. We need more of them!

And a special big thanks to my publisher and fellow data modeler, Steve Hoberman.

The list goes on, and many will see themselves reflected in the stories included in this book.

Thanks to all.

Foreword

Once in a VERY great while, you meet an almost mythical person. In the case of John Giles, I met him through a mutual friend, Juha Korpela, who told me John was a rare force of nature in data modeling. Since then, I've had the pleasure of getting to know John, and I have always been impressed by his ability to sensibly and thoughtfully bridge the gap between data modeling, business, and IT. In his previous books, John briefly mentioned the "Data Town Plan." Now, in "The Data Elephant in the Board Room," he takes it a step further by diving deep into the concept of a Data Town Plan.

One of the things I appreciate most about this book is that it is not just theoretical. John provides numerous real-world examples of how Data Town Plans have improved business outcomes. These examples range from small businesses to large organizations and cover various industries.

I also appreciate that John does not shy away from the challenges of implementing a Data Town Plan. Data modeling - and data management in general - is notoriously challenging, especially when working with "The Business." People talk past each other with different vocabulary and intentions, which often stops data modeling efforts dead in their tracks. John acknowledges that getting business and IT people to work together can be difficult and provides practical advice on overcoming these challenges.

Finally, John writes, "Data Town Plans are (ideally) technology agnostic." Technology changes fast. Data Town Plans - and the language of the business - move less quickly. And they should be technology agnostic. But here's where the tension lies - operational systems sit at the front of most IT systems. Analytics, machine learning, and other use cases are derivative from these operational systems. However, operational systems aren't primarily focused on analytics and other downstream use cases. These operational systems are often critical to an organization's day-to-day operations and need to be integrated to ensure that data is accurate and consistent. A Data Town Plan provides this cross-sectional blueprint of shared vocabulary and understanding that's so often missing from technology-first approaches.

This book is not just a must-read, it's a must-have for any organization serious about data management and modeling. It's a treasure trove of insights and strategies tailored to the needs of business and IT professionals. It provides a clear roadmap for creating a Data Town Plan, making it an essential resource for anyone looking to enhance their data management practices.

I encourage you to read this book and to consider how a Data Town Plan can benefit your organization.

Joe Reis

Author, Educator, Data Engineer

Is this how the business sees the world?

Many business managers are told that data is a valuable asset, but they don't want to get involved in "technical" stuff. And that's how many of them see "data."

Conversely, some information technology (IT) people are told that they are there to serve the business, and that they *should* engage with the business folk, but a number of these IT folk don't really get involved.

There may be many reasons. For example, some members of the IT community are drowning in a sea of technology challenges and struggle to find the bandwidth to meet with business people. Others are remunerated for keeping the (technology) lights on and are not invited to collaborate with business folk.

Now, this next excuse for IT people living apart from the business community might make you smile. I've encountered more than a few IT professionals who have fun playing with technology, but a few of them are hesitant to step into the business world. And that's understandable. We humans come in all different shapes and sizes, and some who understand technology may feel uncomfortable sitting at the boardroom table. We smile, but some of the technical professionals who enjoy embracing the latest technologies assume these tools might somehow deliver value to the business, but instead sometimes end up costing the business lots of money while delivering little business value.

So, back to the business folk. A number of them tend to look at how to make value for the organization, now, and into the future (well, at least the shareholders hope that's their focus).

We often see this business/IT gap. So, do we insist that the business folk become more IT literate, or alternatively insist that the technical types become more business savvy? Nice theory, but often, "it isn't going to happen."

Instead, let's build a bridge. We start with the business articulating how they want to see *their* data managed in a manner that's not steeped in technical detail. The IT team can subsequently leverage this bridge to shape technical solutions that can deliver tangible value for the business.

The changing data landscape, from micro to macro

I remember when data integration wasn't a major issue. My first job was at a rope company, and they had a computer with a debtor's system, and nothing else. Absolutely zero integration required! And be careful not to drop the Debtor's Master file or you would have to spend hours sorting the punched cards.

I'm guessing you're possibly sick to death of people saying how much IT has changed, and I don't want to add to unnecessary comparisons. But here's one area of change that's biting organizations and biting them hard: they've now got lots of IT systems, lots of data, and lots of challenges as they try really hard to get meaning from it all. In addition to the tsunami of data from within, this connected world is offering them lots more data from outside than they can consume, let alone understand. What the business wants is "simply" to integrate the shared data in a way that they can understand.

And I can almost hear the pained groans as I mention a frequently pedaled solution: "Let's build an Enterprise Data Model to drive data integration." I'm not trying to cast doubt on the good intentions behind Enterprise Data Model initiatives (and the like), nor their value if they "work." Surely, it's a good thing to have a model that expresses data concepts (customer, product, and so on) in business terms rather than in IT terms, and that also describes business-centric relationships between these concepts? It's just that the mechanisms behind such projects and the shape of what ends up being delivered can give a bad name to enterprise-level data modeling. Please, I'm not saying that certain methodologies simply cannot work. Hey, I've seen a screw driver used as a chisel. It sort-of works, but it's not ideal.

The good news is that there is a better way. Let's call it Data Town Planning. At its heart is the idea that if you're building a new city or making major changes to an existing city, having a town plan (also known by many as an urban plan) that communicates the vision for the future makes a heap of sense. Imagine the opposite. You collect a small army of skilled tradespeople and equip them with the best of tools. You drop them in an open area and tell them to start building, but without any plans at all. Insanity. But sadly, a similar scenario is sometimes observed in IT's management of the data of an enterprise.

So, what's a Data Town Plan?

The back cover of this book briefly introduces the core ideas behind a Data Town Plan. I will say a little more here, then leave the rest of the book to delve deeper.

For a city, or a Data Town Plan, you start top-down with the big picture. Too many Enterprise Data Model initiatives get buried in costly and unnecessary detail. Instead, embrace the helicopter-views of the business leaders and leave technical details to IT professionals who actually need nuts and bolts particulars.

Leverage patterns. For a city, there are patterns for shopping centers, hospitals, schools, residential estates, and more. For data integration across the enterprise, there are patterns for customer data, product data, event data, task data, and more. Importantly, these patterns:

- Form a bridge, making it easy for business people to talk about broad concepts, while IT professionals have a clear path from business concepts to implementation.

- Are proven, flexible, and extensible.

Town plans describe not only what the city will contain (one hospital, two shopping centers, three schools …), but, importantly, how these elements fit together. For data integration, we likewise need to see how each of the data patterns fit together to form the integrated whole.

Town planners look to the future. Their work is intended to be a beacon, guiding developments in a way that today's investments will contribute to the future vision. It's similar for data. In his excellent book titled *Data Model Storytelling*,[1] Larry Burns suggests our data work "… can drive conversations about what could or should be, rather than simply what it is …"

We've already spoken about the unfortunate gap sometimes observed between IT and the business. Put simply, a Data Town Plan articulates the way the <u>business</u> wants to see its data managed, which in turn makes life easier for IT to deliver solutions that meet business expectations.

A quick example of a starting point follows of a Data Town Plan for a water utility.

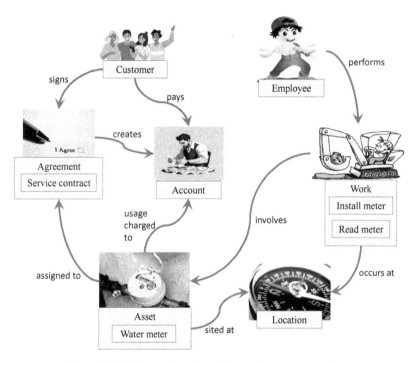

Figure 1: Model-on-a-Page Data Town Plan for a water utility

Too easy? Yes, but I did say it's only a starting point. There's a whole book still to be read!

About the book

The first major section of this book presents <u>the case for Data Town Planning</u>. We want **business** people to understand what a Data Town Plan is and what it can do for them. Rather than giving

---

[1] Burns L. (2021) Data Model Storytelling: An Agile Approach to Maximizing the Value of Data Management/

arms-length support to some IT initiative, we'd like them to realize that a Data Town Plan captures *their* views of today's business data and *their* dreams for the future. It is all about them and their importance.

Next, we want the readers to <u>get a level of comfort with some of the building blocks</u> for creating a Data Town Plan. We call these things "data model patterns," but don't feel threatened by technical terms. Just like tradespeople need to learn the tools of their trade, we want those who participate in designing their Data Town Plan to have *sufficient* understanding to be able to contribute to considering design alternatives, but without having to become experts (they can leave detailed use of these patterns to more technical people who might also like to perform a deeper dive in the Appendix on data model patterns). The business folk just want to have fun creatively tossing ideas around.

Having hopefully demystified the wonderful world of pattern-based building blocks, our next step is to use them to <u>assemble a Data Town Plan</u>. This includes looking at helpful preparation, hints on running the workshop to create an initial unified view, and then looking at how we handle the reality that the path to a single "unified" view might involve grappling with a number of divergent views that are anything but unified.

We close off the heart of the book by standing back and <u>reflecting on the creation and use of a Data Town Plan</u>, including seeking to debunk some of the myths around high-level data models, and we touch on some other topics that might threaten success.

That's the essence, aimed at business people taking control of their own data future in a not-too-technical way. But the goal is always to build a bridge between the business world and the technical world. We want the business' vision that's contained in the Data Town Plan to be embraced by the technical people as they seek to deliver tangible value through technical solutions. The first appendix looks at just some of the ways this might be achieved. The list is not comprehensive, and as is typical of "technology" elements, the items in the list may start to show their age. Nonetheless, use the list to initiate discussion on <u>some options for taking the Data Town Plan and realizing IT solutions</u>.

Finally, the second appendix provides more technical detail for those interested in <u>digging deeper into the data model patterns</u> that sit behind the "building blocks."

Isn't there an overlap with another book?

In 2012, I published a book titled *The Nimble Elephant: Agile Delivery of Data Models using a Pattern-based Approach*.[2] It helped people deliver "agile" projects at the velocity required by the development team and with the quality required by groups such as head office data governance. "Good and fast" was its mantra. These apparently opposing goals are accommodated through the use of proven, published data model patterns.

It is noteworthy that the same patterns that were used to facilitate quality-at-speed delivery for discrete projects are the same patterns used in this book to deliver quality-at-speed for enterprise-wide data perspectives for the business.

In 2019, another book was published, titled *The Elephant in the Fridge: Guided steps to Data Vault success through building business centered models*.[3] Its focus was on a Data Warehouse approach known as Data Vault.

- The intended audience for *The Elephant in the Fridge* was experienced IT practitioners who wanted an outline map for developing the town-plan view. The book you are now reading is a more in-depth training manual to make Data Town Planning accessible to a much wider audience.

- The primary focus of *The Elephant in the Fridge* was Data Vault, with a Data Town Plan being a means to that end. In contrast, this book focuses on the Data Town Plan in its own right, with only a passing reference to Data Vault.

If your main objective is to do Data Vault better, reading *The Elephant in the Fridge* is still recommended, but you may nonetheless enjoy this book if you want to dive deeper into the development of the prerequisite Data Town Plan.

---

[2] Giles J. (2012) The Nimble Elephant: Agile Delivery of Data Models using a Pattern-based Approach.

[3] Giles J. (2019) The Elephant in the Fridge: Guided steps to Data Vault success through building business centered models.

PART 1

The Case for Data Town Planning

When people design a new city, or seek a major upgrade to an existing city, town planners get involved. Importantly, the citizens or their representatives should also get involved. Likewise, when there's a need for a whole-of-enterprise view of an organization's data, we need not only the data equivalent of "town planners", but we also absolutely need "business" people involved. After all, it's the way the business sees, or wants to see, _their_ data, that is important.

Now here's the catch. Sometimes business people and technology people talk a different language. We need a bridge between the two. And we need to build that bridge in a way that is quick and cheap to assemble from the perspective of the business, and yet is of such high quality it can facilitate delivery of technical solutions.

But is that even vaguely possible? The answer is a resounding "Yes." Some good news-stories follow to generate discussion on what might work for you, followed by some lessons-of-experience warnings.

Let's call this bridge between the business and technology a Data Town Plan, and let's have a sneak-preview of what it might look like.

CHAPTER 1

Bridging the Management-versus-IT Gap

When management is wishing that IT gets it right

There was a song that was made popular in the 1960s by Dusty Springfield. It was about Wishing and Hoping. My message is that if corporate management is just wishing and hoping that IT can and will deliver what they want, that's a poor strategy.

> *Some organizations, rather than being enabled by IT, find themselves in trouble because of the technology.*

Financial woes are one dimension of "wishing and hoping" failing to deliver against expectations. For me, one Australian bank jumps to mind. It was reported that it invested heavily in IT for a visionary leap of faith to get ahead of the pack, but the courageous and blind trust of the management team in the promises of technology ended up costing lots of money and putting the bank behind the others instead of ahead. I'm sure that you can add your own tales, direct or indirect, of money spent on IT but failing to provide the expected returns.

Statutory compliance is another dimension. Again, I think of an Aussie scenario. A failure on the compliance front hit the press, and the Chief Executive Officer bravely put on a face of "not my problem—it's an IT issue." You hear of people jumping before they are pushed? Well, this apparently bright individual embraced the ostrich head-in-the-sand position. Shortly after, they were kicked hard in the body part exposed by the "ostrich" stance. Ouch.

I actually felt sorry for this individual. After all, it is reasonable for a CEO to delegate certain authority to the head of IT. How on earth can anyone expect the CEO (or other senior managers) to have a detailed working knowledge of technology, especially when even smart, competent IT professionals must run hard and fast to try and keep up?

Finally, naïve wishing-and-hoping may mean that the managers miss out on massive opportunities due to their ignorance or fear of technology.

Houston, we have a problem.

When management's little knowledge of IT is dangerous

Let's jump straight into a comparison between a business investing in its future versus someone investing in a home for their family's future. Of course, any analogy has some gaps. Nonetheless, comparisons can be informative. They can also be like visiting a dentist—a little painful in the short term as identified problems are dealt with!

Let's start with the home investment scenario.

Extremes can shine a spotlight on issues. The first extreme might be a person who knows vaguely what they want but knows very little about building. They want a house with a view that won't get flooded. Perhaps the following might reflect their design.

Figure 2: Novice house design

We can chuckle and hopefully recognize that, as well as being entirely impractical, such a dwelling would never receive a permit from building authorities. It simply won't work to any acceptable standard. The novice designer should admit to their shortcomings and engage a professional. However, this new strategy of engaging an expert could potentially lead to another extreme.

In the second scenario, the future home owner still knows dangerously little about house design, but instead of trying to drive the design, they lean on an architect they happen to know. Their brief to the architect is, "I trust you—design whatever you like and get it built for me." No constraints, perhaps not even a budget? For some architects, this is a dream client. I've seen building shows on TV where some architects can work to a budget and deliver a valuable home for the family. However, some architects are truly inspirational individuals and deliver awesome works that will be admired for years to come, but blow the budget by miles—they build a monument to themselves, hang the expense. For some of their creations, I question if their inspiration was driven by unbridled egotism. At this point, some architects may get defensive, but if we put the house that was built under their direction on the market, and if nobody is willing to pay a price anywhere near the cost of its construction, perhaps I might have a point?

> The two key messages are that (1) it can be dangerous for a novice in house architecture to take control of their own future home build, and (2) it can be dangerous for the novice to hand over their housing future to a specialist based on blind trust.

Sadly, such common sense may be missing in some business settings. Again, let's play out the above two extreme scenarios, this time for management instead of home owners. In both scenarios, the managers are playing a hypothetical role of IT ignorance.

But first, let's cut them some slack.

Senior managers quite rightly cannot be expected to have deep and current knowledge of every aspect of the IT platforms that keep their organization going. It's hard enough for full-time IT professionals to try to keep up with change! So, if I, as a consultant, insist that C-level executives absolutely *must* understand the inner workings of technology before they make a decision, I might find myself promptly marched out of the board room.

So, back to the two scenarios. We can dispose of the first one quickly. Just like the humorous case of the caravan-on-a-pole, we're not likely to have an IT-ignorant CEO driving an IT project.

But now comes the very confronting reality of the second scenario of "blind trust." If the managers totally hand over all responsibility for technology decisions to the IT team, they *may* get brilliant and inspired solutions, *or* they may get expensive technical "works of art" that do nothing positive for the financial bottom line. Or these technical masterpieces may even expose management to breach-of-compliance risks.

Nodding your heads in agreement? Doom and gloom? Yes, outcomes can be disastrous if either (1) management take control of their own IT future but based on a seriously flawed understanding of technology, or (2) management naively delegates the organization's future to "trusted" experts.

One solution may be to engage expensive consultants only to discover that some in this category primarily focus on their own partner bonuses rather than client welfare. Just like there are good and bad architects for homes, there are good and bad consultants.

So, here's the first bit of good news. While encouraging business folk to get involved in "IT," I do not suggest that the management team roll up their sleeves on everything to do with "technology." The side of IT that loves shiny new toys is arguably best left to those with the knowledge (and passion) for such things, with management having little more than a broad understanding of the potential of these elements (stripped of the hype), and an understanding of the proper context for such toys. Sure, some senior managers actually do have an interest and flair for all things technical, and I have most certainly encountered some along the way, but the focus of this book is to equip the non-technical manager with the skills they need to set the vision for a wholesome future, and ensure that the IT folk align with that vision and deliver real value.

So, what part of IT might management be well advised to embrace? In a word, "data." Again, I will encourage avoidance of the more technical aspects of managing data, and instead encourage the business to assemble and communicate what *it* sees as core concepts vital to the business.

Which leads to the second bit of good news. This book is squarely aimed at enabling the business to positively and effectively shape the data bits of their organization's IT future that they do care about (and possibly have a bit of fun on the way—who said "technology" stuff had to be boring?) It will hopefully enable the management folk to interact with the IT people without becoming dragged into technology details. As a complementary dimension, the latter part of this book will then offer potential guidance to the IT people to embrace the management team's vision, engage meaningfully with those managers, and celebrate mutual success.

Going back to the home and architect analogy, it's like giving the homeowner *enough* of the right language to communicate with the architect, to meaningfully participate in decisions without getting bogged down in details, and to enjoy the journey towards delivery of value.

I talk of "value." Value may be measured in many ways, including financial, environmental, and societal benefits (remember the "Triple Bottom Line"?), or perhaps it might keep the directors out of jail for breach of compliance. Define "value" however you like.

The "Esperanto" of modern business

One easily overlooked word above was "language." It refers to the right language for homeowners to use to communicate with architects or corporate management to communicate with IT.

In the late 1800s, an artificial language called Esperanto was created. The idea was that if everyone learned Esperanto as a secondary language, everyone in the world could communicate. If I spoke English and Esperanto, and you spoke French and Esperanto, and a third friend of ours spoke Spanish and Esperanto, we could all talk to each other. Even more importantly, if I wanted to translate some work (for example, this book), I could translate it once into Esperanto and then anyone could read it.

The creator of this language, L. L. Zamenhof, had observed a tension between people groups in his place of birth who spoke different languages. He hoped that some of the cultural barriers would be lessened by having a shared means to communicate. Likewise, there can be unnecessary barriers between managers and IT professionals because the two groups "speak a different language." And perhaps it's not just an IT and management issue. Perhaps business folk from different parts of the organization also speak a different language!

For example, just in the world of "data," the IT folk may talk in terms of data models that use the Information Engineering notation or Class models that use the Unified Modeling Language (UML) notation. They may talk of conceptual data models, logical data models, and physical data models. The good news for business managers is that while such topics might excite the IT folk, I am going to strive to leave such topics largely alone. For the business folk, we will focus on what's important to them. Yes, we might capture their thinking in fun ways ("boxes and lines") that the data modeling purist might criticize, but if it works for the business *and* provides communication, that's enough.

It's a bit like a future homeowner doing a house concept sketch on a napkin at a coffee shop—if it's not to scale but communicates with the architect, it's done its job. And hey, the homeowner is probably enjoying tossing around ideas and providing direction on *their* destiny!

Planning and patterns for cities

In my part of the world, town planners (or what others may call urban planners) design new cities or major upgrades to existing ones. They design for the important bits, such as residential areas, hospitals, schools, universities, and commercial zones.

Water supply is one of those important bits. If we're looking at what we need for a new city, we're going to need water. At the macro level, the town planner might suggest we need a massive dam. At the micro level, the plumber will want to know exactly what type of taps will be installed. Both groups of people have valid perspectives, but their views are miles apart as far as the scope of their interests goes.

Figure 3: Cities need water, from dams to taps!

In theory, when designing a new city, you could get every house design in absolute detail, find out how many occupants are in each, how long they each take for a shower, and calculate the amount of water for each person, each house, and the whole city. I did say, "in theory." In practice, town planners will gather the big picture requirements, consider how all these bits and pieces might interconnect, and from there assemble the town plan. They can leave decisions such as whether the front door to the town hall swings left or right, or what color tiles will be used in the kitchen, for someone else, later. Much later!

In the 1800s, my home country, Australia, was a loose collection of somewhat independent states. In 1901, we became a single, federated nation. We could have then called ourselves the United States of Australia, but another country had already grabbed the "USA" acronym!

One of the first problems facing the well-intentioned folk was where to put the new national capital city. The most populous states suggested *they* should be the center of the new national government, in either Sydney or Melbourne. A compromise was reached—some farmland sort of half way between the two state capitals was chosen to be the site for a new seat of federal parliament, to be called Canberra (thought by some to appropriately reflect an Aboriginal word for "meeting place").

Figure 4: Australia's national capital, Canberra

For a moment, let's consider a hypothetical scenario—what if we dropped the best tradespeople, with the best tools, on that farmland, but with no town plan, and told them to just start building the city? Most agree that would be disastrous.

So, what actually happened in Canberra? Sadly, close to that scenario. In 1911, we started building—a few timber buildings, lots of tents, and a plant nursery! In 1913 the authorities *started* planning, and the "final design" wasn't tabled until 1918—years after we started to build!

We can laugh at that true story. But do we ever do the same for IT projects? Get good developers with good tools but don't provide a "town plan"? Some IT practitioners seem to adopt the "Why isn't everybody coding?" attitude. As Dr. Phil McGraw of the Dr. Phil show might say with a wry smile, "What could possibly go wrong?"

Many mums and dads are consciously, or unconsciously, aware that there are patterns for home windows (sliding, awning, casement …) and doors (sliding, bi-fold, French …). Christopher Alexander inspired the explicit recognition of patterns in architecture for regions, towns, homes, furniture and even doorknobs. I gather that he offended some of his fellow architects by suggesting that less experienced (and more affordable?) people could achieve great outcomes by leveraging the established patterns.

> *If you've already got a palette of "micro" patterns for doors and windows, the town planner doesn't have to worry about those details.*

Ah, but the town planner does have to worry about the big picture view. The good news is that Alexander also had patterns for the "macro" thinking. Your town plan needs to include a university and a hospital? No worries—there are patterns for those. Then they will need services (water, power, road networks for access and more), and again, there are patterns for those, too.

It gets better. Not only are there patterns for the components of a city, but there are patterns for how they can fit together.

Now, the really exciting bit. While there will be some experts who know the inner workings of each of these patterns, the patterns can act as the "Esperanto" to aid communication between the highly skilled folk and the wider community.

That's all well and good, but what on earth does that have to do with businesses, IT, and "data"? Please read on!

Planning and patterns for data

You've seen the claims that "data is your most important asset"? You've also seen claims that your customers are your most important asset and your employees are your most important asset. The reality is that all of those and more can be highly valued assets. Data *is* important (as are customers and employees), but the value of data plummets if, for example, it's not accurate, it's not current (if you need it to be, as compared to conscious choices to analyze historical data), or it's not understood.

We'll leave the first two topics (accuracy and currency) aside, and instead focus on the issue of being "understood." What on earth do I mean by that? Let me tell a story.

The CEO of a water utility asked IT to tell him how many employees worked for the organization. IT grappled with what appeared to be several answers. Did the count include only salaried employees but not those senior managers who were on three-year fixed-term contracts? Did it include those who read water meters but were subcontractors who, while wearing company uniforms, were managed by third parties? Did it include the person who mowed the lawns each fortnight? These questions could not be made by IT alone—the "business" needed to be involved in defining terms.

> *IT folk should have a really good understanding of today's IT systems and the data they contain, but they can't be responsible for defining what data might be needed tomorrow, particularly if the business makes some radical changes, such as an unannounced acquisition of another company.*

So, what's the way forward? Taking the homeowner and architect analogy, we've got two players here; the business managers who want things, and the IT folk who understand the grubby technology details that *might* deliver what the business needs.

Both groups need each other. But they need to be able to communicate effectively. Simply:

- The business folk *need* to be empowered to articulate how they want data to be delivered so that they can get value for the organization. That's the core subject of this book.

- The IT professionals *need* to deliver against that requirement. That's the focus of Appendix 1.

The central goal is to make it easier for the business to simply, quickly, and effectively assemble an expression of how their data is to be structured. They (with assistance from IT) will deliver an artifact that I might call a "Data Town Plan." But what do I mean by that phrase?

Let's leverage off this analogy:

- A "Data Town Plan" should capture the bits and pieces important to the business (such as Customers, Products, Contracts, Resources …).

- A "Data Town Plan" should capture the essence of how these bits and pieces fit together. They might start with blatantly obvious things, such as a relationship that states, "Customers buy Products." They might then flesh out some of the more specific relationships that are core to specific, given business processes.

- A "Data Town Plan" should articulate a *small* amount of drill-down into detail (Customers might subtype into Retail and Commercial Customers, or perhaps into National and International Customers, or …).

- A "Data Town Plan" should _never_ include excruciating details that will make it hugely expensive and difficult to maintain.

Most of us can imagine what a city's town plan looks like. Perhaps a copy of Canberra's town plan will give you the idea.

Figure 5: Canberra's high-level town plan

As discussed earlier, underneath this helicopter view, there will be lots more detail. And supporting all of this will be proven patterns for hospitals, industrial areas, shopping centers, and much more.

Likewise, for our Data Town Plan, we will want a high-level view of our organization's data. Figure 6 represents such a view for emergency response to wildfires.

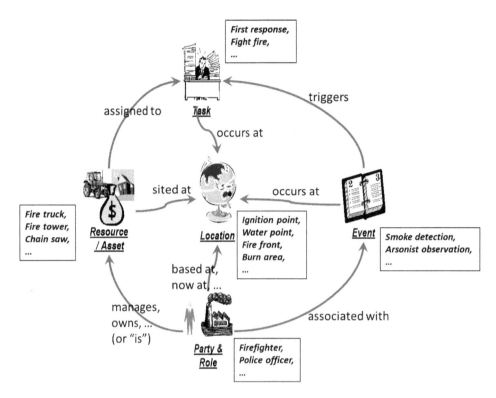

Figure 6: Business relationships

As for a city's town plan, there will be lots more detail beneath the surface. And there will be lots of patterns we leverage off, with some such as Task, Resource/Asset, Event, Location, and Party/Party Role being hinted at in Figure 6.

I'll briefly mention that technology artifacts that look, at face value, a little like a Data Town Plan, come under all sorts of confusing and frightening names, such as a Business Information Model (BIM), an Enterprise Data Model (I really hesitate to even use that phrase as it brings to mind so many horror stories of business data done wrong), or a Conceptual Model (another term that makes me hope you don't throw the book away at this point). Let's cut out the techno-babble from that conversation, and simply talk of Data Town Plan "boxes and lines" that can be the Esperanto of communication on "data" matters.

Importantly, this fun and valuable artifact will act as a bridge, performing in such a way that the IT folk can take this expression as a statement for delivering against business expectations.

Key points

- Management can't afford to blindly delegate responsibility to IT. They must have "sufficient" knowledge of what is happening, or risk being held accountable for consequences (financial, regulatory, reputational, etc.).

- Conversely, management typically can't afford the time to become experts in every shiny new technical toy.

- Bridging the business/IT gap is made easier when both sides share a common language, especially about "data."

- A palette of proven data model patterns can facilitate the development of that common language; broad concepts are understandable by the business, and implementation details are available for technical people.

- Just like cities have high-level town plans, the business (assisted by IT) can develop their own "Data Town Plan."

CHAPTER 2

Some Happy-ending Stories to Inspire You

I'd like to share some real-life stories that might grab the attention of business people who are desperately looking for a straw to clutch. Perhaps they feel like they are drowning in a sea of "techno-babble," and they are crying out for a clear vision of a way forward to bring IT value to the business.

> *At the heart of the following stories is the business expressing how it wants to see its data presented and managed.*

It's a view *of* the business data, assembled *by* the business, *for* the benefit of the business. Almost democratic? (And apologies to Abraham Lincoln for butchering his famous phrase about the government of the people, by the people, for the people.)

Wildfires: When you and others need a shared view

In the United States, there's an initiative known as the National Information Exchange Model (or NIEM for short). Put simply, it's intended to make life easier for a whole bunch of organizations to share data. I haven't been involved in the NIEM development nor its deployment, so I am not in a position to comment on it; I just wanted to mention it as an example of multiple parties wanting to work together on the data front. Now, my own story.

Lots of countries have devastating wildfires. In Australia, we actually name the worst of them. For us, Black Friday isn't just some day of annual sales frenzy, but a reminder of a fire from my parents' era. Then, for me, there's Ash Wednesday. I knew my children were in a danger zone, and the phone lines were down (and this was before mobile phones). I still feel the pain now as if it was yesterday, remembering helplessly sitting at my work desk waiting for some news, and hoping it was good news (which, thankfully, it eventually was).

Figure 7: A wildfire

Now we wind the clock forward to 2009 and look at Black Saturday. The fires destroyed homes and cost many lives. An inquiry looked into the fires, not as a witch-hunt, but to learn lessons for the future.

One story that came out would have been comical in another setting. It went something like this.

An incident controller asked a representative of a volunteer organization how many fire trucks they had in a given area. The answer? "We don't have fire trucks. We have appliances. Is that what you mean?" OK, so this organization prefers to call their fire trucks "appliances." We get that. Now the incident controller, with a hint of frustration in his voice, turns to the representative for the government fire agency and asks, "How many fire trucks, or 'appliances,' do you have?" And the answer comes back, "We don't have either. We have 'tankers' and 'slip-ons.' Which do you mean?" (For your benefit, tankers are big fire trucks, and slip-ons are really just four-wheel-drive tray vehicles with a pump and tank unit "slipped on.")

The incident controller reportedly replied along the lines (with expletives removed), "I don't care what you call them!!! How many vehicles that can squirt water do you have?"

Now, let's get down to the core data message in this story. It is a problem when humans trip over communication issues—imprecise communication could cost lives. But there can also be computer-to-computer communication issues along similar lines. The communication problem was recognized, and I was engaged to develop a data model called a Common Information Model, or

CIM. And when the topic of naming fire trucks came up during a workshop, and I sensed tension in the room, I light-heartedly suggested we call them "big red water-squirting vehicles" as a common, shared phrase. One response? "Ours aren't red." We laughed, and then worked together with an agreed shared vision—to achieve precision in common terminology, with supplements that reflected and respected local names ("synonyms" if you prefer).

> *A Common Information Model can be a bit like the Esperanto language we spoke about earlier, but in this case aiming to bring different "data cultures" together.*

If we apply this Esperanto thinking, every participant in a wild fire response can talk their own "language" but have an agreed common language (for people and computers), facilitating data exchange. The individual organizations are not forced against their will to reprogram their internal IT systems with some new external standard they don't want. All they are asked to do is to shape the data that gets exchanged externally in an agreed form.

Perhaps this story has inspired you that a data model can be used to express a common language between multiple organizations (in this case, up to 17 separate organizations), and also between not just people, but the IT systems they use. Perhaps your organization's needs are simpler, involving few (if any) external parties, but the same approach can potentially assist internal communication and data sharing.

Bank: When we need to look at business processes, fast!

This book has "data" as its center, but another large part of any organization's world is "process."

Some people see data and process as representing two separate, competing worlds. For example, I have encountered people with the role title of Business Analyst who arguably could be better labeled as Business Process Analyst. They don't want to analyze business data, just the business processes. Perhaps that's fine as long as people understand the scope of their responsibilities.

Other people see data and process as being joined at the hip. One argument I've heard is that data doesn't exist in a vacuum; it is created and maintained as part of some business process. While that may be true, unfortunately the reality is that we can sometimes be presented with data as a record of facts, but without the surrounding context of any associated business process.

Are these process-versus-data tensions necessary? I think not.

As background, a well-known Australian bank had launched a six-month business process reengineering exercise. They were well underway when they encountered a problem that was a solid show-stopper for their workshops. At this point, some data professionals may smile; these business process consultants recognized the issue wasn't a process issue, but a data issue, and I was called in to help.

The first thing to note is that the business process consultants had the good grace to realize a data person might be able to help. Kudos to them.

Now, the story has an entertaining twist. A good friend, Damien, approached me to ask if I was available to help. I said I might be able to squeeze in a few days here and there, but it might be a few weeks before I could dedicate a solid amount of time. He laughed, and told me he was asking me to develop an entire Enterprise Data Model for the bank, with drill down into detail on a topic labeled "securitization," and he wanted me to start on Tuesday midday and finish by midday the following day!

Really? Some consultants take months or years to develop an enterprise-wide data model. But one day? And I had never even heard of securitization—what the heck was it?

I like Damien—he's one of the best in the industry. I enjoy a challenge, and I love data modeling. I am also an enthusiastic fan of "data model patterns," where years and decades of experience have been nicely packaged for us, ready to use (I like to use the phrase "fast and good" because these patterns can be leveraged to deliver solid, proven, extensible models, and in record time).

So I took on the challenge. But not without caveats. First, I declared that I was going to leverage the banking patterns of people such David Hay and Len Silverston—why not stand on the shoulders of giants if we want to get a better view? Next, I mandated that the workshop be provided by the best and brightest the bank had. No excuses about them being busy—if they wanted an enterprise model in a day, they had better furnish me with people who could give authoritative and informed answers on the spot. No time for follow-up interviews here! Finally, I set the expectations that the deliverable would be hand-drawn models, copied from a whiteboard. If they wanted serious documentation, that would take a few weeks of follow-up.

Here I go with the town plan analogy again. You want an outline for a new city? And you want it now, not next year?

You'd be well advised to (1) leverage off patterns, (2) work with the best people you can find, and (3) keep the initial deliverables lightweight.

Detailed? Heck, no. Sufficient? Absolutely. Well, sufficient for that moment so they could get the "process" show on the road again. It's a bit like a town planner needing a high-level sketch plan for water infrastructure services. Way down the track, someone will have to decide if the Jones' household wants two taps in the kitchen or one mixer tap. But we *don't* need those details to get the town planning exercise moving.

And the outcome? The project was considered an amazing success. The process workshops were mobile again. I was asked to return to provide more formal documentation over a few weeks, and then stay on for other projects.

Data and process can cooperate. We can now look at more on that, in a totally different story.

Not-for-profit: When we need to pull data and process teams together

The previous story started with a business *process* initiative and ended with embracing a business *data* view. This narrative flips the process versus data story around the other way, starting with the development of the Data Town Plan and ending with the radical reengineering of business processes.

A CIO I knew well contacted me. Larry worked for a highly regarded not-for-profit organization. He wanted a business-centered view of their data. I wanted to help him, but unfortunately, I was full-time consulting for another organization. Ah, but then that organization closed down for a three-week summer holiday break. Even contractors were required to amuse themselves, without pay, for three weeks.

Larry had a suggestion. I could tell my wife that she and I weren't taking a holiday together that year, and instead, I could develop a detailed, fully documented Enterprise Data Model for him in three weeks. What a choice. And my long-suffering and supportive wife was on board with me helping the not-for-profit.

I was comfortable with the project. Three weeks was fine for a top-down data "town plan" with sufficient detail to help them grapple with their IT integration issues. But there was an unexpected challenge, and it was a people-and-process challenge.

The organization had lots of wonderful, caring people in many fields. Some specialized in helping people with drug and alcohol dependency problems, others helped the homeless, the unemployed, victims of domestic violence, or any one of a long list of issues. These delightful care workers often had many years or even decades of valuable experience, providing support in a given field. But they were specialists, delivering services in silos. Larry and the management team had engaged me to assist in integrating data. The very opposite of silos!

I had been briefed on this challenge.

At the very start of what I will call an "integration workshop," I slowly and carefully wrote the following words on the whiteboard: "Let's leverage off what is common and respect what is distinct."

For me, I sensed an immediate easing of tension between these specialists.

As I have stated, these folk were great people: caring, compassionate, and excellent at communication. We had a wonderful day together, working collectively on how *data* might be shared for the common good. A scenario was presented to me where a person is asking for help to buy a meal. They're obviously hungry, but a little digging reveals they have been forced out of the family home. The reason? They had been convicted of a domestic violence offense. It went further. It's absolutely not an excuse, but a complicating factor was that they had been retrenched, and, in a depressed state, had turned to alcohol. So, who's going to help them? A specialist in homelessness, or employment assistance, or alcohol dependency support, or …? The answer was "All of the above," and more, each with its own specialist, each with their own case file.

From my perspective as a data modeler, the *data* sharing for multiple case files was simple. But collectively, we had a light-bulb moment. What if, instead of sharing case files, there was a change of *process* with just one case file, managed by just one "case worker" who coordinated across all the areas, calling in other specialists as required, but still under one holistic case management plan? Of course, you, the reader, probably saw that coming. But the deeply entrenched business processes had hidden the obvious.

As one of the participants put it at the end of the workshop, she had initially assumed there was 20% in common and 80% distinct. At the end of the day she concluded it was still an 80/20 ratio, but flipped—80% in common, 20% distinct.

There were two very positive outcomes from the workshop.

The first was a change of not only the internal business processes, but case management across multiple complementary organizations, including other not-for-profits and government agencies.

The second outcome caught me by surprise. The senior management team was so delighted with the positive changes being wrought by a data and process integration effort that they offered me a most unusual contract: they wanted me to commit to a contract for 90 minutes a month to sit in on their executive board meetings, along with Larry and his right-hand technical person, Tony. So often, people talk about how hard it is for IT and management to engage with each other. This story declares it is more than possible. It actually can happen, and can be a delight.

Medical practitioner registration: When we need IT and Business strategic alignment (isn't that "always"?!)

Put simply, organizations may want to look ahead and consider where they might want to end up in the future.

The scope of strategic planning is much bigger than just looking at data strategies. However, data is, nonetheless, an important element. I'll share a story of how this worked in practice at one site.

For a number of years, a certain organization had been responding to today's crises by applying patches to hold things together. Perhaps you've heard the saying that people are so busy trying to wrestle with the alligators that they don't have time to drain the swamp. They were surviving in a challenging world, largely not of their own making, and I actually admired the way they had kept things running as they tried to build on shifting sand. But they were desperately keen to stop applying short-term fixes to things and instead wanted to take a breather and commit to a longer-term, well-architected way forward.

Another consultancy had been engaged to manage the overall strategic plan, but they wanted me to take the lead on the data strategy front. We can summarize my responsibilities as follows:

- Step 1: Develop a top-down Data Town Plan that represented the <u>future state</u> based on how the business wanted things to be, *not* on how current IT systems forced the business to operate.

- Step 2: Work alongside their IT people to express the <u>current state</u> of application data, but seen through the lens of the future state. This was fundamentally a mapping exercise—if the future state referred to "Suppliers" and the current IT systems used the term "Providers," then map the old term (and its related current IT systems) to the new term. OK, it was a bit more complicated than that, but you get the idea.

- Step 3: Join with the larger team of business managers and IT professionals in a fun and action-packed workshop considering <u>alternative paths</u> for getting from today to tomorrow on all fronts (data, IT applications, IT technology, and business aspects).

- Step4: Finally, support the presentation to the decision makers.

Did this take a year or two? No, just a few months, with Step 1 (the Data Town Plan) only being allowed to take a few weeks. Was this enough time? Absolutely—remember that "the devil *is* the details." The phased *implementation* of such a grand plan for totally restructuring all parts of the entire organization would take years, but the strategic *plan* allowed for incremental stages of delivery, each realizing value.

Multiple clients: When we need day-to-day operational integration

I'm going to have a little fun at this point, and also be a little controversial. Lots of consultants make lots of money helping deliver data warehouse solutions, but what if we didn't need data warehouses at all?

What if all our operational systems held history? What if they were on compatible platforms so you could throw queries at them in a technology-agnostic manner? What if these queries could be processed in the operational environment without negatively affecting transactional performance?

Now comes the million-dollar question from a data perspective: what if all these operational systems integrated data in such a way that (1) there was only one source of truth for any given subject area such as customer or product, and (2) all these systems directly mirrored how the business actually saw their world?

Finally, what if all this (and more) was true and you could guarantee that new systems introduced tomorrow wouldn't break this wildly optimistic (and unrealistic) hypothetical? Then, perhaps you could throw away the idea of a data warehouse. Such a wishful-thinking utopia was sometimes attempted in the 1980s under the banner of "corporate databases." These projects were typically expensive and commonly failed to deliver the wished-for dream. A re-run of this vision in the 1990s was rumored to have threatened the very existence of one of Australia's largest banks.

So, why have I teased you with something so unrealistic? Because too many people think data integration can only happen in a data warehouse, and they won't even consider applying effort to get integration in the operational systems. It is a laudable achievement if you can build a data warehouse that provides an integrated, business-centric view of an organization's data, but these data warehouses are often primarily intended to support analysis and reporting functions, while the day-to-day operations of front-line workers continue to be plagued by integration pain.

I'll give a simple example. Let's say an organization has several (or dozens of) places holding customer data. In the worst case, something as simple as a change of address can be an error-prone nightmare. It's not good enough to consolidate and rationalize at the data warehouse level if communications from different operation systems still send out letters to old addresses because the new address was only applied to some records.

A so-called Master Data Management (MDM) solution may help. But some forms of MDM, like with data warehousing, may leave duplicated and inconsistent data in multiple sources while providing a reference point for a consolidated view. That's an improvement *if* the operational systems go to this consolidated reference point.

Another variation of MDM architecture may appoint just one operational system's data as the single source of truth and use it to propagate copies back into multiple source systems. That's arguably better again. Either way, our operational front-line workers will benefit.

But here's the punch line: no matter what form of data integration your organization aims for, you *need* a Data Town Plan that expresses the organization's data in business terms.

I've already shared the story from wildfire emergency response where an agreed definition for fire trucks was needed (whether they were called appliances, tankers, slip-ons, or perhaps big red water-squirting vehicles).

A very common subject area of master data management centers on customer data. You might think getting a clear, unambiguous definition of a "customer" would be easy. That's not always true.

For example, one client of mine operated a cemetery. If a person has a pre-paid funeral plan, they're probably the customer. But in the unfortunate situation where this individual develops some form of memory loss and a family member is granted power-of-attorney to act on their behalf, is this power-of-attorney person now the customer? And when the person with the original funeral plan dies, and burial is to occur, are they still the customer?

Let's take another example from my experience. You've got a health insurance company that offers dental benefits. What if a grandparent is paying the health insurance fees, a parent is bringing in their child to visit the dentist, and the child is sitting in the dentist chair with mouth wide open in obedience to the dentist's instructions and eyes wide open in fear? Who is the customer—the grandparent, the parent, or the child?

So let's concede getting agreement on definitions may not be easy, but also concede it's worth the effort.

If you've got a robust Data Town Plan, with precise definitions, and, where appropriate, supported by synonyms (an Appliance is also known as a Tanker), plus hierarchies of classifications (Tankers and Slip-ons are types of Fire Truck), you've got an agreed foundation for managing data. For the wildfire example, the proposed operational solution was data sharing via a common information model. For other clients, some form of master data management was chosen. The clear message in all cases was that the central, agreed Data Town Plan was used to drive a solution with the potential to positively impact operational staff.

We've looked at several examples of organizations that need day-to-day operational integration. We now look at one more, and it happens to be the same organization as was at the focus in the previous section, 'Medical practitioner registration: When we need IT and Business strategic alignment (isn't that "always"?!)'.

Australia historically had a dozen or more health practitioner registration groups (for doctors, nurses, dentists, chemists, chiropractors, etc.). What was worse, these agencies were typically duplicated across most states and territories, with a little bit of sharing for the smaller ones. In total, there were more than 80 separate organizations. I shudder to think what the numbers might have been if we had 50 states like the USA.

Then to really mix things up, each of these agencies typically had at least three core IT applications. Now you've got a few hundred IT systems holding data on health practitioners. Perhaps this would be manageable if one practitioner could only ever appear under the watchful eye of one agency. But here's a hypothetical (but realistic) scenario.

Chris was a nurse in my home state of Victoria. Some patients complained that Chris, at times, seemed to be under the influence of alcohol or drugs. An inquiry was made, and substance abuse was confirmed. Chris participated in an appropriate rehabilitation program, and was allowed to continue to practice, but under strict supervision, and with the condition that random drug tests came back with zero traces of the problematic drugs.

Chris was now a model nurse, moved to the adjoining state of South Australia, and not only continued to practice, but was also on the Nurse Board, overseeing other nurses. The "Nurse" records are now spread across two states.

Chris works hard and studies hard, and is subsequently registered as a student doctor. The one state, South Australia, now has two sets of records, one for Chris as a Nurse and one for Chris as a Doctor-in-training. During ward visits, a patient reports concern relating to apparent drug or alcohol impairment. As it turns out, an investigation concludes Chris is "only" fatigued. It's a serious problem, but different from a reappearance of drug abuse.

The important theme behind this story is that the records of health practitioners needed to be accessed across different professions (doctor, nurse, etc.), different states, and different IT systems.

Australia's national government mandated that all of these registration groups would be consolidated at the end of July 2010. The operational consolidation of some 300 IT systems was critical. The goal was crystal clear—the front-line workers of the new, national organization (the Australian Health Practitioner Regulation Agency) needed the business and IT to work together to create operational integration. It didn't happen overnight, but a Data Town Plan was foundational in steering the efforts.

Emergency response: When we need flexibility

As you have gathered by now, I have been involved in delivering technology solutions to help in emergency response to wildfires. One much-loved resource is an American helicopter, known locally in Australia as Elvis.

Figure 8: Erickson S-64

An extract from a hierarchy of types of resources deployed in fire response could look something like this:

- If we're talking of things that could get deployed, perhaps we could start at the very top of the classification hierarchy with something as blindingly obvious as Deployable Resource. *[By the way, such an abstract concept is a massive thumbs-up for those who like generalizations, and a massive thumbs-down for those who want to see specifics—another story we'll tackle later.]*

- OK, let's go one level deeper, and we might encounter Vehicles, Consumables (such as diesel fuel for the fire trucks and foam to be sprayed on the fire), and Plant and Equipment (including pumps, generators, chain saws, and much more).

- Following the Vehicle thread, we might have Aircraft, Land Vehicle, and Boat as more specialized subtypes.

- Again, taking just one thread, we could subtype Aircraft into Fixed Wing and Helicopter (or Rotary Wing if you prefer) and go even further into their subtypes.

You get the idea. So, if we want to capture how the business sees its Helicopters in this realm, do we want to model them as a Deployable Resource, a Vehicle, an Aircraft, or a Helicopter (or even more specific like classifying if they have a single main rotor or two). The best answer should be, "Ask the business." But in this case, it depends on who you ask. A person with the title of Logistics Officer may answer that the core business concept is, in fact, a Deployable Resource. A member of the Air Wing is likely to be more specific, and talk of Aircraft. And others might also have their own divergent views.

So who is right? One simple answer is to try and accommodate all major business perspectives. Perhaps we could have a classification hierarchy that represents all their views? In this case, it should arguably include at least Deployable Resource *and* Aircraft.

Now comes the fun bit of this story. The business wanted to primarily embrace generalized concepts such as Deployable Resources (rather than Fire Trucks and Helicopters), and Emergency Events (rather than just Fires and Floods). In fact, a mandate for the IT solution, even though funded by Fire Management, was for the IT system to be flexible enough to be quickly adapted to different scenarios. And the person in charge of eventually testing whatever was delivered warned the IT team upfront that he would ensure we'd achieved this mandate for flexibility.

Ah, but this tester also said he had no intention of declaring *how* he would test the flexibility. He argued that if we knew ahead of time, we might cheat a little and make sure that a less-than-flexible system could be hard-coded to appear to be flexible, and hence pass the nominated tests.

The time for testing inevitably arrived. The first test was introduced by the tester who said something like this: "OK, you've allowed for Helicopters and Fixed Wing aircraft to be deployed to a fire, but now we want to use helium blimps to assist in fire-spotting. We need to be able to key in details of each available blimp, including its registration number, fuel type, air speed, and flight range. Then, we want to be able to immediately deploy them. Initially, all I need from you is an estimate of how long it would take to reconfigure your system to meet these test objectives."

Figure 9: Blimp

The somewhat cheeky developer clarified the tester didn't want the actual changes made yet, but just an estimate of effort. The developer suggested the tester get a cup of coffee, then come back in a few minutes.

In due course, the tester returned to the desk, and the developer, with a mischievous grin, gave him the answer, "About four minutes and 23 seconds." The tester was confused, until the developer said he thought it would be quicker to actually make the changes than spend time with a calculator guessing. The tester was now offered a screen to enter Blimps and deploy them. He was gobsmacked.

But the tester had one more trick up his sleeve. He knew we were prepared to manage emergency response to fires and floods, and probably a few other scenarios such earthquakes and storms, but he wanted to *really* test our flexibility.

Figure 10: Penguin

In Australia, we have a breed of penguins that are so small they probably couldn't reach high enough to peck your kneecap, even if they wanted too. They are super cute and super shy. But the tester's scenario suggested these cuddly little critters had gone rogue, had acquired some boats and weapons, and were heading across the bay to forcefully take over a major city of millions of people. We laughed, but he was serious—that was his test scenario.

It was a bit more complicated than the blimp test and took more time, but it was achieved.

The Fire Management group wanted flexibility long before Australia needed emergency responses to unforeseen events, such as fire ant invasion and a pandemic, reaching Australian shores. Other clients likewise wanted flexibility, but it's a continuum. So, what are some key takeaways for all of us?

First, IT solutions *can* be designed to be flexible (though flexibility doesn't come for free, and not all developers are comfortable with creating generic IT systems).

Secondly, and following on from the above, you should talk with the business about how much flexibility they really want. More specialized solutions are typically quicker and cheaper to deliver (at least for the first few specific targets), and a better fit for today's requirements (if not tomorrow's). It's a balancing act that warrants conscious debate.

The key message is that a business-centric Data Town Plan will likely contain hierarchies for classifying business concepts (as entities in the data model), with generalized concepts at the top and more specific classifications at the bottom.

That's good, and these hierarchies can be used to trigger conversations with the business that may offer guidance to the IT development teams, including carefully considered statements of requirements for solution flexibility.

Commercial-off-the-shelf IT solution delivery: When we need an objective, independent benchmark

An organization involved in transporting goods had IT systems that were an increasingly poor fit for modern business, and an IT Commercial-Off-The-Shelf (COTS) solution vendor was keen to sell their product as a replacement for the aging software. All of that is pretty standard stuff.

Unfortunately, one scenario that seems to play out too often involves sales people by-passing IT and blowing in the ears of senior management. Management is "sold" on an IT solution that sounds good to them, but when IT implements the shiny new tools, the wheels fall off.

The transport organization very wisely wanted to establish an independent benchmark for IT solution evaluation and involve senior management *and* IT. They didn't want the benchmark to be based on the existing systems because they had already been identified as missing the mark. Nor did they want to be swayed by the glossy brochures from the vendor, which might bias the product evaluation's independence.

The solution? Create a Data Town Plan based on how the organization *wants* to see its data managed in the future, and benchmark the proposed IT solution against this target state.

Step one was to create the Data Town Plan. That was fun, and didn't take long at all.

Step two was to do a mapping from the IT COTS solution's logical model against the benchmark. That was a great theory, but you might be surprised at how many companies whose bread and butter existence is developing and selling software do not have a logical model for their core products. The best they could do was to provide me with a pile of sheets of paper that was a generated model of the physical database.

I took over the board room table to assemble these separate sheets, each representing one part of the total jigsaw puzzle. I literally crawled over the assembled, massive diagram on my hands and knees, following relationships between tables. At one point, I was trying to pinpoint how this software handled bundling of smaller delivery packages into larger packages, starting at individual parcels and ending with aircraft containers. It didn't take me long to find what I was looking for: the required data structure to handle packages-within-packages was in place.

Then came the "oops" moment. An embarrassed representative of the COTS solution software company said he hadn't understood the intended purpose of that particular structure, and had reused that column for something else. The bottom line was that the feature designed for the original model had been thrown away and could no longer be simply reintroduced. The vendor said it would cost a lot of money and take a long time. The discovery, driven by the independent benchmark, saved the transport organization a few million dollars buying something that would not work and cost the IT solution vendor a few million dollars in sales.

A Data Town Plan can be used for many purposes, but one of them is, as shown here, to articulate what the business wants, in its own business terms, as a benchmark for evaluating candidate future IT solutions.

Land titles: When the "obvious" business concepts may not be that obvious!

We've already noted how contentious it might turn out to be trying to define what the business means by a "customer." Shortly before I wrote this book, I heard one person suggest that, in his experience, it is so challenging to try to nail down an agreed definition of "customer" that he suggests it is not even worth trying. I strongly hold a different view. The harder it is to get consensus, the more important I see it as being. Please note that there are ways you can facilitate agreement without being confrontational. You can record synonyms to respectfully note alternative terms. You can create a hierarchy of terms, as demonstrated in the Fire Truck example, where subtypes appear as specializations of more generalized concepts; people can see their favorite term in context with those of others. You can note that certain parts of the business, or certain processes, see things differently, and that's OK. Sometimes, in spite of all the tricks you bring to the table, there still may be roadblocks to reconciliation, but even in such cases you can still document areas where agreement couldn't be reached—well at least not yet!

We've spoken about the concept of "customers." Earlier, we mentioned a water utility that struggled to pin down the definition for "employees."

Perhaps you smile at these examples, and think they must be pretty rare? Sadly, understanding "simple" terms can be challenging, but believe me, it is worth the effort to pin down precise definitions of what a customer, an employee, a product, a contract, and more, really are. I encourage the supporting descriptions to include examples of what they are and examples of what they are not.

Finally, let's look at yet another story demonstrating how a business-centric Data Town Plan can bring value. And this story is pretty spectacular.

In my part of the world, we've got a government body called Land Victoria (Victoria is the state I live in). They maintain a register of who owns what land, as recorded on Land Titles. One of their main transactions is known as a Transfer of Land, when ownership changes. Ask pretty well any data modeler what a central entity might be (based on the opening sentences in this paragraph), and you wouldn't be surprised to hear, "Land."

Let's step back a little in time. I was told that this registry had a problem with their records, and the problem had been known to exist for more than 100 years, long before computer records came into being. In the 1980s, they had formed a team of people to solve the problem. After three-and-a-half years, they dissolved the team, having achieved nothing.

I was not aware of this history. I just did my job, looking for core business concepts, and using data model patterns to drive some of the conversations. The resultant high-level Data Town Plan started to shape up, looking something like Figure 11.

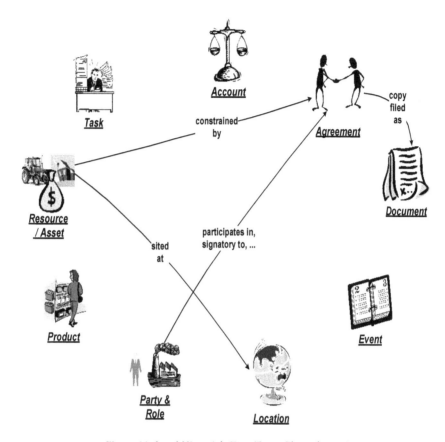

Figure 11: Land Victoria's Data Town Plan schematic

A quick explanation of the diagram is that vendors, purchasers, solicitors and the like are represented as parties fulfilling roles; things like bank loans and sales contracts are represented by agreements; and the property that's changing hands is an asset at a location. That's a gross over-simplification, and as is true for a Data Town Plan, each icon needs drill-down into its details. But it gives a context to start a discussion.

The long story short is that even though the word "land" appeared in the title of their organization and in many of their documents, I suggested that their business was really about "rights," not land—the rights of owners, the rights of tenants, the rights of people to access the property on registered easements, the rights for mining companies to perform exploration, and so on. The rights were assets as much as the land itself. As it turned out, the act of me asking the "dumb questions" and challenging very long-held ideas about their core business concepts apparently led to the 100-year-old breakthrough they needed. Problem solved.

Now here's the humorous part of the story. One of the most senior officers in this organization, upon having a light-bulb moment that their registration was about rights, not land, loudly exclaimed, "We can blame the English." For those not aware of Australia's colonization history, the English established themselves as the colonial masters of this country. Colonization issues aside, Australia owes much to our English forebears. But here's the twist that he explained to me.

Apparently, in old England, long before they had central registries of title ownership, there was a quaint ritual for noting who owned what real estate. If Chris was buying a farm from Sam, the two would assemble the village elders as witnesses. Chris would have money in one hand, ready to buy the farm. Sam would reach down and pick up a handful of soil, representing the farm's land. At the same moment in time, as Chris deposited his coins in the open hand of Sam, Sam would deposit the piece of "land" in Chris' open hand. A "transfer of land" had occurred! My colleague excitedly concluded that the whole traditional emphasis on "land" could be traced back to this old-world tradition.

> *It took a willingness to challenge the apparently obvious to shine a new light on the matter.*

Key points

- No man is an island, nor do business units (or even entire organizations) exist in isolation. There are times when people and IT systems need a common language to exchange information.

- While some focus on "process" and others on "data," they are often interdependent. A better understanding of how business people see their data may assist in understanding processes and improving them.

- Business strategies and IT strategies can both be improved by understanding the current state, the future state, and alternative pathways. Data architecture plays a vital role within this context.

- An integrated view of data can be presented via a data warehouse, but even more basic data integration can occur at an operational level.

- Whatever is today's chosen approach to data integration, the Data Town Plan upon which all of this is based must embrace the business' vision for the future.

- A business-centric Data Town Plan can provide objectivity in benchmarking IT solutions.

- Defining core business concepts (customer, product, etc.) can be challenging. It may require detailed, unambiguous specifications as to what each concept really means, but is definitely worth the effort.

CHAPTER 3

Red Flags

We've just looked at some sunny day scenarios. They aren't just hypothetical scenarios from some textbook on "data" theory. Instead, they highlight actual benefits experienced by real-world organizations. But strewn along the pathway to success are too many traps for the unwary. Some warnings follow.

Let's just start building (or "Why isn't everybody coding?")

Imagine wanting to build a city, but having no plans. Not even outline sketches. A recipe for disaster, and a lot of rework? The parallels for data-related projects are hopefully clear. If you start building an enterprise-wide data warehouse or commence a master data management initiative that is intended to pull together common views from across the enterprise, you'd be well advised to know what a "common view" looks like. Otherwise, as for building a city, you're likely to have lots of failures, rework, and additional and unnecessary costs.

But that all relates to having a vision of where we're going at the macro level. What about at a micro level? Does the same thinking still apply? For example, should "Agile" projects have a big design up-front before commencing an Agile project? On behalf of the "agilists" in this world, the answer is a resounding "No." But what about at least a light-weight sketch?

A fellow consultant at one of my client sites told me a story about an Agile project he led. The team didn't model the data. They just started coding and building tables as required. Their velocity got progressively worse over successive development iterations ("sprints").

What he noted was that tables that were created in the first sprint were changed in the second sprint. This meant re-coding and re-testing the already "finished" functions in sprint 1, plus adding more functionality (and tables) in sprint 2. Sprint 3 involved changes affecting sprints 1 and 2, with subsequent rework. Sprint 4 required rework of functions from sprints 1, 2, and 3. A pattern emerges?!

The scrum master made a bold call. He got a commitment from the product owner to use one entire sprint to build an outline (town plan) of the big picture. OK, they "lost" one sprint, but the measured velocity was 12 times faster in subsequent sprints.

If IT is working on some grand enterprise-wide initiative, they'd be well advised to assemble a Data Town Plan so they get the foundations secure. At the other end of the scale, if they are creating an independent piece of software, even within that project's scope, they still might want to consider a light-weight sketch of where they're going. But I did say an "independent" piece of software. If it's likely to share data with other projects in the future (and that is arguably more common than not), a bit of a Data Town Plan at the enterprise level might save a lot of integration pain later.

Progress by project, leading to auto-magical integration

Figure 12: Silos

This topic and its variations are scary. I understand and sympathize with the thinking behind pushback against massive initiatives that take too long and rarely, if ever, deliver much value in a timely fashion. I get it that you might not be able to get corporate backing for enterprise-wide projects, so why not try the stealth approach of "progress by project"? That can mean we get funding for one manageable project, then for another, and little by little, we end up with the big picture, or so the theory goes.

Here's the catch. If each project has its cost justification tabled in isolation, sure, you may get some returns on the IT investment. But the sum of multiple projects, if they are not aligned with the long-term vision, is unlikely to lead to what I call the dream of auto-magical integration. It's like building a city based on the need for schools, then the need for hospitals, then the need for transport, but without the overarching town plan. The collective whole is most likely less than the sum of the individual parts, the exact opposite of what is intended.

Let's look at some examples of "progress by project" that can go wrong as compared to holistic, integrated efforts.

There's the "business unit" silo. I was consulting with a large organization where the management team had sought to pull disparate operating business units into a coordinated whole. Things were looking good for a while, but one major business unit simply wanted to do its own thing, and refused to come to the party.

The next silo is a real trap. It's the "source system" silo. People want to reinvent aspects of their portfolio of IT systems and do it one system at a time. For example, perhaps they want to create a Data Vault (a type of data warehouse), and want to tackle the creation and loading of the Data Vault one source system at a time, basing the design of the Data Vault on the data structures of each source system. What they may end up with is the much-dreaded and an unworkable "source system Data Vault" where the data reflects today's current IT systems rather than today's *and* tomorrow's business-centric view.

Other ways the big picture is broken up into silos include segmentation according to business process, segmentation according to product line, or …

Ah, some of you may wish to take issue with what I am saying. Perhaps you've seen "progress by project" work, and work well? OK, I'll take a step back. In a preceding paragraph, I talked about multiple projects that struggled to deliver collective value. With emphasis this time, I said that these multiple projects, "… *if* they are not aligned to the long-term vision," can fall short. Now, I'll turn it around. What if we do have a grand plan (including my much-loved Data Town Plan)? And what if we break the strategic direction into bite-sized chunks, and get phased, iterative delivery of a unified whole? I will cheer you on. Yes, you can get "progress by project" in such a setting. At the heart of this approach is still the unified vision. We can portray the approach in Table 1.

Focus	Model type	Data subject area:-								
		Account	Agree't	Doc't	Event	Locat'n	Party	Product	Resource	Task
Data Town Plan (Business)	Model-on-a-Page (Overview model)	x	x	x	x	x	x	x	x	x
	Divergent + Convergent models		x		x		x	x		
Technical design (Solution)	Logical data model		x				x	x		
	Physical data model						x			

Table 1: The T-model approach

I've labeled it the "T-model" approach, and no, I am not talking of the Ford vehicle from the early 1900s. Instead, I am talking of starting top-down with the mile-wide, inch-deep view of the business world (the top of the letter T), and then drill down into more detail on given subject areas. We will cover this more carefully later, but it gives us the picture that we can start with the unified view, then actually achieve progress-by-project within this holistic framework.

All we need is the central vision. This book can help you assemble one—please read on!

"Modeling too small"

Larry Burns, in his excellent book, *Data Model Storytelling*,[4] has a few pages titled "The danger of modeling too small." He tells the story of two "business process" silos within his organization, a vehicle manufacturing company. The first was the group responsible for writing Warranty Contracts upon the sale of a new vehicle. There were also business processes for managing claims against those warranties, and again, the warranty component for the claims process was modeled. One could have

---

4   Burns L. (2021) Data Model Storytelling: An Agile Approach to Maximizing the Value of Data Management.

reasonably assumed that the data structures for warranties were identical across both processes, but apparently not.

My friend got both groups into the same room at the same time to gain a holistic, enterprise perspective rather than a process-centric perspective. Problem solved.

I've seen this siloed approach triggered by people trying to focus on discrete business processes, business units, analytic reporting requirements, urgent "pain point" initiatives, strategic positioning for the future, and more. This less-than-enterprise view is, for example, evident in the practice of "Data Mesh," whose evangelists proudly preach the message of decentralization. The danger is that you may get a disjointed and contradictory view by assuming the sum of all parts will result in a unified view.

Does this mean that approaches such as Data Mesh should be outlawed? No, but with a caveat. If your organization is embracing Data Mesh, with each domain (e.g., a business unit or a business process) having its own domain-driven data model as its private "ubiquitous language," I would recommend that each team leverage off a pre-existing Data Town Plan to avoid the problems Larry speaks of above. I would also recommend interested parties read Larry's excellent 4-part series of articles on Domain-Driven Development from the TDAN.com website.[5]

OK, perhaps we can build the big picture, but starting "bottom-up" with the details we know?

I hope you see the value of a business-centric, enterprise-wide Data Town Plan. I also hope that the previous notes on "progress by project" are starting to suggest that we need to consciously make the effort to construct a Data Town Plan as an explicit exercise rather than hoping it will emerge through accidental integration by pooling the ideas we get from disparate projects. But can we assemble this enterprise-wide view by starting with the details we already know and can access?

---

[5] Burns, L on TDAN. (all four parts available via Part 4: https://tdan.com/domain-driven-development-part-4/29883)

Looking at real-world sample data

Let's look at some real-world stories about deriving data structures by starting with the details close to hand.

Graham Witt, an internationally recognized Aussie data modeler and author, told a story that from memory goes something like this. A junior developer was responsible for delivering an IT system for a school. It included a register of the people involved, including teachers, students, and parents/guardians. That doesn't sound too hard. Apparently, the developer figured there was no need to do a model and crosscheck it with the business.

Instead of using a top-down approach, he used bottom-up practices, basing his view on a limited number of data samples. The developer observed that each student had a family name, and the student, mum, and dad shared that one name. So, to save a tiny bit of space in the computer's storage, why not record the family name once? It worked fine until he encountered a family with members who had different surnames.

> *There's a not-too-subtle message here: when you start doing bottom-up modeling based on explicit examples, they may not be sufficiently representative.*

But before we leave this school system scenario, it had one more terrible outcome. This developer also assumed that all family members lived at the same address. Things got ugly for a wife who was living in a women's refuge for protection from a violent husband (the address of this facility was closely guarded—that is, until the IT system behind this story exposed the refuge address to the husband, based on the built-in assumption that they all lived together). That turned out to be a massively serious outcome when the violent man exclaimed, "Ah, now I know where the so and so lives."

That story was based on a small project rather than an enterprise-wide system, but it highlights the dangers of a limited sample collected by a person with limited exposure to the real world.

Looking at current IT systems

Moving on to modeling for current IT systems, let me share one scenario I was close to. As part of understanding the data behind one organization, it was deemed important to dig into all the existing IT systems. But they didn't know how many systems they had, so before launching the project to build the Enterprise Data Model, they launched a project to build a registry of their systems (along with details such as what technical platforms they ran on, associated business processes, who to contact for more information, and more).

This little project before the big project took 18 months just to get a register built of more than 1,000 IT systems. The resulting project to build the Enterprise Data Model took a sizable team many years.

Even if you can successfully build an enterprise model within a reasonable budget and a reasonable timeframe by drilling down into existing IT systems, there's still a fundamental problem. The systems might at one time have been loved by the business, but may be showing signs of aging. Or worse, the IT systems were *never* a really good fit. Put simply, you cannot trust that the IT systems are a good representation of how the business sees themselves today, let alone tomorrow.

> *I am not discounting the huge value of understanding what you've got, but it is a really questionable place to start this Data Town Plan journey.*

What about Waterfall/Big Design Up Front models?

OK, so perhaps looking at the details of sample data or current IT systems might have real dangers. Perhaps instead, we should invest in a massive, enterprise-wide initiative to create the mother-of-all-data-models for our organization?

IT developers of the "Agile" variety sometimes refer disparagingly to their colleagues who try hard to get the deliverable almost perfect on the very first release.

The "waterfall" analogy draws parallels with a cascading type of waterfall, where, stage by stage, the water eventually reaches the bottom. Similarly, waterfall-styled software development goes through a number of stages. I won't go into all the various steps some people include. Still, as a brief example, the project might start by spending months striving to get a near-perfect statement of requirements, more months of effort pushing for a near-perfect design, followed by near-perfect coding (or at least as close to perfect as one can get after exhaustive and exhausting testing), and eventually, swing the near-perfect solution into operation. That's the dream.

Changes late in this type of process are always more expensive to fix, so the fewer errors in earlier stages, the cheaper the final result. But it is almost impossible to get the requirement specification stage near perfect. Most people need to see some indication of the final result before they can best articulate their requirements. Imagine getting an architect to design (and oversee the construction) of a house based on nothing more than a list of requirements. Most of us want to see some sketches or models before we commit.

Worse, even if the statements of requirements were perfect (and perfectly understood by the developers), by the time the solution is implemented, it may be discovered that the carefully constructed statements no longer reflect what is needed by the business today. Things have changed.

Many in the developer community have moved away from "waterfall" approaches to more iterative/agile styles of working. But, the option to head in more iterative directions is not always recognized in the world of modeling for enterprise integration. In the worst cases, consultants spend years (and I am not exaggerating) looking for data behind every nook and cranny, carefully analyzing existing systems, business processes, and interviewing people from all levels across all parts of the business. They can end up with some unwanted consequences. One can be a massive data model that is hard to understand and maintain. Another can be cost and time overrun.

Behind the bloated data model is an implicit, if not explicit, goal to capture almost *all* of the data belonging to an enterprise. No wonder you can end up with thousands of unnecessary entities in the model and thousands of entries in the business glossary.

Not all initiatives to build an Enterprise Data Model using a waterfall/big design upfront approach are necessarily doomed to failure. I'm just warning that such an approach doesn't come without serious risks.

I'll tell another of my stories here, even though I risk playing my cards a bit early, as you can read between the lines where I want to take this conversation. Nonetheless, let's hear this one out.

A massive telecommunications company spent years with a large team trying to finalize their Enterprise Data Model. I got the impression that it was never going to end, or even get to the first iteration, as the modelers were striving to capture excruciating detail.

An individual left that organization and joined another telecommunications company. They had three projects expected to launch in two weeks' time, and wanted an Enterprise Data Model as the foundation for data sharing. On my own, but armed with Len Silverston's industry model of the telecommunications industry, I delivered a model with "sufficient" detail in the designated timeframe.

Ah, did I say an "industry model"? That topic opens another huge can of worms. Please read on.

Could we buy an "industry model"? (Perhaps, perhaps not)

OK, so building your own massive Enterprise Data Models might now look a bit risky. What about simply buying a ready-made "industry" model off the shelf? Job done?

I'll be quick on this one. For a price (!!!), you *can* buy an industry model that purportedly is so well suited to you (and your competitors) that the hard work is already done. A few comments follow.

They're often far from cheap.

By nature, they are generic. You will typically have to do work to make it "your own." That's not bad in itself. In theory, you can leverage what is common and then tweak the model for areas that make you different (remember, that just might be the bit that gives you a competitive advantage). Some generic models are well received. I consulted with an Australian telecommunications company that embraced the Tele-Management (TM) Forum's Information Framework, known as the Shared Information/Data (SID) model. They did what I just described above—they took the base model and then personalized it. Further, in an altruistic manner, they even went as far as making contributions to the SID for the wider benefit of the telecommunications community.

A great story, but not all engagements with industry models end that happily.

I've consulted with several organizations that have spent a significant amount of money on acquiring an industry model, only to shelve it. Just to underline this message, some of my clients have expressly directed that the industry model must *never* be used. I was warned that if I referred to one such model, the company would walk me out the door!

However, it is critical to note that there is a variation between those love-or-hate extremes of purchased industry models that I will briefly introduce here. David Hay and Len Silverston have published several wonderful books on data model patterns, including some patterns aimed at specific industries. In fact, Volume 2 in Len's series is an entire volume dedicated to the subject. Although Len and David's models may be labeled as "industry models," they should not be confused with commercially available models with the same title. David and Len's models are high-level frameworks and are available for the cost of purchase of one of their books. In my opinion, that's real value.

The bit I don't want to write ("What could go wrong?")

I tend to be an optimist. But let's ask some questions that might expose possible threats to a Data Town Plan project:

- What if the organization has cultures that are isolationist, encouraging turf wars rather than cooperation between various business units? Can we find a way to work within their framework, or would an enterprise-wide initiative be undermined and doomed to failure?

- It's not uncommon to encounter difficult people. Sometimes, they can actually be great assets, willing to unflinchingly expose flaws within the organization and welcoming of people who actually want to deliver a better future. Or they can just be naysayers who will oppose anything and everything. So here's a telling question—do we have individuals in a position of influence who will block a Data Town Plan just because they want to flex their muscles? Or can we work with them, perhaps educate them, and get them to see a better way forward?

- Do we have competing consultancies at a site, each trying to undermine the other? I've (occasionally) seen competitors who will cooperate for the client's good rather than their own short-term profitability, but unfortunately, that's less common. In one rather memorable conflict, different business units had different consultancies, and they (the business units *and* the consultancies) didn't even want to talk to each other. Would any attempt to build a unified Data Town Plan be destined to fail?

• Perhaps the organization has been burned by past "enterprise" initiatives that cost a fortune, took ages, and never delivered value (and I truly mean "never"), but surely we can loosen the purse strings this time and get funding for something so obviously of benefit? (Or am I dreaming?!)

• Some technical people have traditionally appeared unwilling (or unable) to engage with the "business," but now that we've told them about the importance of showing love towards non-technical executives, perhaps they will change?

So what's the answer to such questions?

I didn't want to write this section. I would like everyone reading this to think that if they follow the advice in this book, they simply cannot fail. But if I take that position, I would deserve pushback from those who have genuinely tried but can't deliver to expectations.

I've completed something like 20 enterprise-level data models in one form or another. Most have delivered real value, and the clients have recognized this. Many times, people I met in one setting have moved to another organization and actively sought me out to do whatever I did last time, but in their new workplace. Sometimes, I have worked alongside brilliant people, yet one (or several) of the factors mentioned in the bullet points above have come into play and devalued the project. Or killed it off!

Here's the tricky on to make a call on. What if one or more of the threatening factors are at play, but we can gently turn things around? I've also experienced that outcome. You don't *have* to run away just because there might be some challenges. Is there some foolproof checklist that will determine whether an initiative can be nudged towards success, or is it best to stop flogging a dead horse? I suggest you look at the "happy ending" stories and the "red flag" warnings shared above, and have a conversation. Identify the strengths and weaknesses, and threats and opportunities that are present in your organization. Openly discuss the risks and mutually decide whether to proceed or not.

If you're going ahead, keep an eye on the risks, and think ahead of time about how best to respond if some of the risks materialize.

Now, what if you decide to *not* go ahead? I go back to the town planning for cities. Have some cities grown organically rather than having a visionary outline to guide development? Yes. Can that approach work? Yes, in a fashion. Might the final results be less than ideal? Yes, but perhaps workable.

… that's the conclusion I didn't want to put in writing. I strongly recommend a short, sharp, focused development of a Data Town Plan, but if, for whatever reason, that isn't going to be feasible, be aware of the consequences and communicate them. Then, live with whatever reality you are given. Play the cards you're dealt.

Now, let's look at the Data Town Plan idea, and perhaps some of what lies ahead will convince the naysayers.

Key points

- Even one small IT initiative performed without the guidance of a Data Town Plan can lead to painful rework as the larger picture emerges.

- Some organizations try to avoid enterprise-wide initiatives and instead embrace the project-by-project philosophy, with each independent project cost justified in its own right. Unfortunately, there is a very real risk that the multiple projects simply won't play happily together.

- Perhaps the goal is to address the needs of discrete business units or business processes, again only to discover that subsequent necessary data sharing between systems (that are focused on discrete business units or processes) have incompatibilities in data structure and meaning.

- Perhaps the perceived solution to silos is to have an overall framework for enterprise data sharing, but it is to be assembled "bottom-up," based on a detailed analysis of today's data samples or today's IT solutions. If this work is intended to create a holistic perspective, multiple discrete views may not provide a unified understanding. The sum of the parts may be significantly less than the desired whole! Bottom-up is a dangerous way to develop a holistic view.

- An extreme response to the above risks is to invest lots of time and money assembling the big picture before commencing any projects that might actually deliver value. Agile enthusiasts shudder at the idea of "big design up front." Typically such initiatives deliver too little, too late.

- Alternatively, vendors of "industry models" are happy to sell you their complete solution. Unfortunately, these generalized solutions are often expensive and need more money spent on making them fit the specifics of a given organization.

- Last but not least, any initiative can fail, including attempts to create and apply a Data Town Plan. We need to evaluate the threats and see if they can reasonably be mitigated.

CHAPTER 4

A Closer Look at this "Data Town Plan" Thing

Navigating our way forward

I've done a fair bit of bushwalking ("bushwalking" is an Aussie term for what others might call hiking). Much of this has been in remote areas. The arrival of GPS devices (especially now that they're embedded in smartphones) has made navigation easier these days, but earlier my basic tools-of-trade included a paper contour map and a compass. I still like the old-fashioned tools as a safety net because they don't have batteries that can go flat, and you aren't affected by mobile phone or GPS "black spots" where you can't get a signal. Yet I also like the accuracy and convenience of modern navigation aids.

It reminds me of my boss from years ago. Prior to getting into IT, he was a merchant seaman responsible for navigation. One of the young blokes on the ship challenged Mike to see if he could still navigate the massive ship from England all the way to Australia without any reference at all to the electronics on board. Mike rose to the challenge. The crowning glory was calling the youngster up to the bridge and Mike announcing that, if he was correct, they would see the Australian coast within five minutes. Sextants and charts won the day. As Mike told me, he had to always keep the traditional tried and true way as a safety net.

OK, here are the three basics of navigation. First, know where you are. Next, know where you want to get to, i.e., the target destination. And finally, pick a good path from A to B.

For building a city, the town plan represents one image of the target destination. I am suggesting that for many IT initiatives, the Data Town Plan, as expressed by the business, fulfills a similar role. It describes one dimension of where we want to be. But you may well ask, what on earth does a Data

Town Plan look like? By the time you get to the end of this book, I hope you will be capable of developing a Data Town Plan yourself, but let's look at some snippets of one of these artifacts so we are all on the same page. Put simply, I want you to be comfortable that you have an initial feel for where we're going together.

A Model-on-a-Page to start the Data Town Plan

I refer to a "Model-on-a-Page," where you can typically comfortably fit an overview of the entire (business-centric) perspective of an organization's core data onto a single sheet of paper or a single PowerPoint slide. This summary view is a little like the context map for a street directory (you might remember how we used them before we navigated using our smartphones). The context map sets the scene for a city (or perhaps a state), and then you drill down into the details of the address you want to find.

We've spoken about the value of a Data Town Plan sketch of data that's deemed to be important to the business. But what might that look like? We'll dip our toes in the water to give you a feel for where we're going. Let's start by looking at a real-world example, namely the data required to support emergency response to wildfires.

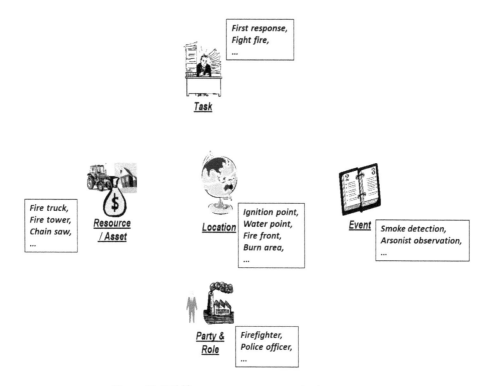

Figure 13: Wildfire emergency response business concepts

At the outset, we identified certain items that best represent the business view, portrayed above as labeled icons. We also noted the subtypes of each (examples of Events include the event where smoke is detected and the event where activity of an arsonist is observed).

Next, we talk about business process scenarios. Importantly, they not only put business concepts already identified in context, but they may also introduce some new business concepts not originally identified. Examples could include the following:

- A fire spotter (a Party in a Role) in a fire tower (an Asset) observes smoke (a smoke detection Event). Another person in a second fire tower also observes smoke. By noting the compass directions of these two smoke detection observations, a bit of mathematics can be applied to calculate the Location of the ignition point.

- The smoke detection Event triggers action—a Task is created to dispatch a first response crew involving firefighters (Parties in Roles) and a fire truck (an Asset).

- When the crew arrives, they observe an individual running away, carrying a jerry can that they assume might have contained combustible fuel. A video of the suspected arsonist and his car is captured and forwarded to a police officer (a Party in a Role), who subsequently tracks down the individual and makes an arrest (another Event), which triggers work (another Task) to prepare a submission to a court.

Not all elements of these scenarios are represented in the diagrams. Still, hopefully, they give you an idea of how a relatively simple picture of core business concepts and their inter-relationships can be formed.

We might refine and extend the subtypes or even add more business concepts. Importantly, we can now start to capture a representation of business relationships between these core concepts.

I can share with you that Figure 14 is not some artificial example to make real life look simple just for the purposes of a book; it actually is a fairly close representation of the top-level "Model-on-a-Page" developed as a part of a so-called Common Information Model targeted at emergency response agencies.

It is to be noted that the full specification of the business concepts and business relationships requires supplementary artifacts to capture more detail, but it is vital that these supplementary exercises do not get into too much detail.

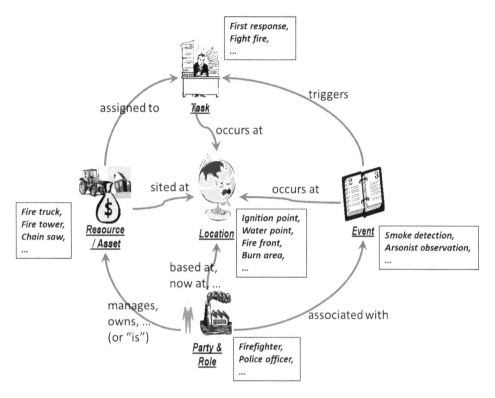

Figure 14: Business relationships

All we want is "sufficient" detail to deliver business value. That's the main game of any Data Town Plan!

OK, we've applied some elements of common business concepts to just one business (that of responding to wildfire emergencies), but how might they be used in a totally different setting? I'll take another real-life example, this time from a well-known and much-loved social care agency. Looking at their case management subset, we have a representation as shown in Figure 15.

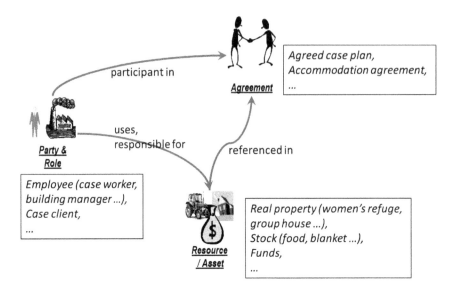

Figure 15: Case management subset of a social care provider

Again, we use some elements from a palette of common business concepts. Party (and Party Role), as well as Resource/Asset, were used in the previous example, but Agreement is new here, and we didn't use some of the palette items (Location, Task, and Event) from the previous case here. Importantly, while some of the palette items may be common, the identified subtypes are unique to each organization. Party/Role subtypes for fires included Firefighter and Police officer, whereas for the care agency they were Employee and Case client, with Employee further subtyped into Case worker, Building manager, and more.

Some people push back against highly generic concepts, and in many cases, their concerns are completely valid. I say "many cases" because, occasionally, the high-level generic concepts represented by the palette directly map to how an organization actually talks and thinks. That aside, even if we use these generic palette entries as nothing more than conversation starters, and drill down (and record) the specific subtypes applicable to a given organization, we can get real value from them.

Isn't a Model-on-a-Page too simple to be useful?

You may question if such a high-level view has any value to the business.

- One of my clients, a state police force, loved the unifying aspects of this view so much they actually had mouse mats manufactured which captured this view.

- I still smile at an interaction from another of my clients, this time a health practitioner registration and regulation agency. While getting a coffee in the kitchen, I overheard a C-level executive chatting about the Model-on-a-Page that had emerged from the previous week's workshop in which he had actively participated. He boasted to a colleague about the model _he_ had developed. How's that for ownership?!

- As told earlier, the exercise of developing the model had such a positive impact on another of my clients (a social care provider) that I was asked to enter into a contract for 90 minutes a month for the next three years so that I could attend their board meetings. That was by far the most unusual contract I have ever had, but it's reflective of how much value the business saw that this exercise delivered.

Further on the value question, I have encountered statements from a military perspective along the lines that "Plans are of little importance, but planning is essential" (Churchill?) or "Plans are worthless, but planning is everything" (Eisenhower?). The above bullet-point snippets seem to suggest that the artifact really is valuable. However, thinking about the military quotations, perhaps the _process_ of developing the understanding is also of immense value.

Going beyond the Model-on-a-Page view

We've had a sneak peek at samples of a Model-on-a-Page. It is the starting point of the Data Town Plan. But the exercise of capturing definitions of how the business sees their world doesn't end there.

The police force supplemented their model with a series of "scenarios" that presented hypothetical examples that showed how a unified view of their data could support day-to-day operations.

The social care organization had a detailed model under the high-level schematic, but additionally presented how different parts of the organization intersected with the core common data structures. For example, they had complementary subsets that reflected the data requirements needed to support those responsible for asset maintenance, aged care delivery, job training for the unemployed, and more.

David Hay, in his book *Achieving Buzzword Compliance,*[6] provides what I believe to be a useful classification of data models. What I have lightly called a "Model-on-a-Page" is close to his Overview Model. It can be presented as a graphical representation of the most important concepts in the business. Its target audience is corporate executives.

David then talks about how different groups within an organization might have their own unique, specialized views. They are unlikely to quickly and easily align at the first attempt at assembling a unified view, and he rightly calls them "divergent models" (he also uses the term "Semantic Models").

Having carefully and respectfully gathered numerous "divergent" views of the organization, David ends with *one* Essential Model. To separate it from the "divergent models," I sometimes refer to it as the "convergent model." Or the Data Town Plan!

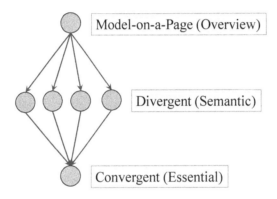

Figure 16: Drill-down for a Data Town Plan

I'll share a few warnings at this point. We will go into more detail later, but I want to ensure we avoid misunderstandings from the outset if we can.

- Some practitioners figure it is going to be too hard to get all the key stakeholders in a room for a few hours to thrash out the construction of the single "Model-on-a-Page" view. After all, we're probably seeking time from some of the busiest people. It can be hard, and at times impossible. There can be internal politics, turf wars, personality clashes, time pressures, and more. But I strongly recommend that you assemble as many willing, ready, and able people as you can muster. Tell them the truth—they have a golden opportunity

---

[6] Hay, D. (2018) Achieving Buzzword Compliance: Data Architecture Language and Vocabulary.

to shape their organization's future, whereas those who erect separationist barriers will likely be at a disadvantage later. Sorry, but for them, that's the probable consequence.

- It's all about the "business." Ideally, the attendees will have some representation from senior management levels through to hand-picked representation of front-line workers. Oh, and by the way, some IT folk will be invited, too, but we really want the business perspective from all participants. At this stage, we're not focusing on technology solutions.

- After a short, sharp (and fun) drafting of (1) the initial Model-on-a-Page view, we want to (2) dive into the multiple divergent views across the organization, and (3) unite them in the consolidated view. We *could* try to collect <u>all</u> the divergent views in one phase, and then perform a single, massive consolidation exercise. My recommendation is that the process is best handled iteratively. You get a new "divergent" view, and it is integrated into the emerging consolidated view before tackling the next divergent view.

A little story on the above points. I was consulting at a mine site in a remote part of Australia. Using standard commercial routes (rather than direct flights on an executive jet—nice in theory, but …), flying from my hometown was about 4,000 kilometers (well over 2,000 miles) each way. I had to pack in as much interaction with the business as I could in each visit. Instead of getting the key personnel together for a kick-off meeting, the well-intentioned client contact arranged a series of 1-hour meetings, up to eight per day, with individual stakeholders.

The first negative impact was missing out on that initial gathering of the minds, as addressed in the first bullet above. One consequence was I was being fed contradictory views, and I absolutely had to have that meeting of all stakeholders, albeit at the end of all interviews. We did get to the end goal, but delaying the group meeting until after all the individual meetings were finalized was a painful and unnecessary waste of time, as so much had to be reworked.

The second impact was also painful, for me at least. Each evening, I would review the six to eight interview note sets to weave them into the progressively emerging consolidated view. The next night I would take another set of notes and rework and re-consolidate the emergent unified view. That would typically take another eight hours. One evening, at about midnight, I needed a break to freshen myself up. We were beside a beach, and in the soft moonlight, I was jumping from one dark, flat rock in the sand to the next. All went well until the next dark, flat rock, which was actually a deep rock pool. Apart from embarrassment, I was now wide awake and ready to press on!

Later, we will go into the processes behind assembling the final convergent model, but for now, it is enough to say that the "Model-on-a-Page" is a great starting point for achieving unity on how all parts of the organization see the business data and that the "Model-on-a-Page" is valuable in its own right, but really leverages its value as it is usefully extended into a more detailed representation of the multiple divergent views.

A vision of the Data Town Plan end-point

A Data Town Plan typically captures core business concepts (types of customers, types of products, types of resources, etc.) and their core relationships.

It represents the entire organization, not just a department, branch, or a single business process within the organization. And it most definitely does not represent a logical view of an IT system, no matter how central and important that system might be.

It is business-centric, not technology-centric.

It is not limited by the constraints of IT systems that may not necessarily closely align with how the business works or wants to work.

It represents not only the core business concepts of today but also of tomorrow.

It has many potential uses, not the least of which is giving people a common, unambiguous language. You might be surprised by how much variation you might get when asking different people innocent questions such as "What is a Customer," or "How many people work for us?"

It also can act as a bridge between the language of the business and the language embedded in IT solutions.

We looked earlier at the starting point for a Data Town Plan, calling it a Model-on-a-Page. That's the first element. We also briefly mentioned the second element being the set of multiple "divergent" models representing a variety of views from across the organization, and the third element being the single "convergent" model that brings the diverse views back together again. Please note that the steps involved in developing these elements are not linear one-at-a-time steps to be performed in a waterfall-like sequence.

We'll take snippets from a real-world example, cut down to size to fit in this chapter, but that reflect aspects of the deliverables you can expect to develop.

In the animal kingdom, people may want to classify the different types and subtypes of animals. One vastly simplified (and less-than-perfect) subset might look like Figure 17:

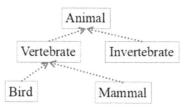

Figure 17: A subset of an Animal kingdom taxonomy

Many will (quite correctly) call that a "taxonomy." Perhaps you might feel more comfortable calling it a classification hierarchy, and that's fine.

Now we can have a bit of fun. Let's say we want to drill down a little deeper, perhaps looking at various types of birds and mammals. What say we find something that has webbed feet, loves to swim, has a bill for a mouth, and lays eggs? Perhaps it's a "Duck," a subtype of the "Bird" entry. Or perhaps, for an Aussie, it's a "Platypus" fitting under the "Mammal" entry? Yes, we have several creatures that breast-feed their young (a feature of all mammals) and that lay eggs! Welcome to Australia.

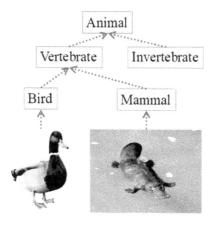

Figure 18: Is it a 'Duck' or a 'Platypus'?

Now that we are hopefully a little more comfortable with the idea of a taxonomy, let's look at how taxonomies might work in the business world. Let's take the case of emergency response to wildfires. Some of the resources deployed to a fire are displayed in Figure 19. Yes, boats (with water cannons) can be used to fight fires, too.

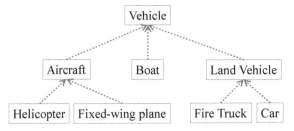

Figure 19: Emergency response vehicle types

When we talk to the business about fires, we are told that Forest Fires are also known (in Australia) as Bush Fires—we have synonyms for what is essentially the same thing. In addition, we might be told that emergency responses aren't limited to fires. Our firefighter heroes also respond to floods. Our taxonomy for emergency events might look like:

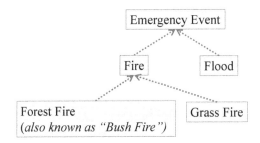

Figure 20: Emergency Response taxonomy

There was a subtle phrase in the paragraph above—we spoke about talking to the business. I had a reason for earlier introducing that little bit of an unexpected twist about a Duck versus a Platypus. It's easy to make assumptions, such as believing that the little critter with webbed feet and a duck-bill is a duck. You need to talk to someone who understands this stuff. Similarly, when we do a Data Town Plan for an enterprise, we must talk to the business. Who would have guessed that firefighters might get involved in flood rescues, too? We should note that the identified business concepts, such as Fire Trucks, should have some other information about them recorded. A light-weight sample follows.

Entity Name	Fire Truck
Synonym(s)	*(none yet identified)*
Taxonomy	Fire Truck is a subtype of Land Vehicle
Description	A Fire Truck is a heavy vehicle equipped with fire-fighting equipment such as a water tank, water pump, and hose. It has two specialized subtypes, being: 1. A Fire Tanker - a large, dedicated vehicle, often with a water tank capacity of the order of 3,000 litres (approximately 700 gallons). 2. A "Slip-On" - a multi-purpose four-wheel drive tray vehicle with a "slip-on" tank + pump + hose temporarily fitted to turn the vehicle into a fire-fighting unit. The water tank capacity may be more like 1,000 litres (a bit over 200 gallons).

Table 2: Description of the Fire Truck entity

The business may also want to describe important attributes against each concept (entity). For example, does a Fire Truck record its Registration Number, and is this used by the business as an identifier, or is the identifier the Roof Number that's painted on the cabin roof? Does the business see it as important to capture Fuel Type? And what about ...? So, perhaps the supplementary documentation for a Fire Truck might include attribute specifications like in Table 3.

Attribute Name	Attribute Description
Registration Number	For a vehicle registered for use on public streets, this entry captures the value as displayed on the registration plates attached to the vehicle e.g. "ABC-123".
Roof Number	An optional record of the number painted on the cabin roof e.g. "21". Although often referred to as a "number", it may also contain alphabetic characters to indicate vehicle type (or the home-base area or...) e.g. "AB21".
Litres Water	The maximum capacity of the water tank, expressed in litres. Note that this maybe different to the number of litres actually loaded into the tank at a point in time.
Litres Fuel	The maximum capacity of the fuel tank, expressed in litres. Note that this maybe different to the number of litres actually loaded into the tank at a point in time.
Fuel Efficiency	This attribute is intended to record an indicative number of litres typically consumed when travelling 100 kilometres. WARNING: This attribute may need to be generalised to accommodate different units of measure (e.g. miles-per-gallon), supplemented with a record of the unit-of-measure being used.
Range	A computed / derived value of the expected reasonable maximum distance that can be driven on a full tank of fuel.

Table 3: Description of the Fire Truck's attributes

OK, we've looked at "taxonomies" to discover entities (and perhaps some of their attributes). The next thing we want to look at is how the concepts might relate to each other. We're interested in recording the interrelationships between things. We've been introduced to the concept of a Fire, and also to the concept of a Fire Truck. The business tells us that Fire Trucks are deployed to Fires. We could put that information on a diagram like in Figure 21.

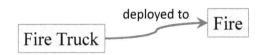

Figure 21: One simple relationship in our Data Town Plan

That's pretty basic, but at least we are starting to build out our Data Town Plan. Relationships can be recorded in diagrams like the one above. It can also be helpful to capture relationships in simple tabular form. This is especially true during workshops where you want to capture business perspectives on the fly rather than taking time to draw them. A simplified example for recording relationships follows (with the first line of data approximating the relationship in Figure 21):

Participant 1	Participant 2	Relationship
Fire Truck	Fire	Deployment
Water Meter	Location	Siting
Project	Employee	Management
Project	Employee	Personnel assignment

Table 4: Sample of basic entity-to-entity relationships

Note that the identification of a relationship needs more than just the nomination of participating entities. There are two distinct relationships between the Project entity and the Employee entity, one identifying the project manager and the other identifying possibly lots of employees assigned to the project as more general resources.

We might want to record more details for each relationship, such as stating if one Fire can have more than one Fire Truck assigned to it at the same time. What appears as one line in Table 4 now has a single relationship defined in two lines in Table 5, one for reading in each direction.

Derived description	Participant 1	Optionality	Verb phrase	Cardinality	Participant 2
Each Fire Truck may be deployed to one Fire	Fire Truck	Optional	be deployed to	One	Fire
Each Fire may have deployed to it many Fire Trucks	Fire	Optional	have deployed to it	Many	Fire Truck

Table 5: Sample of extended entity-to-entity relationships

A little side note: The relationships portrayed in Table 5 are so-called binary relationships because they involve just two entities. For the more technically minded, you can have relationships involving three or more entities. But let's not get bogged down here.

We will want to record many more relationships before we dare call this an enterprise-wide Data Town Plan. We talk to the business, and perhaps look at some business processes to see how things glue together, and before you know it, more and more relationships are discovered.

We end up with lots of diagrams representing different perspectives. Remember I talked about "divergent" views? You might get one set of ideas from the Logistics Officer, another from the Air Desk, and most certainly some down-to-earth feedback from front-line firefighters. As each view is respectfully captured and integrated into an emerging whole, we can call that consolidated view the single "convergent" model.

… and some important elements from that detailed convergent view may be reflected back in where we started, with the Model-on-a-Page view. To replay what was presented earlier for fires, it could look like:

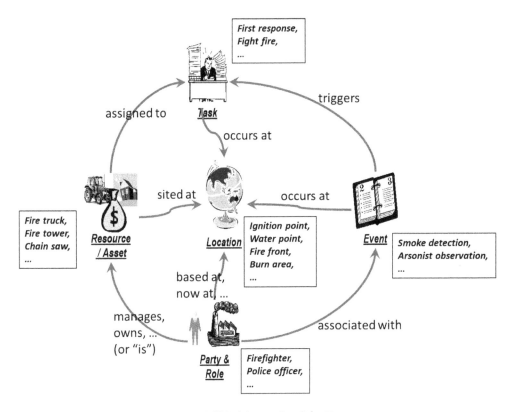

Figure 22: "Model-on-a-Page" for Fires

That's a flying visit to the contents we might expect to see in a fire emergency response Data Town Plan's model.

Some data modelers will react negatively here. They might see the Data Town Plan as a "conceptual" model and argue that such models should not capture attributes. For a Data Town Plan intended to aid communication with the business folk, I recommend capturing the attributes that the *business* thinks are important to *them* and that aid in *their* understanding. I'll take the idea of a Product entity as an example.

If I include a Product entity on the Data Town Plan for an electric vehicle (EV) manufacturing company, what does it represent?

To one audience, each "product" is one item in their catalog. One item might be described as the "Excelsior Model Long Range." Attributes against it might include Recommend Retail Price and the Stock-On-Hand Quantity currently available.

For another audience, each "product" is one physical item that was manufactured. Attributes against it might include Vehicle Identification Number (VIN), Actual Sale Price, and Date Sold.

Inclusion of attributes against the Product entity may help clarify what a "product" really is.

Key points

- A Data Town Plan often provides a vision of where we want to be as far as our organization's data is concerned.

- The first high-level view of a Data Town Plan can be portrayed as a single model-on-a-page.

- The model-on-a-page view can deliver value in its own right, but typically requires drill down into more detail. This can include:

  - Multiple views that represent divergent views from across the business, but most if not all of them expressed (eventually) in common terms.
  - A single converged view representing the amalgamated detail from the multiple divergent views.

- The complete Data Town plan encompasses the model-on-a-page, the multiple divergent views, and the single convergent view. Details include specifications for the core concepts, important attributes for each concept, and relationships between them (such as Suppliers are the source for Products).

PART 2

Getting Comfortable with Building Blocks

If an architect designs a new house, they will leverage proven patterns for doors, windows, bathrooms, kitchens and more. If a town planner designs a new city, they will leverage patterns for hospitals, universities, housing estates and more.

Importantly, these patterns can be understood at a conceptual level for home owners and city residents; the home owners and citizens don't need to understand the engineering details. Equally importantly, the patterns do have the details built in to actually deliver what is designed.

Similarly, there are patterns for "data". They include patterns for how to record details of people and organizations. There are patterns for how work gets done. There are patterns for mapping the locations of important things. And the list goes on. Importantly, the business can have sufficient understanding of these patterns to communicate what they want, and the IT teams can use the "engineering" details in the patterns to deliver technical solutions.

This next part of the book introduces some common building-block patterns in a manner aimed at the business people. The technical people can read the appendix on data model patterns if they want to!

CHAPTER 5

Introducing the Core Building Blocks

We've spoken about Christopher Alexander and his patterns for everything from small items such as doors, to whole buildings such as universities, and town plan patterns for cities and regions.

Patterns are used widely, not just for traditional architects and engineers who are responsible for designing buildings and bridges. For example, I sometimes light-heartedly ask people how many differentials are in a car. (For those unfamiliar with this component, it basically allows power to come into the differential on one drive shaft, and then transfer that power to two shafts coming out of the differential. Importantly, the two drive shafts can potentially turn at different speeds; this feature is needed for a car going around a corner.) Some say cars have one differential—that's the correct answer for most standard two-wheel drive cars. Others suggest a vehicle might have two differentials, which is the correct answer for a part-time four-wheel-drive with a transfer case. And others suggest a permanent four-wheel-drive needs three differentials.

I use this fun question to highlight the reuse of a common design pattern. If you want to build your own farm vehicle, you can grab one or more differentials and bolt them in wherever you want them. Even professional automotive designers can pull the design for a differential off the shelf (and perhaps pull actual differentials off the shelf to try out).

The pattern is proven. It is flexible—for example, you can have options to selectively lock a differential when you're bogged in sand. You get productivity because you don't have to go back to fundamental design thinking to work out how cars can push power to wheels that turn at different speeds on corners—the thinking has already been done for you. You get improved quality because variations have already been tried and tested. And importantly, when talking with automotive engineers, you only have to mention the name of the "differential" pattern, and all the stakeholders are already on the same page.

It goes further. If you have patterns for car differentials, engines, gearboxes, clutches, and more, you can combine them in proven ways. The patterns are valuable on their own. The value multiplies when you use proven patterns in proven combinations.

OK, so patterns can help us build homes and cities, and even cars. But what about building data structures for an organization? Can data model patterns deliver benefits similar to those experienced by using patterns in other applications?

David Hay and Len Silverston have written multiple books on data model patterns. In the foreword to David's first book on data model patterns, Richard Barker states:

> *"… using simpler and more generic models, we will find they stand the test of time better, are cheaper to implement and maintain, and often cater to changes in the business not known about initially."*[7]

Similar encouraging comments come from the object-oriented (OO) community. Their "design patterns" are different from the data model patterns of David Hay or Len Silverston, but the benefits of patterns still ring true:

> *"Strict modeling of the real world leads to a system that reflects today's realities but not necessarily tomorrow's. The abstractions that emerge during design are key to making a design flexible"*[8]

… and one of my favorite quotations on modeling comes from another patterns book, and has a touch of humor:

> *"People often react to a simple model by saying 'Oh yes, that's obvious' and thinking 'So why did it take so long to come up with it?' But simple models are always worth the effort. Not only do they make things easier to build, but more importantly they make them easier to maintain and extend in the future. That's why it's worth replacing software that works with simpler software that also works."*[9]

---

[7] Hay D. (1996) Data Model Patterns: Conventions of Thought.

[8] Gamma E., Helm R., Johnson R. and Vlissides J. (1995) Design Patterns: Elements of reusable Object-Oriented software.

[9] Fowler M. (1997) Analysis Patterns: Reusable object models.

A palette of patterns

I run two opposite risks at this point.

The first risk is that I might lose some technical readers, especially those who are passionate about data modeling and have their roots in physical models (or perhaps logical models) for the implementation of a single piece of software in a tightly focused context such as in an "Agile" project. I will quickly try to put them at ease by saying (1) those more traditional data modeling skills are still hugely valuable, but (2) I've observed a massive shift in emphasis to now embracing data integration that's sourced from multiple places, in addition to modeling for just one area.

The second risk is that I might lose some readers who are business-centric. And, after all, I'm trying to reach them in this book. Some business folk want nothing to do with "data" and might fear that this conversation is starting to become too academic and theoretical. I want them to see that they can have fun being involved rather than being afraid to get involved. Please hang in as I try to also put those business-centric readers at ease.

We'll briefly go back to the home-building analogy. The homeowner probably has some basic understanding of architectural patterns. Most people will understand about windows and doors; some understand the difference between sliding windows, awning windows with hinges at the top and casement windows with hinges on one side.

In a similar way, if we have some basic "patterns" for data, the business can talk about them without worrying about the technical implementation details. Hopefully I can ease the business people into feeling comfortable with effectively communicating their perspective to IT folk, and perhaps even enjoying the journey and the opportunities this approach can open up for them.

House architects have a palette of patterns they draw from (as we've noted already, these can include small items such as windows and doors but there are many more patterns they use). For us, here's a data palette to get you started.

Figure 23: My 9-pillar "Palette" of business concept patterns

Here's a brief introduction to each of the patterns that form my nine pillars of reuse.

Account	You probably know this one already—it covers financial things like debtors and creditors, transactions, and account balances.
Agreement	This can range from formal contracts down to informal hand-shake agreements. It is any type of agreement that the business deems worthy of recording and managing.
Document	Anything from electronic "documents" such as Word documents, spreadsheets, or PowerPoint diagrams to scanned images, photos, or videos from your phone. And yes, good old-fashioned pieces of paper, too.
Event	Something noteworthy that happened. An unwelcome example might be an employee hurting themselves at work, or a more positive example could be an exploration company finding precious minerals needed to make batteries for electric vehicles.
Location	Just think of some item appearing on the map in your smartphone. Perhaps the "line" representing the shortest route to the park you want to visit, a "point" representing a charging station along the way you need for your electric vehicle, and an "area" representing the boundaries of the park.
Party and Role	This can be controversial in some quarters, so for now, think of people or organizations in your address book, some of them playing specific roles (employees, customers, suppliers, etc.).
Product	The goods and services you sell.
Resource (or Asset)	Anything you want to manage as a noteworthy asset, from your laptops through to the multi-million (billion?) ore body noted in the discovery "event" above.
Task	Any noteworthy piece of work to be done, from minor jobs through to massive projects.

Table 6: Description of nine common patterns

Please note that I occasionally referred to "noteworthy" things. We look to the business folk to tell us what is important to them. If going with a colleague for a cup of coffee isn't a noteworthy "event" in their opinion, we don't want to hear about it and unnecessarily clutter the view of core business concepts with an entry named "Coffee Meeting." Conversely, if they've been successful in arranging a coffee with their country's supreme leader, perhaps that's a noteworthy event. Too many initiatives that come under banners such as "Enterprise Data Models" drown in trivia, and hence cost a fortune and take forever to develop, and end up delivering too little value, too late. We need to focus on what's important.

A side issue relates to the implementation of these patterns. The good news is that others have already done the hard work required. This technical detail does exist, and the publications by luminaries such as David Hay[10] and Len Silverston[11] have already addressed this issue. For you, just relax, understand the purpose of each item in the palette, and assemble the business-centric view.

Leave any concerns about how business concepts might be implemented to those who get paid to do technical stuff.

A parting comment on the nine pillars: Is a set of exactly nine patterns the perfect or complete collection? No, it isn't. I have found that these nine have served me well over the years, but others use more patterns, and others use less as their default set, and that's OK.

No man is an island and no pattern lives on its own

Remember how we spoke of car components fitting together? I'm not a motor mechanic, but there are relationships commonly found in most cars. For example, in your car, you might have the engine up front providing the power, then an automatic transmission gearbox, followed by a rear differential, and finally, drive shafts to two rear wheels. Just as there are patterns for the individual components (the engine, the gearbox, and so on), there are patterns for how these things work together. Likewise, cities not only have patterns for each component (universities, hospitals, parks,

---

[10] Hay D. (1996) Data Model Patterns: Conventions of Thought and (2011) Enterprise Model Patterns: Describing the World.

[11] Silverston, L. (2001) The Data Model Resource Book, Volume 1: A Library of Universal Data Models of All Enterprises, (2001) The Data Model Resource Book, Volume 2: A Library of Universal Data Models by Industry Types, and [co-authored with Paul Agnew] (2008) The Data Model Resource Book, Volume 3: Universal Patterns for Data Modeling.

housing estates, sewage treatment plants, and more), but there are patterns for how they do, or don't, fit together. For example, placing the sewage treatment plant in the middle of a housing estate is probably a very bad idea!

The same is true for data model patterns, including those introduced as the nine Pillars. For example, Party is one of the pillars, and Agreement, another. It is quite common to have people participating in an agreement, possibly as signatories. If the agreement is for buying a house, the parties may involve not only those selling and buying the house, but perhaps banks, solicitors, and more. Figure 24 shows a pictorial representation of common relationships between the nine Pillars, including the one we've just mentioned for Parties participating in Agreements. It may appear a bit daunting. Please don't panic—we will untangle all this complexity a little at a time. But what I wanted to do now was to introduce this diagram as a reference point that you can come back to.

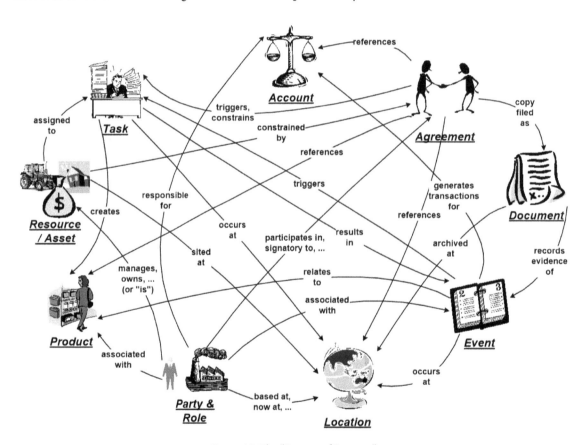

Figure 24: The "Pattern of Patterns"

Preparing handouts for participants

We've just introduced the Palette of Patterns, plus the Pattern of Patterns. Before a workshop begins, I suggest that you print out one copy of each for each participant. As the workshop progresses, they may like to refer to their own copies.

They may also find it helpful to write up their own subtypes on the Palette of Patterns sheet, and add or remove relationships on the Pattern of Patterns sheet.

Data model notation

This document contains a number of data model diagrams. There are quite a number of notations that could have been chosen, but many diagrams in this book use the Unified Modeling Language (UML) notation for Class diagrams. This was chosen rather than a more traditional data model using entity-relationship diagram notation, in part to deliberately create a distance between modeling business concepts and technical implementation, often in a relational database. A sample class diagram follows, with notes on key aspects of the notation.

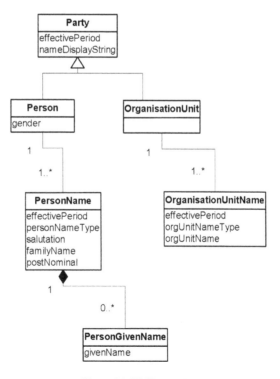

Figure 25: UML notation

- Each rectangle identifies a "class" which represents a collection of similar business objects. For example, the Party class represents the parties of interest (customers, employees, etc.). The class name appears in the first box in the rectangle. Optionally, the second box lists data attributes, and the third lists operations (not included in this model).

- A class at the head of an open arrow (e.g., Party) is a 'superclass'; the classes at the other end are 'subclasses' (e.g., a Person or an Organization Unit). Any aspect of the superclass applies to all subclasses. For example, because a Party has an attribute called "name display string," this attribute applies to both people and organization units. Conversely, aspects of a subclass are unique to them. For example, people have a gender, but organization units don't!

- A diamond indicates containment. In this case, a Person Name, with attributes such as Person Name Type (birth, married, etc.) and family name may "contain" multiple Given Names.

- A simple line between classes indicates an association relationship. Organization Unit Names are associated with Organization Units. The line may optionally be labeled to give it more meaning (not shown in this example).

- The containment and association lines may have multiplicity notation at each end. For example, the relationship between Person and Person Name is to be read that each Person must be linked to one or more Person Names, and that each Person Name must be linked to one and only one Person. Notation descriptions follow:

  o "1" (or blank)—Exactly one
  o "0..1"—Optional (zero or one)
  o "*" or "0..*"—Many (zero or more)
  o "1..*"—At least one, but may be more

Key points

- Patterns are used in all walks of life. For example, patterns for windows in homes and for mechanical devices in cars. There are also patterns for how to structure data.

- Patterns (be they for data, houses, etc.) should be understandable at the concept level, and also physically implementable.

- We can assemble a "palette" of common data model patterns for things like organizations, people, events, locations, products, tasks, and more.

- Just like the patterns for car components (engine, gearbox, differential, etc.) have common ways for joining them together, so do data model patterns (in what I sometimes call a "pattern of patterns").

CHAPTER 6

Resources and their Classification / Composition

Figure 26 shows the Palette of Patterns, with Resource/Asset highlighted as the first pattern we will look at.

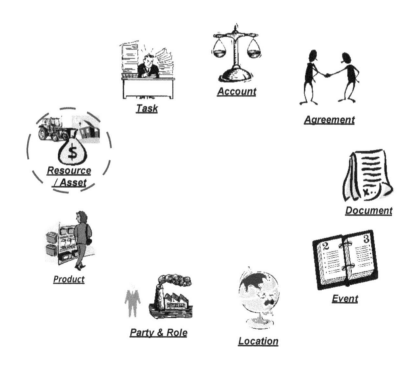

Figure 26: Progress on the patterns - Resource

Introducing the idea of classification

In life, we tend to find it helpful to classify things. Sometimes the classifications are a bit vague. For example, I might say it was a big storm that went through last night, but what on earth do I mean by "big"?

Other times, we use quite precise classifications. A friend buys a new car, and I ask, "What make is it? Ford, Toyota, Audi, Tesla …?"

In between the vague classifications, such as "bigness," and the precise classifications, such as "It's a Tesla," there is the statement by my friend that its color is grey. OK, but is it steel grey, slate grey, charcoal grey, or any one of a long list? My friend also tells me that his new car is a certain model—it's a Tesla Model 3, so perhaps I can pin down options for the grey color (I think their colors at the time included Stealth Grey and Midnight Silver).

In business (the focus of this book), classifying things can also be hugely beneficial. We might sell thousands of products, and each product might be classified in all sorts of ways. We might have thousands of customers, but again we might classify them. If we want to get sales trends for major customers, we better know what is meant by "major."

I've got some good news and some bad news.

First, the bad news. It can be really hard getting agreement between business people from the same department let alone across the enterprise. There can be debates on what a "major" customer is, let alone the more fundamental definition of "customer." You might think the concept of a customer is obvious. Not always so. A simple example springs to mind that might highlight this issue. I had a client that provided care for the elderly. Is a person on a waiting list a customer, or are they not a customer until they are placed in residential care? And what if they progressively are showing signs of dementia and a family member has power-of-attorney to make decisions on their behalf? Is the authorized decision-maker now a customer? Smile if you like, but I've actually been in such conversations.

Now, the first bit of good news. Even if it's hard to pin down definitions, it can be massively valuable to make the effort to get clarity. In the example above, how can you count the number of customers if you can't agree on what on earth a "customer" is?

And the second bit of good news is that this book will help you navigate the minefield of getting business consensus. Another story might help here.

I've already told the story of multiple emergency response agencies working together when we get wildfires, and how one agency called their fire trucks "appliances," while another agency called their big fire trucks "fire tankers" and their small fire trucks "slip-ons" (a four-wheel-drive tray vehicle with a water pump and water tank slipped on), and how I worked on creating a so-called Common Information Model (a data model that reflected common terms). So, what did the agreed classification look like? We'll go into more details later, but for now, it used two simple mechanisms:

- Use of _synonyms_ to capture different words that mean the same thing. For example, one agency's "Appliance" could be seen as a synonym of the other agency's "Fire Tanker." Both agencies can have their preferred terms recorded and respected.

- Use of a _taxonomy_ (a classification hierarchy) that specifies relationships between generalized phrases such as "Fire Truck" and more specialized phrases such as "Slip-on."

Some people may tend to shy away from a term such as "taxonomy," but don't let it frighten you. Earlier, we looked at hierarchies in the animal kingdom (animals subtyped as vertebrates, then further subtyped as birds and mammals)—see 'Figure 17: A subset of an Animal kingdom taxonomy.'

Let's briefly go back to the real-world tension over how to name a Fire Truck, using the taxonomy approach from above, plus a visual but clunky way of recording synonyms.

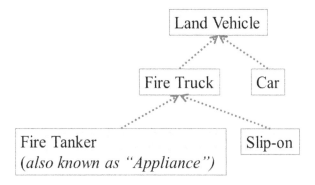

Figure 27: Making peace over Fire Truck naming

In this simple diagram, we can hopefully keep everybody happy. The two agencies that initially disagreed over the term Appliance versus Fire Tanker versus Slip-on can now see "their" important concepts represented. They feel loved and respected. The fact that one agency's Appliance is not just a Fire Truck but is more precisely the same as another agency's Fire Tanker is clearly captured, along with the notion that they are all just Fire Trucks of different shapes and sizes.

You may question if it is worth the effort to seek consensus on what might seem the trivial exercise of finding agreed names for things. Your situation is almost sure to be different from the Fire Truck versus Appliance story, but perhaps you can empathize with the story I've already told of a frustrated CEO who couldn't get a straight answer on how many employees worked for the organization because no one could agree on a definition for "employee." Whether your organization's debates are about precise definitions for employees, customers, products, or whatever, well-understood classifications are almost guaranteed to be important.

Without explicitly calling it out, the previous paragraphs touched on two ways of classifying things:

- Reference data: The example of my friend buying a grey Tesla can kick off this discussion. We can classify vehicles by Make (Ford, Toyota, Audi, Tesla …), Model (such as a Tesla Model 3 or a Model S), or Color (perhaps White, Black, and Grey, then Grey more finely identified as Steel Grey or Stealth Grey). These examples represent what some more technical people might label as reference data. Some people talk about implementing reference data as "type tables"—types of vehicles, types of fuel, types of vehicle bodies, and more.

- Taxonomies: The examples of taxonomies involving duck and platypus entries represent what some more technical people might call supertypes and subtypes in a data model, or superclasses and subclasses (or "inheritance") in a class model.

That's *technical* stuff, and it does have some relevance, but let's focus for now on what's important from a *business* perspective, starting with the supertypes and subtypes as they appear in a so-called taxonomy.

Taxonomies versus reference data

The Logistics Office in a wildfire setting is responsible for a number of types of resources. In a real-life situation, about 200 resource types were identified, but let's assume that, in a conversation, the following subset of resource types were initially identified (listed in alphabetical order):

- Aircraft
- Boat
- Consumable (diesel fuel, fire retardant chemical, etc.)
- Fire tanker
- Firefighter
- Food
- Fire truck
- Fixed-wing plane
- FLIR (Forward-Looking InfraRed) plane
- Fuel
- Generator
- Helicopter
- Rakehoe (a garden rake and a garden hoe combined into one implement sharing a single handle—one way up it's a rake, and then twist the handle 180 degrees and it's a hoe)
- Slip-on unit (the tank-plus-pump resource we discussed)
- Slip-on vehicle (a four-wheel-drive tray vehicle with a "slip-on unit" attached)
- Vehicle
- Water bomber (aircraft specifically equipped to drop water on a fire)
- 4WD (four-wheel-drive) tray vehicle

Remember earlier we looked at a hierarchy of classifications (a "taxonomy") for birds, ducks, mammals, and more? Instead of looking at the taxonomy in Figure 28 for firefighting resources you might like to go through the bullet list above and have a go at creating your own? Or just look at one solution I have put together on the next page.

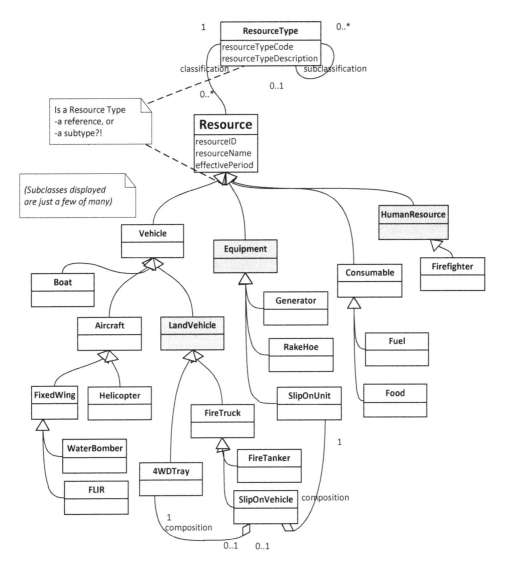

Figure 28: Firefighting resource taxonomy

I'd like to share a few comments on this diagram:

- In earlier examples of taxonomies, I created the diagrams using a simple drawing tool, with an open-headed arrow pointing from the subtype (e.g., Fire Tanker) to the supertype (e.g., Fire Truck). The diagram above diagram was created using a tool intended for more serious modeling that presents a similar idea using a closed arrow. The notation is a bit different (it's a Unified Modeling Language' Class Diagram if you're interested, with further explanation in the 'Data model notation' section of this book), but the idea is similar.

- A supertype called "Resource" has been added to collect all the things together. The remaining white boxes under it match the bullet list above, arranged into a classification hierarchy.

- Three new boxes (shaded) have been added.

  o The Land Vehicle and Equipment boxes were not mentioned in the interviews with business people, but the modeler felt they might be useful. Such suggestions need to be tabled for discussion with the business people, as does the whole diagram.

  o The "Human Resource" addition was controversial and represents a real-world debate. Some Logistics Officers felt that people such as firefighters were just resources to be deployed, the same as fire trucks. After all, people need fuel (food), and trucks need fuel (diesel), too. They both need servicing (rest for people, an oil change and grease for trucks). Folk from the Human Resources department disagreed that there was very little difference between a truck and a person!

Lastly, there is the addition of a Resource Type entry, plus a note questioning whether a sub-classification should be a "reference" entry or a "subtype." What on earth do I mean by this? A full, precise answer gets a bit technical, so let's only lightly look at the topic.

If we started using helium blimps as resources to assist in spotting fires, we might add Blimp as a new entry, perhaps as a subtype of Aircraft. In this case, we might argue that Fixed Wing aircraft, Helicopters, and Blimps, are sufficiently different to get their own classification entries. (From an IT professional's point of view, they might consider this approach if each of these things had different attributes and/or different relationships, or in an Object-Oriented world, they might also have different "methods," but let's leave such technical stuff at arms' length.)

Conversely, let's say that fire trucks came painted in red or green. Would we want to clutter the taxonomy diagram with a box called Red Fire Truck and another called Green Fire Truck? Probably not. Instead, we might simply add an attribute called "Color" to the Fire Truck entry, and when this thing gets implemented, a data entry person can put in Red or Green as the color. And we may have a specification of allowable colors in, for example, a table of allowable colors. That might be called a "reference" table—the focus of a separate section after we've dealt with the basic building block patterns. But let's look quickly at a simple example.

Code	Description
R	Red
G	Green
B	Blue

Table 7: Sample reference data (Color)

For now, let's simply say that we want the business to tell us what types of things are important to them. If they want to suggest that these things are pretty fundamental to the business, we can put them into the diagrams as subtypes (in "taxonomies" if you prefer). If they want to simply suggest that the core concept needs an attribute such as Color, and perhaps document this attribute with examples, that's fine. Some data professionals object when high-level models include attributes, but if the nomination of attributes helps the business to understand and communicate, I am actually quite comfortable with including important attributes.

And what attributes might we consider to be "important"? My cheeky but serious answer is, "Ask the business."

Composite items

Let's have a bit of fun extending the fire truck scenario by looking at resources that are assembled from smaller resources. We'll start by revisiting this idea of a "Slip-On":

Figure 29: Slip-On Vehicle

You might remember that a Slip-On Vehicle was actually made up of:

- a four-wheel-drive tray vehicle, plus
- a Slip-On-Unit attached to its tray.

(Out of interest, the slip-on unit is itself made up of components, including a water tank and a water pump, but we're not going into that level of detail at this point.)

Now here's an interesting twist on the idea that resources can be made up of finer-grained resources. An underground mine I visited had four-wheel-drive passenger vehicles that transported people and small loads down the underground tunnels. To keep the dust down, these tunnels were kept watered. Unfortunately, the soil had a high salt content, and the vehicle bodies rusted out quickly. However, the engines were often driven only relatively small distances and outlasted the bodies.

The mine also had four-wheel-drive passenger vehicles used by people who, for example, inspected the water bores scattered at enormous distances across the countryside. The bodies of these vehicles spent all their time in the dry desert air and probably could have lasted for decades, but their engines took a pounding, traveling vast distances every day, and wore out quickly.

One time, my car broke down on something less than a multilane highway. It was aptly named Bore Track—an access route for mine workers to inspect the bores. Thankfully, a mine worker was out doing his regular inspections, found me, asked me what the heck I was doing in this remote part of outback Australia, and then kindly arranged for my rescue by heading back to town (*many* kilometers away), and returning two hours later with a car trailer. The local police came back with him, too. I think for them it was a highlight of their day to encounter someone who actually thought their dry, flat backyard was worthy of a visit by a tourist! Apparently, my plight became the talk of the quiet little town. (And yes, I did have back-up plans in the event of an emergency, but the help of this mineworker, including generously putting my wife and me up for the night at his place, was hugely appreciated.)

Figure 30: Bore Track rescue

Now, back to the heart of this story. The practice was to take good engines out of the underground vehicles and put them in the good bodies of the surface vehicles. So why am I telling this story?

If we modeled important concepts for this mine, "Vehicle" would be a prime candidate. For all but the motor mechanics, "Engine" and "Vehicle Body" probably wouldn't be worth mentioning. Now, let's take a leap. Let's assume that one use of this Data Town Plan is to shape a Data Vault implementation, with Data Vault "Hubs" based on business concepts. Each Hub needs a business key. For a Vehicle, Registration Number sounds like a good candidate until you realize that vehicles that never leave the mine site aren't registered. The Vehicle Identification Number (VIN) stamped on the body is another candidate, as is the Engine Number, but this apparent solution only works until you realize that bodies and engines are interchanged all over the place. So, one Data Vault solution (and I won't get side-tracked into nuances here) is to identify the Engine as one Hub and the Vehicle Body as another, with the idea of a Vehicle as a derived concept based on time-stamped associations (Links) between an Engine and a Vehicle Body.

That's a long way of saying that, in this case, the motor mechanics might get a win and see their Engine and Vehicle Body represented as core business concepts in the Data Town Plan. And it's just one example I have seen of the need for the Data Town Plan to capture not only a "thing" of the business, but also its associated concepts. Another example from a few years back was for a water utility. The water meter was a real thing, but an attached remote reading device (useful for cases when a vicious dog guards the water meter) had interchangeable associations. A water meter could break and be replaced and attached to the old remote reading device. Likewise, the remote reading device could fail and need to be replaced. These two "things of the business" had relationships coming and going over time.

The Resource pattern

This chapter has been focused on resources (or assets as they may also be named). The reason we started here was to use a very simple data model pattern to introduce the idea of classification, either by a reference data set or by using a taxonomy (subtyping). The idea of a reference data set supplementing a taxonomy of types and subtypes is what forms the core of the Resource pattern (with the subtypes not shown in the core because it is up to each individual organization to determine their specific subtypes).

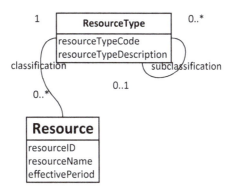

Figure 31: Resource pattern core

<u>Note</u>: The entities (and their attributes and relationships) in this pattern are described in the Appendix on *Data Model Patterns* (as are many entities from the following pattern diagrams).

As will progressively become clear, these patterns do not live in isolation. For example, Resources (and Resource Types) can be assigned to Tasks, where Task is an entity in another pattern. For example, to get some work done, a Task labeled "Initial response to emergency wildfire 1234" might have a generic Resource *Type* of "Water Bomber" assigned, plus a *specific* Resource of "Fire Truck ABC-123."

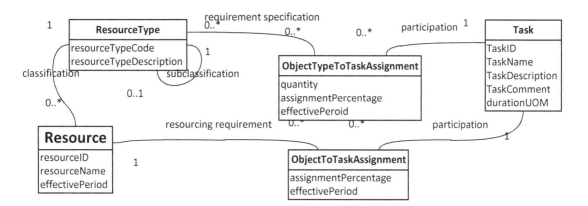

Figure 32: Resource assignment to Task

Again, these additional entities and relationships are described in the appendix on data model patterns.

Key points

- This chapter introduces the idea of "classification."

  - In business, there is real value in classifying things (types of customers, types of products, and so on).
  - Sometimes, getting agreement across the stakeholders can be tricky, but there are mechanisms, such as the use of synonyms and the establishment of classification hierarchies, that can help us represent everyone's views.
  - There are a couple of major technical ways we can express a classification hierarchy (as reference data or as taxonomies), but the business folk don't need to get into the finer points of this technical distinction!

- This chapter also introduces "Resource" as the first data model pattern from the Palette of Patterns.

  - Larger, aggregate physical resources can be assembled from smaller physical resources.
  - Resources, like all of the building block data model patterns, can have relationships with other data model patterns, such as "Task."

Your turn: Resources at a mine site

I've done some work at mine sites. Their investment in machinery is massive. In fact, their machines are massive.

Figure 33: Haul truck and utility vehicle

I remember asking why the passenger vehicles at one particular site had enormous flags on tall poles. The answer relates to driver safety. Apparently, one person had parked his car behind a haul truck, and walked away. Later, the haul truck driver had climbed up the ladder at the front of his cabin, started the truck, and reversed. He felt a small bump and wondered what he'd run over. It was the car. He had completely flattened the car. Oops. After that, flags were fitted to all cars so the flag could be seen even if the car was too "small" to see!

Below is a list of some of the resources associated with a mine. It's not in any particular order, as we might have generated the list from a brainstorming session but not yet collated the responses:

- Haul truck
- Car
- Seaport facility
- Train
- Railway rolling stock
- Pump
- Generator
- Excavator
- Refueling truck
- Single-cab utility vehicle
- Twin-cab utility vehicle
- Dump truck (also known as a Haul Truck)

You are encouraged to assemble the items in the list above as a taxonomy.

- Create a multi-level hierarchy starting with a generic "Resource" supertype. Use any tool you find easy (e.g., a spreadsheet, a modeling tool that accommodates supertypes/subtypes, or a good old pencil and paper).

- Just as was done in production of the sample firefighting resource taxonomy, feel free to introduce new categories that might serve as supertypes for two or more subtypes.

- In the diagram labeled "Making peace over Fire Truck naming," the categories of Fire Tanker and Appliance were considered to be synonyms. Likewise, can you find categories in the above list that could be considered equivalent? If so, pick one as the chosen phrase and label the other(s) as synonyms.

CHAPTER 7

Selective use of Pattern Elegance
(Let's have a Party!)

We've looked at the Resource pattern to gently introduce one of the nine patterns we wish to understand. The pattern itself was relatively simple; the challenge was to gain an understanding of classifying things, either as subtypes (as part of a "taxonomy"), or as reference data.

Now, we will delve into the Party pattern (including Party Role). Again, we refer to the Palette of Patterns to review progress.

Figure 34: Progress on the patterns - Party

It's certainly a richer pattern, presenting a few twists and turns. Some would say this pattern offers massive flexibility. Others might shy away, feeling it introduces unwanted complexity. We will try to demystify the complexity aspect and leave you with an understanding of the pattern's flexibility so that you can listen to the business and adapt the pattern to what the business really wants.

Introducing the idea of a Party

At its most basic, a "Party" is a collective term for individual people and organizations. The simplest way to understand the concept of a Party is to see it as something like the address book on your smartphone or work computer.

In data modeling terms, Party is the supertype, and Person and Organization are subtypes. Using the UML notation, the arrows point from the subtypes (the UML calls them subclasses) of Person and Organization, to the supertype (superclass) of Party. One subtype attribute is noted for Person (gender). It is just an example, demonstrating that the subtype attribute applies to Person only, and not to the subtype Organization nor to the supertype of Party.

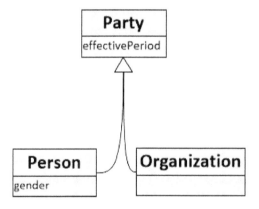

Figure 35: Party and its subtypes (Person, Organization)

A secondary aspect of the Party patterns relates to the multiple roles a party may play. Is this person an employee and/or a customer? Is that organization a supplier or customer? (Note that customers can be individual people or organizations.) Unfortunately, the Party Role pattern is seen by some as being controversial. We'll tackle that head on and hopefully defuse the tension (in part by looking at the perspectives of business people who want to nail down their business concepts as compared to the technical people who have to implement this stuff). For now, let's look at the Party and its address book aspects.

Revisiting naïve simplicity (one family name and address)

Earlier, I shared the confronting story of an inexperienced developer of a school register system whose assumption that all members of a family would share a common name and a single address led to a very serious privacy breach for a women's refuge and extreme risk of danger for the woman and child.

In contrast to this youngster's over simplification of name and address structures, the Party pattern in Figure 35 offers significant flexibility. Let's dive into the pattern's flexibility and then look again at what it could have meant for the school register system.

Name flexibility

The following diagram may look a bit daunting and somewhat technical, but we'll leave those details for the technically minded folk who want to read the Appendix. Relax and think of this as little more than the under-the-cover structures that might sit behind how names are stored in your mobile phone or your company's customer relationship management system.

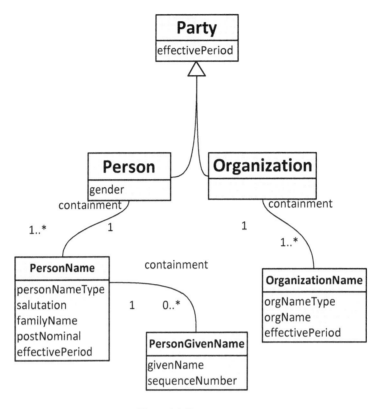

Figure 36: Party names

Using a couple of different technical data structures, each name can have multiple given names (my mother had one, my sister had three). The structure can also optionally record a salutation (e.g., Professor), and a post-nominal entry (e.g., Fellow of the Royal College of Surgeons).

A person can have multiple names, such as a birth name, a married name, and perhaps a pen name (pseudonym) as a writer.

Not all names may be active for the individual's lifetime. For example, a person can have a married name for a number of years, then divorce and cease to use that name. Later perhaps, they may marry again and nominate a new married name. The nomination of the Effective Period is used to record the relevant "from" and "to" dates.

Not only can a person have multiple names of different types, all active at various points in time, they could have multiple names of the same type active at once. A writer may, for example, adopt more than one pen name at the same time, one for each separate genre they use. Or here's a twist. Did you ever see the film *Paint Your Wagon*, where the daughter of a man with multiple wives argued that there should be no problem with her having multiple (concurrent) husbands? This may be illegal in many jurisdictions (and many may suggest polygamy could be ill-advised). But the message is that this flexible pattern would allow multiple concurrent married names to be recorded.

The base pattern offers a lot of flexibility, but if the business desires even more features, the base pattern can be extended. Don't be afraid to ask your technical support folk to expand the pattern. For example, I heard of one culture in northern Africa where the name of a person included the person's career (much like Smith, Baker, or Butcher in an English culture), the names of two generations of patriarchal ancestors (son of X, grandson of Y), the names of all sons and grandsons (again, a male-centric view), whether or not the individual had performed the Hajj (a pilgrimage to Mecca), and more. The base pattern for person names does not cater to this group's requirements, but the pattern could be extended.

Address flexibility

Your address book holds not only names, but also holds information about how to contact these people and organizations using phone numbers (mobile or fixed, or even pager numbers), email addresses, physical and postal addresses, and more. Again, the diagram is somewhat technical, but the message is that it supports flexibility.

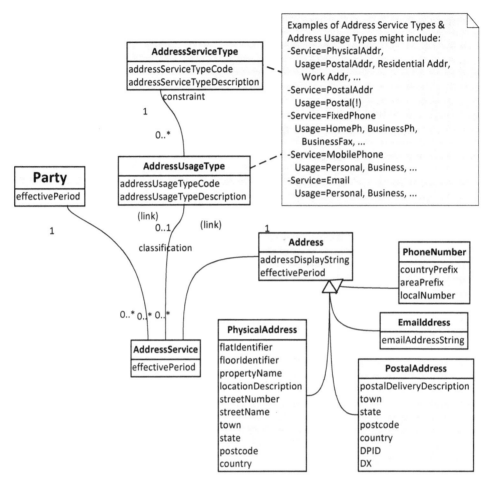

Figure 37: Party addresses

The pattern supports different types of addresses. The ones explicitly presented in this diagram include physical and postal addresses, email addresses, and "phone numbers." Yes, some people really do classify phone numbers as addresses. I personally wonder if the name "Contact" might be better than Address, but I've seen people use the word "contact" to refer to a person rather than their *means* of contact. So I've stuck with Address. But change it if you like. I've also seen pattern variations that include "Electronic Contact." This can embrace email addresses, but also ever-changing variations such as social media contact points.

This pattern also supports one "Address" being used in several ways. A physical street address could, for example, be a home address, a postal address and, increasingly, a work address. Most of the other address types can be nominated for use as a personal contact point as well as, if desired, a business contact point. Postal office boxes are more limited in their use, though I once did nominate my post office box as my residential address because a bank kept on sending mail to my home address rather than the postal address I had supplied. The bank seemed incapable of configuring their records to sort this out, so, in frustration, I changed my residential address to the post office box. The call center operator insisted it was impossible to live in a post box. Still, I held my ground, insisting it also seemed impossible for their software to understand I wanted my mail sent to my postal address. I won, with my records continuing to declare I live inside a tiny post office box. Their problem, not mine!

Now, let's look at a bit of flexibility I have rarely seen used. In this variation of the pattern, the concept of "Address" is treated as a primary business concept, not just some descriptive entries embedded in a person's or organization's details. A few organizations I have consulted with actually treat an address as a thing in its own right rather than as attributes of a person or an organization. One was a water utility, where a whole heap of services "belonged" to an address, whereas the people at an address were treated as being a secondary consideration as they may come and go over time. Another organization was the government department responsible for recording land titles, though this position was challenged. Then, there was the organization that delivers mail to Australians, and they keep central records on addresses, including street addresses, but also other "delivery points" (post office boxes, road-side-delivery points, etc.).

Some things to take away from this story

We return now to the real-life story of the developer over-simplifying the school records for names and addresses:

- The developer assumed that all family members involved in the school shared one "family name" (or "surname" or "last name" if you prefer) and lived at one "family address." A simple dialogue with people who lived and worked with the school data on a day-to-day basis could have exposed the flaws in his assumptions.

- His design was simple, in fact, too simple. By looking at established patterns for name and address data structures the developer should have been prompted to question whether at least some elements from the enormous flexibility offered by proven patterns might be required for the school system.

- A word of caution is due here. Just because the patterns can offer flexibility, they may offer too much flexibility, leading to unnecessary complications. Again, ask the business what they want!

- A word of advice. Whatever position is chosen between over-simplification and over-complication, document the thinking behind your position. This may have multiple benefits:

  o In the future, another person might wonder if the original modeler had considered certain other positions on the simplicity/complexity spectrum. Having the reasons documented can save people from researching an option that has already been considered and rejected.

  o Things change. What might have been a "good" decision at one point in time might well deserve to be challenged later. Seeing the absence of certain considerations may help the conversation.

  o Last but not least (from a selfish point of view) is that the documentation of the thinking at a point in time can offer protection from unwarranted attack! Do yourself a favor and capture the collective thinking at that point in time.

Party interrelationships

We've compared the Party pattern to the underlying data structure behind your address book. At the time of writing this, the address book in my phone handles the names and addresses of people and organizations quite well, as we've talked about already. What it doesn't handle, though, is interrelationships between entries. Here are some examples of relationships I may wish to record:

- I have entries for Chris (Christine, Christopher?), Dan (Daniel, Daniela?), and Sam (Samantha, Samuel?), but I can't record that Chris and Dan are married, or that they are the parents of Sam.

- I have entries for the organizations Acme and Excelsior, but I can't nominate Excelsior as the subsidiary of Acme.

- Nor can I note that Chris is employed by Acme and several other organizations by simply recording a relationship between those separate entries.

Sure, I might be able to make entries on these relationships in some "Notes," but it's not the same. I want to record these relationships in a structured manner so that I can ask to see all the employees of Acme, and all the personal relationships of Chris.

To achieve all of this, I need to be able to formally define types of relationships, and to assign these relationships to involved parties. The following (somewhat technical) snippet from the Party pattern supports this.

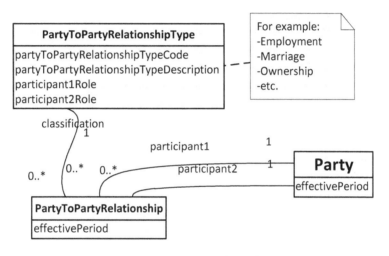

Figure 38: Party interrelationships

When people (and organizations) play many roles

Introducing the Party Role pattern

We've looked at how the foundations for the Party pattern resemble your phone's address book (perhaps extended a little to accommodate the recording of interrelationships between your contact people and organizations). Now, we delve into a more controversial part of the pattern, relating to the fact that one party may play several roles.

One simple example relates to work I did at a water utility. In my part of the world, the supply of clean water to households and businesses (and the task of taking away less-than-clean water) used to be a government service. Someone decided long ago to privatize these services. In theory, it's all about bringing efficiency through competition. What still puzzles me is how there can be competition when all those dwelling in nominated suburbs have no choice about their service provider. Ah, perhaps economists understand the logic. I don't.

What that means, though, is that many *employees* of a given water utility live near the organization that employs them, and hence, they are not only employees but also *customers.* In theory, we could record the details of a given person once as part of the Party pattern (their name, address, contact phone number, etc.) and share these facts with those company records dealing with customer details, *and* those company records dealing with employee details. Hey, if they change their mobile phone number, that is recorded centrally and immediately reflected against their separate customer and employee roles. What a bonus. Well, at least until the human resources (HR) department explained that the company policy was to keep the records separate, especially where a customer may be on a hardship scheme to help with overdue debts, but it would be seen as a breach of privacy to have this knowledge exposed in their employment role. (There may be technical ways to allow selective sharing while also protecting privacy, but that's another story.)

Another similar example comes from my work at a telecommunications company. Many of the companies that are *suppliers* of goods and services are also *customers* because they use phone and Internet services provided by the telecommunications company. One interesting story that came out was of an organization that, as a supplier, successfully sued the company. Later, after settling the amount, it was discovered that the same organization, as a customer, had a large outstanding debt. The telecommunications company wished they had joined the two roles of supplier and customer to one central Party record. Too late!

Here is the pattern for Party Role:

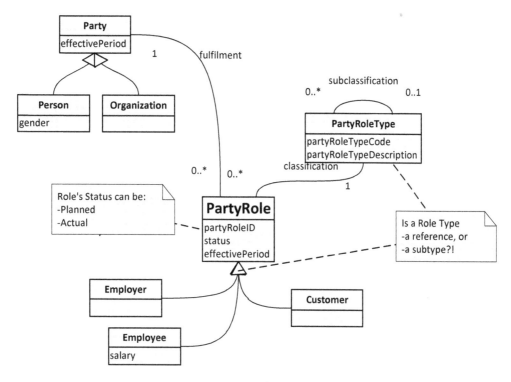

Figure 39: Parties and their Party Roles

Put simply, this pattern says that one Party can play a number of Party Roles, and that each role can be classified either by formal subtyping (as shown in the diagram for Employer, Employee, and Customer), or by using a Party Role Type reference table.

I've spoken about examples for a water utility and a telecommunications company. In Australia (and I certainly hope in other countries, too), we don't let people declare they are doctors and start practicing. There is a central register of health practitioners. The following diagram uses white boxes to portray elements from the standard pattern for Party and Party Role (here simply named as "Role" to reflect that organization's preferred naming). The shaded elements show the subtype hierarchy for some of the roles played by health practitioners and others of interest to the health practitioner regulation agency.

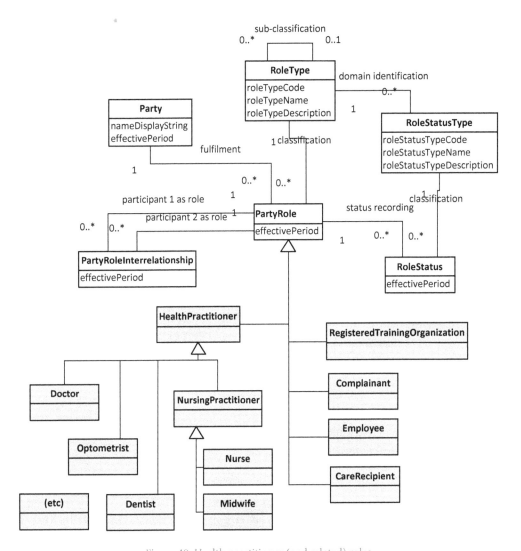

Figure 40: Health practitioner (and related) roles

You may note that the Health Practitioner role is further subtyped, and that one of the subtypes (Nursing Practitioner) is also even further subtyped. Also, the Party Role entity has an attribute for the Effective Period. For example, one individual may have previously been a Nurse, is now a Doctor, and may be in training for yet another related career move. Further, they may be an Employee of the registration organization. They may also be a board member on the Nursing Board (not shown here as a type of Party Role). And a care recipient (doctors get sick, too), and a Complainant who has reported worrying behavior of a colleague.

Now, here's the important message from this organization. In contrast to the water utility where one person who was both a customer and an employee had a mandate from the organization that those records must be kept separate, this health practitioner registration organization mandated the opposite. If a person played multiple roles, they must all be associated with the central "Person" record. As a simple example, if a Nurse had been subject to complaints relating to alcohol-induced impairment in the work setting, and they were now a doctor and similar complaints had been lodged, it was vital to see the whole picture, over time, and across multiple Australian states.

Love or hate the Party Role pattern

I'll make an observation here. I've come across people who love the Party and Party Role pattern, and I've come across those who hate it. There can be a number of reasons for this diversity. I suggest that one of them relates to the physical/technical implementation as compared to how the business sees things. Again, perhaps it's time for a story or two, starting with Figure 41. (Please note that some of the elements in Figure 41 are *not* detailed in the Appendix, as they are presented only for discussion on alternative models.)

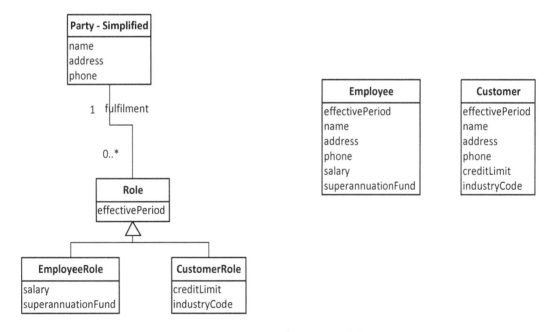

Figure 41: Love or hate Party Role?

I had one client state the business saw Employee and Customer *conceptually* as associated roles of a single Party, but their IT *implementation* had separate systems for each (for example, a Payroll system for employees and a Debtors system for customers). I had another client where the business saw Employee and Customer *conceptually* as discrete concepts with no benefit in sharing Party data, but IT had a single system for recording their details.

Oh dear. No wonder we can get tripped up here. But I am going to suggest a simple way forward.

- Start by realizing that it is common in the real world to find a given Party (person or organization) that plays several roles of interest to the business.

- Work with the business to identify the roles that are important to them. Also include subtypes of these roles, if appropriate—see "Figure 40: Health practitioner (and related) roles."

- Here's the crunch point—ask the <u>business</u> how they want to manage parties that play multiple roles. Does the business want:

  - to have those roles associated with a single, common record for the party, or
  - to have each role related to a separate entity in its own, independent right, or
  - to have a hybrid scenario, with some roles sharing a common party and others as independent entities?

- Suggest that the IT folk take note of the business requirement, and seek to move to align IT implementations with the business perspective.

Declarative and Contextual Party Roles

In Volume three of the series on data model patterns,[12] Len Silverston and Paul Agnew brilliantly articulate an important variation on the topic of parties and the roles they play. They categorize the roles parties can play as either Declarative or Contextual.

- A Declarative Role appears when the organization declares that a particular party is playing a particular role. For example, a person is declared to be an "employee" or an organization is declared to be a "supplier."

---

[12] Silverston, L. and Agnew, P. (2008) The Data Model Resource Book, Volume 3: Universal Patterns for Data Modeling.

- A Contextual Role is the role of a party within a specific business process, event, relationship, etc. The party's involvement within that context provides information about their role. For example, if Chris buys a house from Dan, Chris may be nominated as the "purchaser" and Dan as the "vendor."

Declarative roles tend to be more stable. Someone who is declared to be a nurse may fulfill that role for many years. Conversely, while Chris might be the "purchaser" in one land transfer, they may also briefly be a "vendor" in another land transfer but may never buy nor sell land again for decades, if ever.

Here's an interesting twist: a given type of role may be seen to be declarative in some cases within the organization but contextual in other cases. I consulted with a cemetery. If someone entered into a contract for a pre-paid burial plot, they were declared to be a customer and managed as such. However, if someone bought some flowers from their shop, they were also seen as a customer, but just within the context of that single transaction.

So, how do we manage these two types of roles?

Declarative roles can be handled more formally. We've looked at numerous examples of Customer, Employee, Nurse and more, and I believe we are well equipped to manage them in the ways described above.

Now, we're left with contextual roles. There's a two-part answer to how we manage contextual roles. First, handle the transactions, events, or relationships as they would be managed traditionally, even if we weren't thinking about contextual roles. There's a lot more to come on topics related to events, transactions, and also to business process execution as part of tasks performed. We'll leave those details to later in this book. But the second part of the approach for handling contextual roles is to build on the simple recording of these events, transactions, or whatever. Once the foundational facts are recorded, we can *derive* contextual roles from the base facts. For example, if we have the names and credit card numbers of the people buying flowers at the cemetery's florist shop, we can create a *virtual* view of these customers based on the "context" in which we find them. We don't have to explicitly "declare" them as customers and store the results in some database.

Of course, we need business rules to specify where to find the contextual facts and how to derive roles. But the good news is that you can change the rules. For example, at some point in time you can state that a person buying flowers is now also considered to be a customer just based on their credit card number, even if they don't supply a name. I encountered similar scenarios for "employees" at various client sites. Most agree that salaried staff on the payroll system are employees, but the list of those "employed" by the organization can be extended to include, for example, contractors/consultants such as myself. If our details are recorded in some contract management system, we can relatively easily add these "contextual role" folk to the list of employees from those already "declared" to be employees via the payroll system.

The consolidated pattern

We've looked at various snippets from the Party/Party Role pattern. Figure 42 shows a consolidated model.

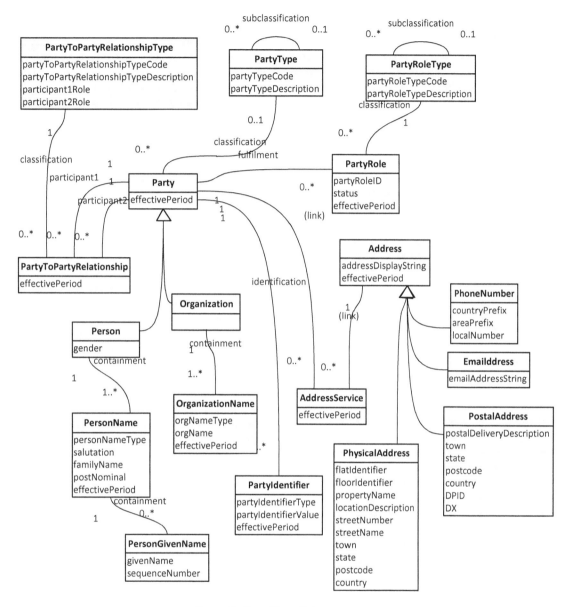

Figure 42: Party/Party Role core pattern

One small bit you haven't seen yet is the Party Identifier. There's not much to it. If a Party entity was implemented as a table in a relational database, it would need one primary key as its (technical) identifier. In this model, the message is that it's not uncommon for the concept of a Party to have multiple identifiers. For a person, this might include their driver's license number (if they have one), perhaps a passport number (again, if they have one), some form of citizen ID if they live in a country with a national identity system, and more.

Base pattern extended for Position

Some simplistic models for reporting hierarchies within organizations depict employees reporting to employees. For example, if Alex is the manager of Brooke, an Employee entity can have a simple self-referencing relationship from the subordinate employee's record to that of their manager.

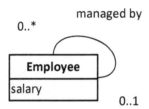

Figure 43: Simplified Position pattern

A widely recognized variation of this model is to explicitly model a Position class.

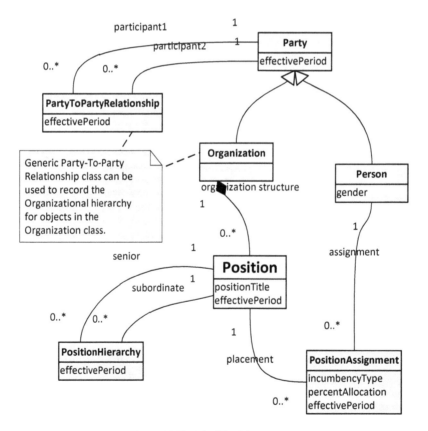

Figure 44: Enriched Position pattern

In this alternative model, Positions are created within an organization, and Positions have a hierarchy. Employees are then assigned to these positions. In this model, rather than a person reporting to their manager (as portrayed in the opening paragraph in this section), a person is assigned to a position that reports to a position to which their manager is assigned!

This may appear to be a bit more abstract and difficult to grasp, but arguably, it has greater flexibility. For example, at a given point in time, a position may be vacant (i.e., it has no employee assigned), while at another point in time, it may have more than one employee assigned (e.g., in job sharing, or for "acting" roles during the absence of the primary person). Similarly, one person may fill multiple positions at the same point in time. Such occurrences would not be able to be easily accommodated by the simpler model.

A couple of comments follow.

Firstly, many of the standard patterns assume positions exist within a formal, relatively static organization structure. In an emergency response scenario (e.g., formation of a crew to respond to a wildfire or flood), such static "day-job" positions, of course, do still exist but are supplemented by emergency response positions within crews. These positions are often structured around practices for incident management, and templates may guide their construction.

Secondly, the common employee/position pattern assumes that people assigned to positions are actually employees. However, it is possible to have people who are not necessarily considered "employees" in the traditional sense, nonetheless assigned to positions. That is why the above model links the person entity to the position assignment rather than a more specific employee entity.

Key points

- A "Party" is a collective term for people and organizations as may be found in an address book (for example, on your mobile phone).

- One Party may play many roles. For example, Dan might be both an employee and a customer of your organization.

- The Party pattern has been developed to handle many different scenarios and has significant richness and flexibility. Perhaps the business doesn't need all that fancy stuff, or perhaps it does but hasn't yet realized it! We can look at the options the pattern offers and selectively embrace those bits that the business indicates are of value to them (now or in the future). And throw away the rest!

- The address book on my mobile phone caters to recording details about parties, but doesn't allow me to easily record inter-relationships such as marriage and employment. The pattern allows for this and may be important to your organization.

- The interrelationship between an employee and their manager may be better handled by a "position" model.

- We need to recognize that there are those who resist the Party/Party Role pattern. Their concerns need to be listened to respectfully. But if their perspective reflects a technology/implementation focus, and the business puts forward a convincing case to embrace certain elements of the pattern, sorry, but the business wins!

Your turn: A pizza delivery Address Book

Outline of requirement(s)

A small pizza shop wants a simple IT solution to record the details of those customers who (1) phone in to place orders they will pick up from the shop, or (2) want delivery to their home or workplace.

Considerations for you

Please mark up the Party/Party Role pattern to highlight the elements of the base pattern to be used, extended, or discarded to meet the stated requirements. In preparing your design, please consider the following:

- Perhaps over time, some people may provide multiple contacts, e.g., a home phone number plus a mobile phone number (or two).

- There may be several people from one address who place orders for delivery. Is such an address to be kept as just descriptive data for each person, or do you think the business may wish to associate and manage all people at one address? If the latter, might this be a breach of privacy?

- How do you suggest that the business handles the scenario where Alex places an order for delivery from a public phone and then comes to the shop to pick up the pizza but pays for it in cash (i.e., there is no credit card to be recorded)? Is such an individual to be recorded as a "customer"?

Please articulate the thinking behind your design decisions.

Your turn: Emergency Response role types

Outline of requirement(s)

The Department of Environment is a government agency that has wide responsibilities, including providing resources for emergency responses (such as wildfires). But they don't act on their own. In an emergency response scenario, many more agencies may be involved, including the Country Volunteer Fire Authority (a wonderful group of country people who volunteer their time to protect others), the State Ambulance Group, the State Police Force, and more.

These other support groups are organizations in their own right, and we want to be able to record details about them, including contact details for the organization, plus a list of people who work for these organizations and who have been nominated for contact in emergencies.

Considerations for you

Please prepare an adaptation of the Party/Party Role pattern. In preparing your design, please consider the following:

- Let's think about various organizations, such as the State Police Force.

- o Is the State Police Force simply an instance of the Organization entity rather than a subtype in its own right? If the State Police Force was a subtype, how many records might appear in the entity? Just one?

- o Even if the subtype has only one instance, might it be important to the business to include it as a subtype to aid communication, even if never implemented that way?

- o As an alternative, might there be merit in introducing a subtype of Organization, named something like Emergency Response Organization that collectively included the police force, the ambulance service, etc.?

- The stable, long-term organizations such as the State Police Force are clearly some form of "organization," as debated above. But what about the organization that exists for the duration of the fire? It is formed from selected organizations and their people. It acts like any other organization while the fire is going (it has a name, one or several contact addresses, etc.). It has staff that look like employees (they report to hierarchies, fill in time sheets, etc.). Eventually, it disbands when it is no longer needed. This pseudo-organization needs to be recorded and managed. Extend the model to accommodate it.

Remember that there is often not just one "right" answer but instead multiple answers with relative merits. Please note the options you considered and describe why you chose your final recommended model.

Your turn: Who is the Customer?

Outline of requirement(s)

We've spoken about "declarative" roles and "contextual" roles. For a telecommunications company, there are all sorts of parties that buy their goods and services. Here are some scenarios to be handled:

- A person enters into a 2-year contract for a mobile phone plan where the purchase of a new phone is included as part of the package deal.

- As a variation of the above, the person paying for the plan is a parent and the adult child is the registered user of the phone.

- A person brings their own mobile phone into the store and signs up for a 12-month plan.

- A person brings their own mobile phone into the store and simply pays cash for a pre-paid SIM card (in the country of purchase, let's assume that they are just a visiting tourist and the country does not require any identification details to be captured and recorded).

- A person comes into the store and pays with a credit card to purchase a protective holder in which they wish to place their mobile phone. They do not provide any personal details.

Considerations for you

Please think about the scenarios above and suggest how you might hold the data. If you think the party is to be "declared" as a customer, show how the Party/Party Role model might be articulated to accommodate the type of customer represented in the scenario. If you think what is really needed is to capture the context as an event, transaction or similar, jot down the sorts of elements you might expect to find in a data model that captures the context.

Your turn: Mix 'n' Match (fun with Resources and Parties)

Outline of requirement(s)

It's understandable that training manuals offer simple case studies so you can learn the basics before being confronted with real-world complexity. But if the training stops there, things can get confusing when you're hit with curly problems.

We've laid the foundations for the relatively straightforward Resource pattern, and then dug a bit deeper into patterns by lifting the lid on the Party pattern with all its variations. Now, I want to invite you to look over my shoulder at a challenge I faced with these two patterns.

We start with the fact that the fire crew is a vital part of emergency response to wildfires. So what's a "fire crew"? Basically, it's a fire truck and a team of firefighters.

If you look at published patterns for Party, its specialization typically involves the Person and Organization (or Organization Unit) pair of subtypes. A common variation is to extend this baseline to include things like "Business Unit" and Family, but believe me, defining a "family" can be tricky. Let's weave in Fire Crew as well and see what we might end up with. (Please note that some of the elements in Figure 45 are *not* detailed in the Appendix as they are presented only for discussion on alternative models.)

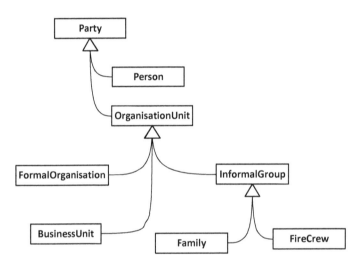

Figure 45: Some extensions to the baseline Party pattern

In this model, a Formal Organization can be, for example, a limited liability company that is registered by a state or national authority. In contrast, a Business Unit can be a department, a division, a section, or whatever classification an organization defines for its internal hierarchies. Then we've got Informal Groups that typically exist outside the more structured elements of a business. A family is one example. And we've added Fire Crew as another group.

But is it "informal"? In some aspects, most definitely. Picture this true story. I'm living in a small town in the country. I'm at the fish and chip shop when the bell at the local fire brigade starts ringing. George had been serving me, but he is also a volunteer firefighter. As soon as the bell rings, he tears off his apron, literally leaps over the counter, runs to the fire station, and minutes later is on the truck as it heads off with whoever are fellow members of the fire crew. All very spontaneous. His wife quietly comes out from the residence behind the shop, picks up a frying basket of assorted foodstuff, asks who had ordered the contents, and takes over running the shop as if this is a normal occurrence. Thank God for these brave and selfless volunteers.

Ah, but let's look at the definition(s) for "Fire Crews." As is common with seeking to assemble an enterprise-wide view, different folk have different definitions. In my state, the virtual organization formed to respond to a wild fire can be made up of up to 17 organizations and their people, so we can expect some divergent opinions.

First, we talk to the business representatives from the volunteer firefighting organization. They define a Fire Crew as a Fire Truck plus its Radio. The Crew Leader is whoever jumps into the driver's seat of the fire truck, and the Crew Members are whoever else piles into the truck before it pulls out! The Fire Crew identifier is the truck's Roof Number. A specific model for their Fire Crew could look something like the following, with the center of the focus on the Fire Truck. [Please note that the elements in Figure 46, Figure 47, and Figure 48 are *not* detailed in Appendix 2 as they are presented only for discussion on alternative models.]

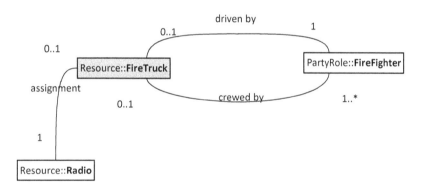

Figure 46: Fire Crew for the volunteer organization

You might notice in this particular diagram that the names of the entities are prefixed by the "pattern" to which they belong. So perhaps a Fire Crew is not a subtype of Party and its Organization, but it's a Resource?

We then interview business representatives from the government organization also responsible for helping fight wildfires. They claim that a Fire Crew is fundamentally a qualified Crew Leader plus their personal Radio. In their emergency response setting, Crew Members and a Fire Truck are then assigned to the Crew Leader. The Fire Crew identifier is the leader's Radio Number. A specific model for their Fire Crew could look something like the following, with the center of the focus on the Crew Leader:

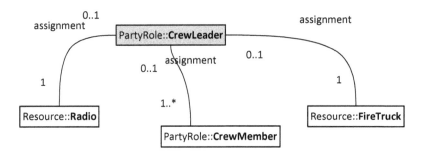

Figure 47: Fire Crew for the government organization

OK, so the focus has shifted from the Resource pattern back to the Party pattern, but this time it's Party Role at the center. Are you getting confused? Welcome to what sometimes happens in the world of resolving differences. But please, don't shy away from differences. If they exist in the real world, they need to be openly and respectfully discussed. Avoiding the issue simply won't make it go away and only adds to what needs to be sorted and resolved later.

So, what was the way forward in this case? We chose to see if we could come up with a mutually agreed upon but slightly more generalized model. Both definitions had Fire Trucks. Both definitions had Radios (albeit one assigned to the truck and one assigned to the Crew Leader), and both definitions had Crew Leaders and Crew Members. One candidate shared model follows.

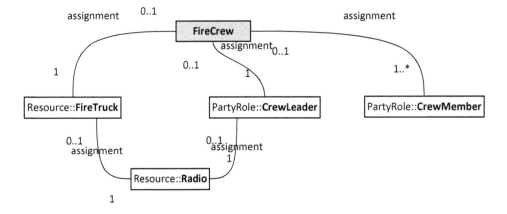

Figure 48: A consolidated Fire Crew model

Note first that the "0..1" multiplicity on the association between a Radio and either a Fire Truck or a Crew Leader means the Radio *can* be assigned to either thing. This little compromise accommodates the two views.

The other thing to note is that the Fire Crew isn't tagged as belonging to either the Resource pattern or the Party pattern. This was initially left open for discussion. At the end of the day, the Logistics Officers said that, as business representatives, they wanted Fire Crews to be seen as a Resource that, along with pumps, generators, and helicopters, could be deployed to a fire. Again and again in this book, you will hear the message that we want to listen to the *business* view. Of course, we can challenge their views, and sometimes a new perspective can help the business see things differently, but if we challenge them, it is always to be done gently and respectfully.

Considerations for you

The above scenario didn't ask you to prepare candidate data model solutions. Instead, it presented a journey from a real-life scenario. What you are asked to do is to comment as follows:

- Comment on the various models as they appeared over time

- If possible, share a similar challenge you have faced and comment on how the lessons from the above scenario may have contributed to either reinforcing the direction you chose, or alternatively how the scenario might have triggered a different response in your setting.

CHAPTER 8

Documents and Agreements

As marked in the solid circles in Figure 49, we've laid the foundations for Resources (also known as Assets), and for Parties and their Party Roles. The pattern for Party and Party Role was arguably important but challenging. Now we can ease back a little and look at the Agreement and Document pair of patterns.

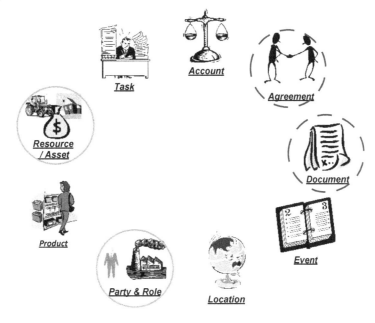

Figure 49: Progress on the patterns—Agreement and Document

Introducing the Document and Agreement pair of patterns

Let's start this chapter with a gentle introduction to a pair of patterns that can sometimes be seen as close cousins. We'll start with the Document pattern.

To kick things off, let's think about the sort of things that might be included as attachments to an email. They might include a Word document, a spreadsheet, or a set of slides for a presentation. Also in this set might be images of documents, such as a PDF generated either directly from a Word document or as a scan of a printed copy. These are examples of traditional "documents."

With the advent of smartphones, we also see photos and videos increasingly appear as attachments to emails. These can also be classified as "documents."

The above are examples of what I will loosely call "electronic" documents. We need to accept that, in some settings, hard-copy documents are also important. For example, a solicitor's office may hold paper copies of signed contracts and land titles going back many years, but they need to be safely retained.

Throughout this book, the default position is that the Data Town Plan identifies things of importance to the business but does not get into the technical details of how an IT solution might be implemented. The Data Town Plan should identify the types of documents deemed to be of importance to the business. Implementation of document management can often be left to commercially available off-the-shelf solutions that might be labeled as Document Management Systems or Content Management Systems. However, some of these focus on electronic document management and do not necessarily facilitate central indexing as to the locations of physical documents.

OK, so it seems Documents are not that hard to understand. What about the Agreement pattern? Again, it is not complex. In essence, an agreement can range from more formal things, such as binding contracts to less formal "handshake" understandings. If I agree to buy your house, that will require an unambiguous and enforceable contract. If we agree to meet for a cup of coffee this afternoon, we probably don't need a formal contract for that! So, how do we decide what "agreements" to include in the Data Town Plan?

You may now guess my answer: talk to the business and find out what things they deem worthy of managing.

If scheduled meetings for chats over coffee are nominated as essential for inclusion, sorry, but they are on the list! Unlikely, but you understand what I am saying.

OK, but why have I paired these two patterns together in one chapter? The answer is that they are often joined at the hip, and sometimes it can be easy to get the two confused.

Let's look at some examples of where they *don't* overlap:

- If an organization has a photo of its head office building, that may well be a Document they deem worthy of recording and managing, but there may be no associated Agreement.

- If the CEO of the same organization has a handshake commitment to join with CEOs of their customers at a friendly game of golf, that may be deemed to be an Agreement worthy of recording even if there's no associated Documentary evidence of the agreement.

Now, the overlap. I return to the contract for the purchase of a house. Perhaps the vendor and purchaser had lots of discussion and bartering and finally reached a mutually acceptable agreement. In some parts of the world, that agreement, even if verbal with a handshake, is legally binding. Still, even so, it can be hard to enforce it if details (or even existence) can't be proven by having documentary evidence. You need the agreement (and that may be recorded first), and you need it documented (possibly days later).

Looking more closely at the Document pattern

This data model pattern represents data constructs typically found in a document/records management system, used to safely store and retrieve important documents. Even though such software is typically purchased as an off-the-shelf software component, this pattern is useful for inclusion in a high-level enterprise model as it represents concepts the business may need, even if its physical implementation is via a purchased solution.

As already noted, the subtypes of Document include electronic documents and physical documents. As shown in the diagram below, electronic documents are, in this pattern, divided into "structured" documents (where computer programs can easily find bits and pieces within them), and "unstructured" documents such as photos from your smartphone (though increasingly clever image recognition software can discern elements even within "unstructured" documents). One could expect that electronic documents could be directly retrieved via document management software, but for physical documents, while a given document's location can be identified, you will need a human being (or robot?) to retrieve the hard copy.

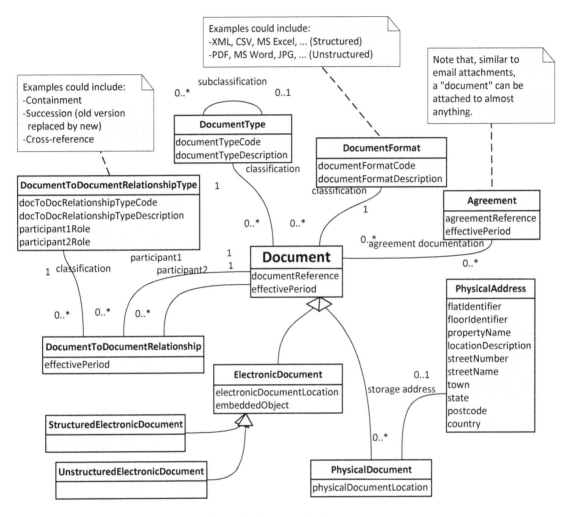

Figure 50: Document pattern core

Document management systems can also manage things such as versioning, represented here by the Document To Document Relationship entity (to identify the old version and its replacement). It also manages other relationships, such as containment of one document within another, and cross-referencing.

You might note that the diagram refers to the Agreement entity. An example of this relationship might be, as discussed, a contract of sale for real estate, where the Document entity provides documentary evidence for the Agreement. This is just one example of how a Document may be associated with the other patterns from the palette of patterns (Party, Resource, etc.). So, how does all of this get used when we're building a Data Town Plan? It's not too hard actually. The business identifies the types of Documents that are important to them and what other things they connect to, and that's the foundation laid. Leave the technical implementation details (including those implied by the pattern above) to others!

Looking more closely at the Agreement pattern

An Agreement (or "contract") represents some formal or informal arrangement, typically involving participating parties. Examples of formal Agreements might include lease contracts for vehicles, or employment contracts. An example of an informal Agreement might be the recording of Dan's willingness to chair tomorrow's design review meeting.

Figure 51 portrays the heart of the Agreement pattern. It's not too complicated, just showing Agreements that are classified either by subtyping (an Employment Contract shown as an example) or using a reference data set. There's also an Agreement Item that might, for example, handle an Order and its Order Items. And then there's our good friend, Document; this association between Agreement and Document was already presented within the previous diagram that was centered on Document. It's just a mirror of the same relationship.

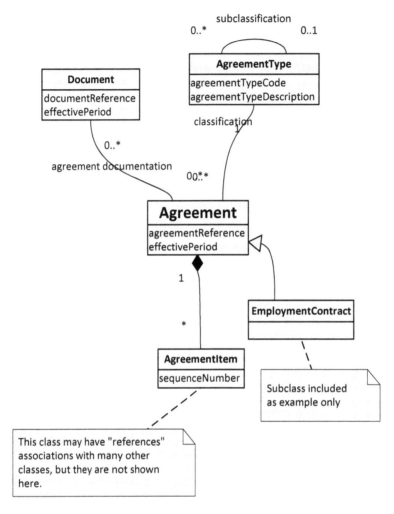

Figure 51: Agreement pattern core

Figure 52 then demonstrates that, just like Documents had interrelationships (e.g., for versioning and cross-referencing), so do Agreements.

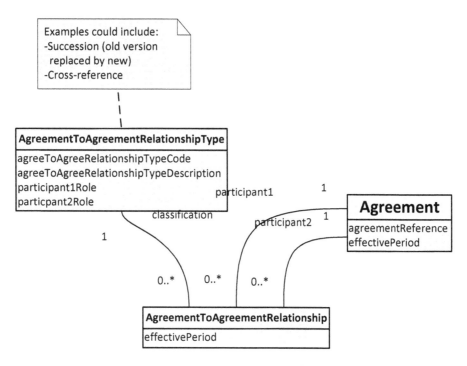

Figure 52: Agreement pattern—interrelationships

Again, the pattern has hints for the implementation team, but for the Data Town Plan, all we need from the business is articulation of the types of Agreements of importance to them and their relationships.

Next, as shown in Figure 53, Agreements typically involve parties. For the scenario involving a real estate contract of sale, this might include the vendor, the purchaser, both their solicitors, perhaps two banks, and, of course, the real estate agent who worked hard for a commission! The example in Figure 53 is a simpler example of an employment contract between the Employer and Employee.

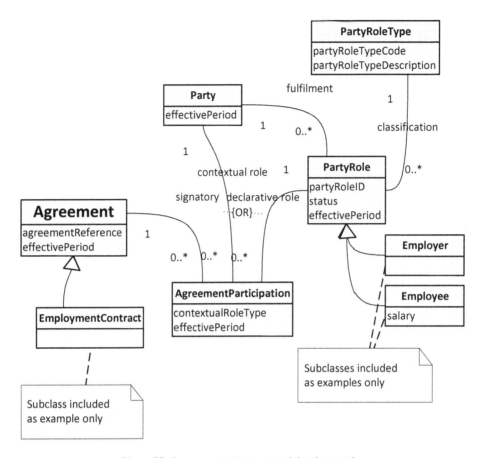

Figure 53: Agreement pattern—participating parties

Key points

- Documents include physical things like printouts and fax copies, and electronic things like Microsoft Word documents, Excel spreadsheets, and PowerPoint slide packs, but also things like smartphone images and videos, PDF forms, emails, SMS texts, and much more.

- Agreements can range from things like informal handshake agreements to massive, formal contracts.

- The "Document" and "Agreement" patterns are often closely related. Where an agreement (such as a formal contract) has documentary evidence of its details, there can be a record in both the Agreement pattern and the Document pattern.

- It is important to note that not all documents, nor all agreements, need to be recorded and managed; just those that the business deems to be noteworthy.

Your turn: Is it a Document, or an Agreement (or both?)

Outline of requirement(s)

We talk to people from the fire emergency response group. They tell us about the following items that they want managed as documents and/or agreements:

- Photos and videos taken by first response teams of suspected arson (e.g., of a person running away from the fire, carrying a jerry can).

- A commitment made over the phone by a logistics officer who agrees that two more fire trucks will be on site tomorrow morning.

- A lease agreement for an Erickson Air-Crane helicopter, signed by Australian authorities and co-signed by the leasing company in America.

Considerations for you

Please articulate whether these items are best considered to be:

- Just a type of Document.

- Just a type of Agreement.

- Better handled as a type of Agreement that has an associated Document.

For the sake of the exercise, hand-write your recommendation as subtypes on a copy of the 9-pillar diagram. You do not need to be concerned if the items might be represented as subtypes or as reference data.

Your turn: Extending the Document pattern

Outline of requirement(s)

A government authority is responsible for filing information related to mineral resource exploration. Some of the records go back many decades or even centuries. Many more recent exploratory results are captured in digital forms, but of course those from the distant past are only in paper form.

The hard copy reports are stored in a massive storage facility. But here's the twist. The facility holds not only paper records of field surveys but also holds physical samples collected, including dirt samples, rocks collected at the site, and core samples taken by drilling at the site.

From a records management perspective, the business wants to capture descriptive details such as what the item is, when it was provided, who provided it, and, especially for physical samples, where it came from (a two-dimensional or even three-dimensional locator). For these purposes, the business sees no difference between a contour map drawn in 1860 and held on a shelf, and a rock sample also collected in 1860 and sitting beside the contour map on the same storage shelf.

Considerations for you

It is not uncommon to find a given pattern offering more richness than the business requires. It is also not uncommon to discover that the business wants more from the pattern than the default baseline offers.

This is a real-life scenario. I also encountered a similar requirement for a government authority responsible for the unpleasant task of researching the cause of death in suspicious circumstances. In the files are more traditional documents (police reports, witness statements, etc.) but also items found at a crime scene. All these items must be carefully tracked.

Please comment on the merits (or otherwise) of treating rock samples (or crime scene evidence) as "documents."

CHAPTER 9

Events that Trigger Actions and Tasks that Manage those Actions

Again, we will look at a pair of patterns, this time Event and Task.

Figure 54: Progress on the patterns—Event and Task

They have a delightful synergy, each relating to the other in a way that enriches both.

Introducing the Event and Task pair of patterns

Let's have a look at a scenario where Event and Task play interrelated roles.

An employee slips on a wet kitchen floor and hurts themselves. That's a noteworthy Event. This Event triggers a series of tasks that are performed, including an evaluation by a doctor. The doctor, unfortunately, diagnoses some serious damage. That conclusion from the "diagnosis" Task is considered to be another noteworthy Event. That new Event triggers another series of Tasks related to setting up compensation for the Employee.

The way the Events and Tasks interacted in the above scenario can be modeled as:

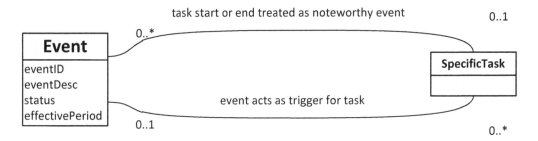

Figure 55: Event and Task synergy

Looking more closely at the Event pattern

The idea behind an Event is "something noteworthy" that happens at a point in time. Perhaps going for a cup of coffee is an event of importance to me, but it is probably not considered to be noteworthy from a corporate perspective. In an emergency response setting for wildfires, the outbreak of a fire is a major event.

When something happens that the business deems to be "noteworthy," a record of that event is created. The essence of the Event pattern appears in Figure 56.

The Event pattern is pretty simple. The business identifies types of Events of importance to them, and they are added to the diagram as subtypes of Event, or alternatively added to a list of reference data for management by the Event Type entity. The pattern also caters for relationships between

Events. The diagram below gives one example, where one Event is an inquiry about a product the organization sells, and there is a subsequent product demonstration Event.

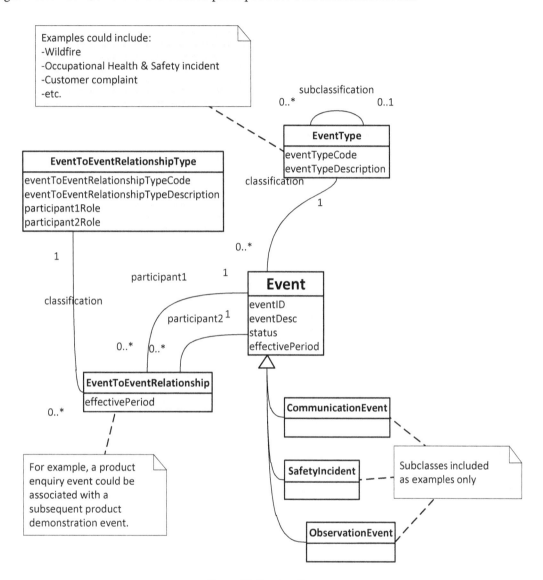

Figure 56: Event pattern core

Looking more closely at the Task pattern

The Tasks pattern is a bit more complicated.

The idea behind a Task is typically some work to be done. A Task can represent a small unit of work. An example might be a simple checklist item ("make sure that someone rings the client back to notify them of a delay," "perform a credit check on the prospect," etc.). A Task can also represent a large and complex unit of work, such as a major project or even an entire program of work comprising multiple projects. Of course, some of these may require specialized attributes. For example, a project may have a budget and a project manager. Nonetheless, they are all represented by a generic Task, which can be extended by appropriate subclassing.

Figure 57 portrays the core of the Task pattern. Those familiar with software like Microsoft Project may see certain features that they are already familiar with.

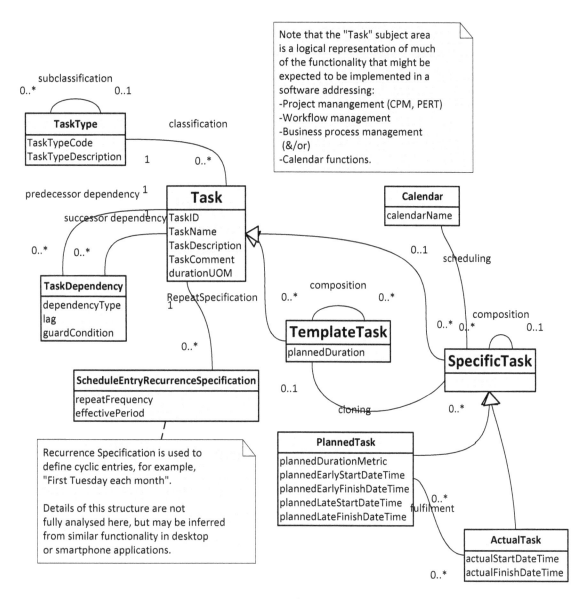

Figure 57: Task pattern core

Each Task has a description and a duration, e.g., "We expect that it will take one week to erect the house frame."

Tasks have dependencies on each other, the most common being a "Finish-to-Start" dependency where, for example, the pouring of a house slab must be finished before starting the erection of the house frame. In this example, there may be a lag of seven days after finishing the slab pour before starting the frame erection. Without getting into details, the dependency may also have a "guard condition" that sets a rule that must be met or else the subsequent Task cannot commence.

The pattern caters for Template Tasks and Specific Tasks. A Template Task represents a standard piece of work, along with its standard subtasks. In the fire management scenario, there may be a standard task for the first response to a fire. That's a template. Template Tasks will have durations reflecting the standard expected time taken to perform the Task.

A Template Task can be picked up, cloned, and turned into a Specific Task with actual dates.

Specific Tasks can also be subtyped into Planned Tasks (something we intended to do) and Actual Tasks (something we have commenced doing and perhaps even finished). In this pattern, one Planned Tasks can be realized as one or several Actual Tasks. Conversely, one Actual Task can be the realization of one or several Planned Tasks. In a simpler variation, both of these subtypes are just a single Task but with planned dates and actual dates as appropriate.

The pattern also has a placeholder to enable the scheduling of recurrent tasks.

Finally, though not shown in Figure 57, there will be relationships to entries under the Resource pattern so that we can record the assignment of resources to Tasks.

An example of Events and Tasks

Let's look at an example of how Events and Tasks might interact, with the Events identified by the <Event> label, and shaded differently. First, we look at the big picture:

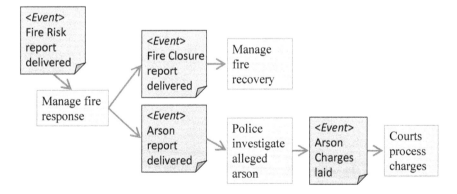

Figure 58: Event and Task example: Macro view core

The background (prior to the Events and Tasks in Figure 58) is as follows:

- Two fire towers spot smoke and record the compass bearings.

- Simple mathematics, based on the position of both towers and their compass bearings to the smoke, quickly identify where the new fire is located.

- Within a very short time, supporting computer systems collate the following information:

  o The land owner at the fire point.
  o Wind speed, wind direction, air temperature, and air humidity based on extrapolation of weather bureau stations.
  o Contour maps (fire typically travels faster uphill than downhill).
  o Access roads, dams, and the like that can be used to fill water tankers.
  o Current location and availability of fire crews and aircraft.

- Using the above, a fire danger is calculated and a Fire Risk report is delivered.

The delivery of this Fire Risk report is the first Event shown in the diagram above. A whole set of tasks (and subtasks) are initiated in the form of a fire management response. In this particular case, the fire is relatively small and a fire crew is close by. Upon arrival, two things happen. The first is that they use their phone to capture a video of a suspected arsonist running to his car, carrying a fuel can. Thankfully, they are able to capture his registration number. The second thing that happens is they squirt a bit of water on the fire and put it out.

Upon return to the office, they file a Fire Closure Report (the report itself is a Document, but the filing of the report is recorded as an Event) that says a picnic table was damaged. The Fire Closure Report Event itself triggers a series of Tasks to manage fire recovery, one subtask being the repair of the picnic table.

They also file a report on suspected arson. This Event triggers a series of Tasks by the police force to investigate the alleged arson, which results in an Event related to the delivery of a charge sheet, which triggers Tasks related to laying charges, which results in an Event where the court finds the person guilty (an Event), which triggers consequences for the arsonist, which …

That is the macro picture. Now, let's look briefly at a more detailed "micro" view of Events and Tasks within the earlier "macro" view.

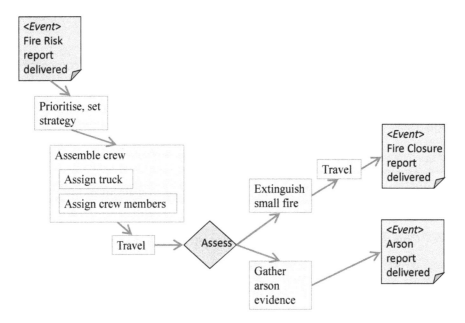

Figure 59: Event and Task example: Micro view core

Let's look at some aspects of the "micro" diagram in Figure 59.

The first thing to note is that the three Events shown are identical to those surrounding the "Manage fire response" single Task from the earlier diagram. The difference is that the single "Manage fire response" Task is now expanded. The Task pattern allows for Tasks-within-Tasks, and all the Tasks shown directly above are effectively sub-tasks of the single bridging Task.

But the Task-within-Task nesting doesn't stop there. The "Assemble crew" Task is itself broken into even more detailed Tasks.

In the Task pattern, the Task Dependency entity has an attribute named "Guard Condition." Its purpose is to capture a conditional business rule used to determine what Task follows next. For example, a business rule might (in long-hand English) be something like "If the fire is small enough for the first-attack crew to simply extinguish it, do so." Another business rule may declare, "When you arrive at the fire ignition point, if it looks suspiciously like the fire was deliberately lit, then gather evidence to help in a subsequent arson investigation."

This example demonstrates the flexibility of the Task pattern and its interaction with Events. It might represent elements of a richer, full-function workflow management system. The goal is not for business people to get into implementation details, but rather to grasp the basic concepts and discuss what types of Events and Tasks are important to them. They can leave the actual implementation to their IT colleagues.

A peek at "how big" Events and Tasks might be

We speak of recording "notable" events. But do they have to be big events?

At one end of the scale, we might decide that every sales order is worthy of being managed. We get (hopefully) lots of orders each day, but for each one, we want to kick off standard workflow actions to make sure every order is processed so that no customers are disappointed.

At the other end of the scale, we might have an industrial accident with loss of life. Such a tragedy should most certainly get attention and be managed. Maybe there is no regular, common "standard" workflow for such an event—who wants to plan for workplace death as if it is something we expect? Nonetheless, we may want to manage large and irregular events using the same Event and Task framework.

Further on the topic of "big" events, some organizations embrace aspects of scenario planning, looking at what might happen and how best to respond if certain major scenarios such as outbreak of war unfold. There are almost certain to be some scenarios which everyone hopes won't be realized, but identification of such Events, and resultant Tasks, may be worthwhile.

Assigning Resources, Parties, and Party Roles to Tasks

We have introduced patterns for tasks. Now we look at what we need to do to assign "resources" to tasks. The following diagram presents a somewhat technical representation, which is then followed by a more business-friendly explanation.

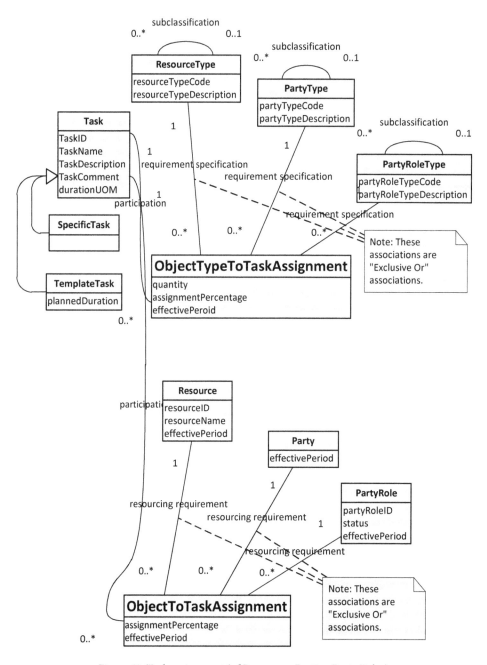

Figure 60: Task assignment (of Resources, Parties, Party Roles)

Those familiar with project management tools such as Microsoft Project will be aware that, in that context, the term "resource" is inclusive of physical resources (such as cars and computers) and human resources. In Figure 60, a subtle distinction is made between the resources represented by the "Resource" entity, what we have modeled as parties, and their party roles. For example, a specific task for firefighting commencing tomorrow at 9:00 am might have assignments that include:

- The fire truck with registration ABC-123 (from the "Resource" entity).

- Acme Catering (an organization i.e. a subtype of "Party").

- Dan in the role of Driver (a party in a "Party Role").

Sometimes a specific task (tomorrow's firefighting task starting at 9:00 am) might have specific *instances* of resources, parties, and party roles assigned, as in the above bullet list of examples. It can also have generic *types* of resources like Party Type and Party Role Type assigned. That is, the assignment of a water pump (from the "Resource Type" entity) without nominating the precise pump.

Figure 60 can cater for the variations described above.

Key points

- Events are things that "happen" and, importantly, that the business considers to be noteworthy. Examples could include small (but important) things like someone slipping on a wet floor and hurting themselves, through to much larger ones, such as the international outbreak of a pandemic.

- Tasks represent work that is to be (or has been) done.

    o Tasks can be small, discrete items such as "Pour the foundations for a garden shed." They can be larger (such as "Build the garden shed") or even larger again such as "Build the entire house," with the construction of the garden shed being just one subtask.
    o Tasks can have dependencies on other tasks. For example, the garden shed must have its concrete foundations poured a week before building the walls.

     o Tasks can be templates that represent typical/standard sets of tasks or actual tasks with specific dates and times recorded.

- The "Event" and "Task" patterns are often closely related. For example, an event such as observing a theft might trigger a response consisting of several related tasks. Completion of one task (arrest and charging the thief) could be recorded as a noteworthy event, and this event could trigger more tasks (a trial in court), with conviction (another event) …

Your turn: Types of Emergency Events

Outline of requirement(s)

Those funding the original fire management IT system were keen for their investment to be able to be used for emergency responses to a wide variety of community situations. We've already looked at the humorous example of protecting the city against the unrealistic attack from feral penguins, but there are several more real-life examples that might spring to mind. Below is a list to consider, not in any particular order, as we might have generated the list from a brainstorming session but not yet collated the responses:

- Landslide
- Flood
- Earthquake
- Cyclone
- Grass fire and Forest fire
- Burst river levee bank
- Outbreak of a pandemic (such as COVID)
- Hurricane
- Tsunami
- Burst dike
- Storm surge (e.g., flooding caused by a hurricane combined with a high tide)
- Livestock pandemic (e.g., outbreak of bird flu in chickens or foot and mouth disease in cattle)

- Volcanic eruption
- Avalanche

Considerations for you

You are encouraged to assemble the items in the list above as a taxonomy.

- Create a multi-level hierarchy. Use any tool you find easy (e.g., a spreadsheet, a modeling tool that accommodates supertypes/subtypes, or a good old pencil and paper).

- Feel free to introduce new categories that might serve as a supertype for two or more subtypes.

- Find categories that could be considered as equivalent. Pick one, and label the other(s) as synonyms.

Further, you are to consider a sample of events that might trigger subsequent tasks and at least provide a name and description for such tasks.

Your turn: Tasks behind building a garden shed

Outline of requirement(s)

Let's imagine you are planning to build a garden shed. While you might ask others to do the actual work, they are looking to you to come up with the schedule of tasks.

Please note that this task is actually part of a larger task for landscaping your backyard.

Also, this "to do" list is to include tasks that will follow the completion of constructing the shed, namely (1) loading the shed's shelves, and (2) scheduling the regular task of cleaning the spouting every 12 months at the start of winter when all the leaves have fallen.

Considerations for you

This exercise is to create instances of tasks. You can use a tool like Microsoft Project or simply hand-draw the plan. Please note the following:

- Each task is to include a name and expected duration.

- The main task is the building of the garden shed, but you are also to include:

  o Subtasks (perhaps foundations, walls, etc.).
  o A "supertask" i.e. the overall landscaping, of which the building of the garden shed is one component (and include at least one more component of the overall landscaping task).

- Show dependencies between tasks (e.g., you can't put the roof on before erecting the walls, and you can't do the walls before doing the subfloor and floor).

- Put a note on the task for cleaning the spout that it is a recurring task.

CHAPTER 10

We Need the Location

The pillar for Location can best be understood by thinking about the mapping application on your smartphone or in your car's navigation system. The technology behind those applications has some complexity, including satellites orbiting the Earth that assist in working out your current location. Thankfully, for the business as it assembles its Data Town Plan, it's easier. We can focus on understanding the potential of mapping software for the business and working out how they want to use it, and then the job is almost done.

Figure 61: Progress on the patterns—Location

Introducing the Location pattern

We've already touched briefly on the story of fire towers spotting smoke. Now, we will dig a little deeper to highlight the role of the Location pattern.

In Figure 62, there's a person in one fire tower who, when they look due east, sees smoke. Another individual in another fire tower sees the same smoke but with a bearing of due north. When you know the location of each fire tower, and each tower's compass bearing for the smoke, you can work out the location of the fire.

Figure 62: Two fire towers spot smoke

Out of interest, the first fire tower pictured was made from two trees bolted together, making a combined height of 100 feet (or 30 meters if you prefer). To get to the cabin at the top, you had to climb straight up, using only steel poles inserted into the trees. Pretty frightening *and* an occupational health and safety hazard! Sadly, this iconic fire tower was destroyed by a fire that threatened my own home in 2020. Pretty ironic for a fire tower to be destroyed by fire?

The management team now wants a tailored map to help them make decisions. Much of this information comes from geospatial "Location" related sources.

They start by looking up our state's land titles system to find out who owns the land at the point of fire ignition. This is important because, in my state, if the government owns the land, then that government agency is responsible for managing the fire. Conversely, a volunteer fire brigade will take primary responsibility if the land is privately owned.

The computer system also contacts our weather measurement and forecasting colleagues to get readings of wind direction, wind speed, air temperature, and air humidity at the nearest weather stations, and estimated measurements at the fire ignition point. Hot, dry air moving fast is what we really don't want for fire suppression. And the wind direction plays into the next location-based piece of information.

Another government system is accessed to get a contour map of the fire location. If the wind at the site blows uphill, fires typically move faster than if the wind blows the fire downhill.

Yet another system provides information on the type of fuel. Is the burn area in grass plains, heavily treed dry forest, wetter fern areas, a farmer's field, or what?

We are far from finished with the need for mapping data. We want to know where the nearest access roads are, where the nearest water points are to refill the fire trucks (in our part of the world, fire response agencies are allowed to come onto private properties and pump from a farmer's dam), and the current location of fire crews and water-bombing aircraft.

Based on all of the above, a fire danger index is calculated and decisions are made.

It's impressive that all of this "Location" information can be assembled in as little as three minutes, accessing IT systems across multiple organizations. At the heart of this ability are some standards for geospatial systems, somewhat reflected in the more technical aspects of the (simplified) Location pattern.

If the fire turns out to be problematic, geospatial information can again play an ongoing role. For example, infrared cameras on aircraft can see through the smoke to map the current fire front. Knowing how fast the fire got there from its previous position, combined with the sort of information considered initially to determine fire risk, other at-risk locations can be identified and alerted.

I tell this story because it is an example of how Location data can provide valuable information, in this setting, possibly saving lives. For the Data Town Plan, I encourage the business representatives to have fun tossing around how they might benefit from easy access to up-to-date mapping data.

Looking more closely at the Location pattern

I left an inspection of the Location pattern until now. I wanted to present a scenario of its use rather than confronting you with the more technical details behind the pattern. See Figure 63.

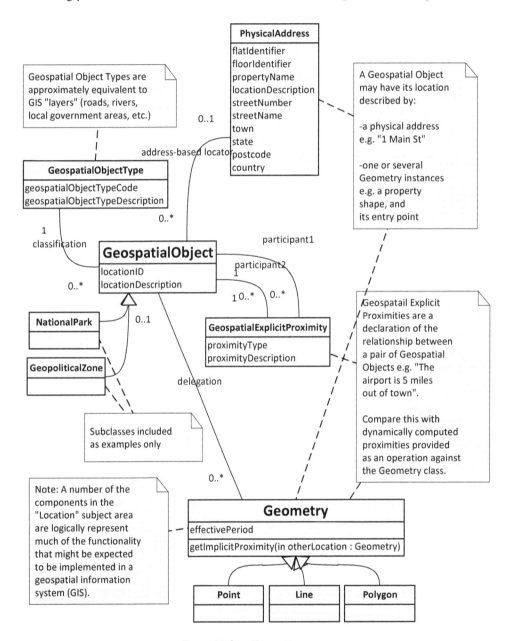

Figure 63: Location pattern core

We won't get too heavily involved in the pattern internals. There are, however, a few things to note:

- For the technically minded, there is a separation between the "shape" element (called the Geometry) and the more business-centered things under the Geospatial Object entity.

- The Geometry entity shows subclasses, namely Point (such as the ignition point for a fire), Line (such as the current fire front), and Polygon, or "area" if you prefer (such as the area burned by the fire). All of these mapping elements are typically assumed to be on the earth's surface. Sometimes the pattern needs to be extended, for example, to cater for:

    o Inclusion of elevation/altitude. For example, a mine may need to record three-dimensional shapes of their open-cut.
    o Extension for the "time" element so that history (and predictions for the future) can be included.

- The Geospatial Object is where the business can focus. Examples are shown of National Parks and Geopolitical Zones (countries, states, shire councils, etc.). Your organization is likely to have its own specialized subtypes of Geopolitical Zone. These are commonly known as "layers" on a map (the road layer, the land ownership layer, the borders layer for towns and states, etc.).

Key points

- Locations are typically described as places on the surface of the earth. Examples could include:

    o The point of ignition of a wildfire.
    o The line that represents the current fire front.
    o An area that represents what has been burned.

Your turn: Wildfires

Outline of requirement(s)

Go through the story in the 'Introducing the Location pattern' section above. Identify elements that *could* be treated as "Location" pattern objects.

Considerations for you

Consider whether the identified objects

- are Geospatial Object subtypes, i.e., they are "location" objects in their own right (such as the ignition point for a fire), or

- are merely descriptors of another, more fundamental object (e.g., a Fire Truck is a Resource that happens to have a location).

Add those items considered to be subtypes of the Geospatial Object entity. For those items considered to be fundamental objects:

- Add them to other parts of the growing Data Town Plan (if not already there).

- Add relationships between the fundamental objects and the Geometry (noting that there may be multiple relationships, e.g., a Fire Event may have a Geometry for its ignition point, fire front, and area burned).

Your turn: Your organization

If you work for an organization (or have done so in the past), consider what "Locations" might be of interest to that organization. (If you haven't yet had that work experience, articulate a hypothetical organization and document its locations of interest.)

CHAPTER 11

Describing the Products the Business Offers

The idea behind a "Product" sounds pretty simple. Isn't it just the stuff the business sells? Well, that's a good start, but there's more. I've participated in all sorts of debates. Do we see the *services* the business offers as "products," as well as the physical *goods*? What about a not-for-profit? They may not "sell" stuff (perhaps they give things away), but are the goods and services they provide to the community also "products"? If an organization sells discrete items as products but also sometimes bundles them up into an attractive package, is the bundle also a "product"? Let's delve into these topics by looking at the next pillar.

Figure 64: Progress on the patterns—Product

Diving into the Product pattern

Products are typically goods or services sold to customers.

Often, people use the word "product" in at least two different ways. One way relates to the items in the product catalog. They might say that the business offers 100 different products, one of which is the Excelsior Platinum Widget. The other way relates to actual instances of products sold. There is only one product description in the catalog for the Excelsior Platinum Widget, but someone might say it's a really good seller—they've sold one million Excelsior Platinum Widgets this year.

Let's be very clear here. They've got one Excelsior Platinum Widget "product" (in the catalog), but they've sold one million Excelsior Platinum Widget "products." We would be better off giving these two versions of "product" a different name. In Figure 65, we call the catalog entry a Product Type and actual instances of things they've sold Product Item. Other data model patterns you might encounter for the product space have different names, and they're OK, too. Pick one that suits the business, as long as the two types of "product" are separately named.

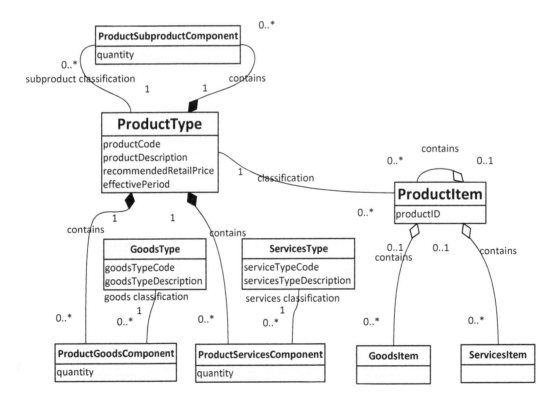

Figure 65: Product pattern core

We won't get too heavily involved in the pattern internals. There are, however, a few important things to note.

First, we've got the topic of tangible goods versus intangible services.

Tangible goods are things we can touch. An example might be a mobile phone.

Intangible services are things we often are willing to pay money for but are less concrete. An example might be a one-year plan for your mobile phone. You can't pick up and weigh the plan, but it is real.

Some models I have seen say that a Product Item is either a Goods Item _or_ a Service Item. The model in Figure 65 is more flexible, saying that a Product Item can be made up of one or more Goods Items (perhaps the mobile phone plus a charger) _together with_ one or more Service Items (perhaps the mobile phone one-year plan plus two hours of "free" education). This same approach also applies to the Product Type catalog entries but with even more flexibility (for example, one Goods Type can be a component in several Product Types). Please don't fret about the technical aspects of the model. Instead, let's focus on the flexibility you can offer the business if they wish to embrace it.

The second aspect of this pattern to note relates to bundling. Whereas a Product Item can be made up of one or more Goods Items and one or more Service Items, a Product Item can also be made up of one or more other Product Items! We just spoke about a Product Item that incorporated a mobile phone, a charger, a one-year plan, and two hours of education. But that Product Item can itself be bundled into another Product Item. Let's say we want a "New Home Starter Pack" Product Item that includes two of the above Product Items plus a Home Entertainment Streaming Service. The model uses the "contains" self-referencing relationship to facilitate bundling, as does the Product Subproduct Component entity associated with the Product Type entity. Again, don't feel daunted by the technical bits that facilitate these features, but just ask the business if they want to do "bundling."

One final topic.

The model in Figure 65 offers flexibility on several fronts but less so on classification and pricing. The Product Type entity has a simple Recommended Retail Price attribute. This may be fine, but greater configurability may be desired for some organizations.

The generic Classification pattern will be discussed shortly. Let's assume you want to buy an electric vehicle. Perhaps you can pick one of several optional body colors and perhaps also select long-range batteries. These are options that can be handled by "Classification." And a relatively simple extension will allow variable pricing on these options.

I've said it before, and will probably say it again, that these technical solutions can be used by IT to guide implementation, but all we need initially is to hear from the business how *they* might desire to embrace the flexibility that technology solutions might enable.

Taking the electric vehicle example, the business might say that each color and battery range option is a totally separate Product Type (Product Code "ACME-Red-LongRange" is one entry in the catalog, Product Code "ACME-Red-StandardRange" is another entry in the catalog, Product Code "ACME-Blue-LongRange" is yet another, and so on).

Or the business might say that there is just an "ACME" Product Type with color and range options (with adjusted prices). As always, present the options that the pattern might facilitate and find out from the business what they want.

Key points

- Products can include physical, tangible goods such as the mobile phone in my hand or intangible services such as an international roaming service that allows me to use my phone anywhere in the world.

- Products can be bundled together to make composite products. For example, I might buy a "New Home Owners" product that includes a TV streaming service plus two mobile phone products for a couple, with each of these products including a phone handset and an international roaming service.

Your turn: Building you own product catalog

Outline of requirement(s)

I have had a love for horses for a long time. Terry, a good friend of mine, didn't understand this attitude. He defines a horse as "An animal that's dangerous at both ends and uncomfortable in the middle." That aside, this exercise is based on a retailer who sells goods and services to those passionate about horses. If the scenario doesn't work for you, perhaps adapt the exercise to a store servicing the needs of dog lovers? (I'm one of those, too.)

The first time I bought a saddle, I was taken aback. I got just a saddle. No girth to hold it on the horse. No saddle cloth to protect the horse. No stirrups for my feet. And even if they had provided stirrups, they didn't include stirrup straps to hang the stirrups from the saddle. It felt a bit like buying a car and being asked if I wanted wheels with it.

The retailer behind this hypothetical story is a bit different. They proactively seek to sensitively meet all your needs rather than leaving you with a useless saddle. They offer free weekend education sessions on a huge array of topics, from nutrition for your horse to care for your saddle and associated equipment. They have affiliations with other service providers, such as veterinarians and farriers. Do you want to learn to ride? That can easily be addressed. Do you want to socialize with other horse lovers? Let me introduce you to like-minded folk. Or are you really starting from ground zero and want to buy a horse and have somewhere to keep it? No problem. They'll facilitate that for you. And, of course, they sell the goods you might need (complete ready-to-go saddles, bridles, horse rugs, food supplements, hay, worming medicine, and so much more).

Your task is to create content for the store's product catalog by populating some spreadsheets (or writing up some tables on scrap paper) with data ready to be loaded into the catalog.

Considerations for you

We will kick-start a few things for you, starting with some sample data in a hypothetical Goods Type table.

Code	Description
WestSad	Western Saddle
JumpSad	Jumping Saddle
Brdl	Bridle
EBSnaffle	Eggbut Snaffle Bit
CurbBit	Curb Bit
Rein	Rein (single) - standard
OatHay	Oaten Hay - small square bale
LucHay	Lucerne Hay - small square bale

Table 8: Sample Goods Type contents

The entries are pretty simple. You may wish to extend this a little for yourself, especially as you get deeper into the exercise.

We've likewise provided some possible entries for a Service Type table.

Code	Description
EduNutr	Education - horse nutrition
EduGroom	Education - horse grooming
EduBrdlFit	Education - fitting a bridle
Vet	Veterinarian
Farr	Farrier
AgntBuy	Horse buying agency
AgntSell	Horse selling agency

Table 9: Sample Service Type contents

Now, the fun begins. The end goal is to provide data for a product catalog for the retailer. Let's look at some candidate data and examine some of its subtle contents.

Product Type

Code	Description	Rec Retail Price
111	Curb Bit	$ 1.23
112	Single standard rein	$ 2.34

(Associated "Component" tables)

Component Type	Component Quantity	Component Code
Goods	1	CurbBit
Goods	1	Rein

113	Pair of standard reins	$ 4.56		Goods	2	Rein
120	Standard show bridle	$ 32.10		Goods	1	Brdl
				Goods	1	CurbBit
				Product	1	113
121	Assisted show bridle	$ 43.21		Product	1	120
				Service	1	EduBrdlFit

Table 10: Sample Product Type (& "component") contents

The left-hand side of the diagram above portrays a simplified form of the Product Type table, which in turn represents core data you might expect in a published catalog.

(Note that the Product pattern has an attribute to manage the Effective Period that a catalog entry is to be considered active. This feature allows old, historic entries to be retained for archive purposes without cluttering the current catalog. It also allows new entries to be loaded ahead of their effective launch date. This attribute is ignored here for the sake of exercise simplicity.)

The right-hand side of Table 10 represents an approximation of three separate "component" tables from the Product pattern:

- Product Goods Component (see rows with "Goods" in the Component Type column).

- Product Services Component (see rows with "Service" in the Component Type column).

- Product Subproduct Component (see rows with "Product" in the Component Type column). This is an interesting feature. It allows a bundled product to be made up of components that include other smaller products.

A horse enthusiast may criticize some of my sample data for being imprecise. Apologies for that. I'm just trying to assist the reader in understanding the Product pattern rather than teaching them the finer points of the equine world. That said, let's look at the sample entries I've provided above as a kick-start for what you may then add.

We start with Product Type 111. It's a curb bit product, and it's got one goods component—a curb bit! That seems a bit redundant, doesn't it? Yes, until you realize that the atomic component can be assembled into all sorts of products, in combinations with other things, and at different prices. Let's move on, and hopefully, this flexibility will become clearer.

People typically buy a pair of reins, one for the left hand and one for the right hand. This requirement is met by Product Type 113 where the Component Quantity is "2" for a pair of individual reins. And Product Type 112 is what the customer buys if they have lost or broken one of the reins and want to replace just one.

Product Type 120 (a Standard show bridle) gets a bit more interesting. It has two "goods" entries, one for a "Brdl" (the code for a Goods Type of "Bridle") plus another for a "CurbBit" (the code for a Goods Type of Curb Bit).

It also has a "product" entry for "113," the code for another Product Type, this time for Product Type of "Pair of standard reins." So we have a bundled product, made up of two goods items, plus this product also contains another product!

Finally, we've got Product Type 121 (an Assisted show bridle), which has a "services" entry for "EduBrdlFit" (the code for a Services Type of "Education - fitting a bridle"). And it also contains another product, the bundled product we just discussed. We can create bundles that include bundles!

Now, here's what I'd like you to tackle, using the shape of the above tables as a template. As a minimum, could you:

- Add a few entries to the Goods Type and Services Type tables based on the stories above about saddles and/or your own creativity.

- Add Product Types with one Goods Item, one Service Type, and multiples of both.

- Add Product Types that include bundling of other more atomic Product Types, including a bundle that includes a bundle!

- Somewhere in the above mix, include an entry with a Component Quantity greater than one.

CHAPTER 12

Accounting for the Money

We're up to the last of the nine Pillars of data model patterns we delve into in this book, though after the Account pattern we will look at one supporting pattern.

Figure 66: Progress on the patterns—Account

This Accounting data model pattern represents data constructs typically found in an accounting package. Even though such software is typically purchased as an off-the-shelf software component, this pattern is useful for inclusion in a high-level enterprise model as it represents concepts the business may need, even if its physical implementation is via a purchased solution.

I don't expect that you will come across too many organizations that don't account for their money. However, I did interact with a colorful character from the fire emergency response setting who might have challenged such a view. His opinion was that he and his colleagues were in the business of saving lives and saving properties, and they didn't care about money. From his perspective, that was somebody else's problem! (I don't believe the business that employed him held the same view!)

The foundational pattern appears in Figure 67.

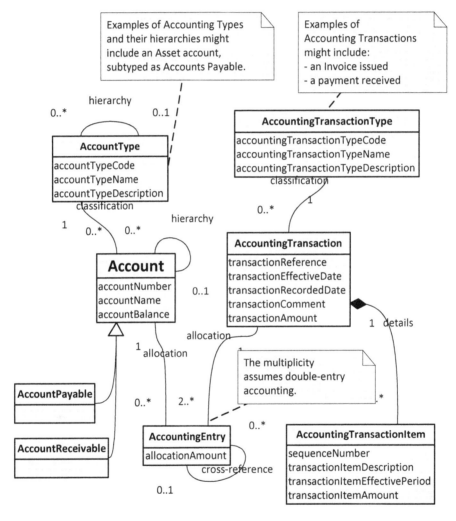

Figure 67: Account pattern core

We are not going to spend much time on this pattern. The foundations for accounting were laid centuries or even millennia ago, including double-entry accounting (as accommodated by the pattern in Figure 67).

Yes, money is important (along with the environment, communities, and more), but those responsible for defining a "chart of accounts" behind the accounting package will already have discussed how to set up their classification hierarchy. We don't have much to do, other than perhaps check the chart of accounts and see how accounts relate to the other pillars. On that last point, an example of how Accounts relate to other patterns is shown for the Party pattern in Figure 68.

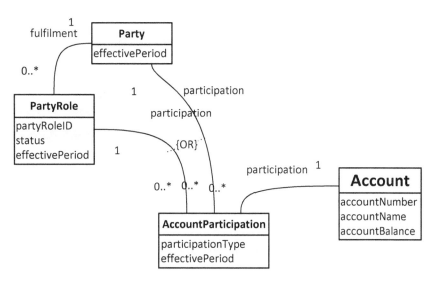

Figure 68: Account-to-Party

One closing comment.

At one client site, we had people from finance referring to accounts. As you might expect, they meant things like assets, liabilities, income, and expenses that you would find in an accounting system as represented by the Account pattern.

Others, from the sales side, also spoke of accounts, but they meant corporations that they sold things to. You might hear them say, "Acme is a big account," or "Excelsior is a new, valuable account." For important sales accounts, they would assign an "account manager."

One of the modelers on the team wanted the details of these corporate sales accounts placed under the Account pattern. After all, it had the right name! The debate was resolved by again looking under the covers of these sales "accounts," only to find company names and addresses, contact people and their emails, and more and more of the stuff that mapped much better to the Party pattern.

The message from this story is simple. While the business people might not care too much about technical details of a given pattern, it can be really helpful to have a broad understanding of the pattern's data model to cross-check where a certain *business* concept belongs.

Key point

- The Account pattern represents the rich features typically found in an accounting software package. While some elements of its (logical) internal workings are presented above, from an enterprise Data Town Plan perspective, we can often leave those to the accountants to sort out!

Your turn

There are no exercises for the Account pattern! We'll leave the establishment of things like a Chart of Accounts to the accountants! Our focus is simply on the underlying pattern.

CHAPTER 13

Classification:
A Supporting Pattern for Reference Data

The so-called "9 pillars" describe some of the more common foundational patterns that reflect core business concepts. Other supplementary patterns may be needed from time to time, and some are quite technical. The Classification pattern is only included here as an understanding of it may help the business reader.

We do go into a bit of detail, but again, the purpose is to equip business people with an understanding of the variety and richness possible.

Introducing the building block

In describing the Resource pattern earlier, we introduced two ways things could be "classified."

Firstly, we spoke about "taxonomies" to more formally (and visually) classify things in a hierarchy of types and subtypes. For example, we looked at types and subtypes of aircraft and fire trucks. Given a suitable modeling tool, it is relatively easy to explicitly identify subtypes in the Data Town Plan. Subtypes are easy to see and easy for the business to understand. One important advantage of this approach is that these subtypes can have their own specialized attributes and associations. We introduced taxonomies early as they were foundational to our subsequent work analyzing business concepts behind each of the remaining core patterns. That's now behind us.

Alternatively, and especially where the subtypes do not need specialized attributes and associations, we can model a "type" entity. For example, we could have an Aircraft Type entity. If this were to be physically implemented as a relational table, we might expect to see rows with descriptions of "Fixed Wing," "Helicopter," and yes, perhaps even "Blimp."

The contents of these "type tables" are commonly known as "reference data." One example of reference data we looked at related to "color." We talked about using this classification set for Tesla cars and fire trucks.

Taxonomies can be nested multiple levels deep. For example, Vehicle can be subtyped as Fire Truck and Fire Trucks subtyped as Tankers and more. Similarly, reference data can be nested. We've just mentioned reference data for color. The simple color of "Grey" could be more finely subdivided. (For the technically minded, this may involve a so-called self-referencing relationship to allow the definition of fine-grained classifications within classifications.)

It is better that a high-level Data Town Plan model is not confused with a physical model. As such, it deliberately avoids prejudging implementation decisions such as taxonomies versus simple reference tables.

But now, let's dig a bit deeper into aspects of reference data to discover flexibility that might be of interest to the business.

Understanding reference data

So here's a story of how money could be lost so very easily. Australia has several trillion dollars invested in superannuation. Yes, that's trillions, not billions or millions. One of Australia's large funds managers paid for advice on share market portfolios. The advisors communicated buy/sell recommendations on a scale that went something like this:

1. Buy the nominated shares at any price
2. Buy if the price is OK
3. Hold the shares
4. Sell if the price is OK
5. Sell at any price

Not too hard to understand? Now, the organization looks at the advice coming in from respected experts in share markets. As you might expect, the advisors had some divergence between their opinions. But some of the advisors seemed to consistently go against the general trend. Why? Because, after some investigation, it turned out that they thought "1" meant *sell* at any price, and "5" meant *buy* at any price—the exact opposite of how those codes were meant to be used. We're talking huge amounts of money here, and the advice received was at complete odds with the message intended, just because the classification had been misunderstood. A *big* oops.

In the buy/sell advice example above, if the data was held in a table in a relational database (or even in a simple spreadsheet), it might look like this:

Code	Description
1	Buy at any price
2	Buy if the price is OK
3	Hold
4	Sell if the price is OK
5	Sell at any price

Table 11: Codes for buy/sell recommendations

Let's look at some vehicles and see if we can extend the discussion on reference data.

Registration Number	Make	Model	Year Of Manufacture	Fuel Type	Body Weight	Body Type
AAA-111	Ford	Ranger	2021	Diesel	2.1	TC
BBB-222	Mitsubishi	Triton	2022	Gas	1.8	SC
CCC-333	Ford	Lightning	2023	EV	3.0	TC

Table 12: Vehicles and their classification

Each vehicle is uniquely identified by its Registration Number. That's easy. In a relational database, the technical people might refer to that as the table's Primary Key, but from a business perspective, it might be enough simply to know how each vehicle is identified. Now, the fun begins.

We have a column called "Make." It might be a simple text string, and for this example set, that might be enough. But even there, what if someone keys in "Mitsubishi" for one vehicle and "Mitsi" for another (did you ever see the advertisement where people exclaim with delight, "It's a Mitsi"?). If there are differences in spelling across the Make column, it might be hard to get a count of vehicles by type (100 Mitsubishis, three Mitsis?), so even in apparently simple cases, a separate set of definitions might be encouraged. The resultant set might look something like:

Make	Manufacturer
Ford	Ford Motor Company
Mitsubishi	Mitsubishi Motors Corporation
Ronart	Ronart Cars

Table 13: Vehicle Make

With this simple reference data set, an IT system that records vehicles and their Make can identify that "Mitsi" is not a valid Make, and enforce standardization. You'll notice the car-maker, Ronart, in the reference data set that doesn't yet have a matching vehicle in the Vehicle table, but we'll come to that.

There's another benefit of having the Make table. Let's look at the Model column in the Vehicle table. Assuming we have a similar reference data set for Model, we can enforce the correct spelling of "Lightning," but can we enforce the rule that you can't have Mitsubishi Lightnings? Yes, and it's simple. In the Model reference data, you include the valid Make column:

Make	Model	Model Notes
Ford	Lightning	Electric pick-up
Ford	Ranger	Live the Ranger life
Mitsubishi	Triton	Nothing frightens a Triton
Ronart	Lightning	British sports car

Table 14: Vehicle Model

And what is used to uniquely identify a Model? It can't be just the Model name, as the same model name "Lightning" can occur in the line-up of other manufacturers (even if you've never heard of the British Ronart Lightning).

Fuel Type is the next topic of interest. In the US, "Gas" is the common abbreviation for gasoline, whereas in Australia, it is the abbreviation for liquefied petroleum gas (LPG), which is typically a mixture of methane and butane. Just to confuse things, gasoline in Australia is called petrol. My Mitsubishi originally ran on gas (petrol) but was then converted to also run on gas (LPG). That's where the agreed reference data set in Table 15 will help define exactly what is meant by vehicle BBB-222 running on "Gas."

Fuel Type	Fuel Description
Diesel	Heavy oil-based fuel ignited by engine compression
LPG	Liquefied Petroleum Gas e.g. butane & methane mix
EV	Electric Vehicle i.e. powered by batteries
Gas	Gasoline

Table 15: Fuel Type

Now, we have come to an interesting role for reference data when used to classify *ranges* of measurements. I am defining that the Body Weight column represents tonnage for the vehicle. *[As a side note, we need to define exactly what we mean by tonnage. Does it represent a "metric ton" (or tonne) of 1,000 kilogram, a "long ton" (or British/imperial ton) of 2,240 pounds, or a "short ton" of 2,000 pounds? For the sake of taking a position, can we please assume it's a metric ton?]* We also need to specify whether, for example, we mean kerb weight (basically the empty vehicle as purchased), gross vehicle mass (maximum total weight with fuel, passengers etc.), tare weight (vehicle plus accessories), payload weight, etc. Again, for the sake of taking a position, I'm using tare weight. With that as a foundation, let's have some fun with measurements.

The business tells us that they want to be able to report the number of Light, Medium, Heavy and Extra-Heavy vehicles in their fleet. They also tell us that they define these classifications as follows:

- Light is up to two ton
- Medium is between two and three ton
- Heavy is between three and five ton
- Extra-Heavy is more than five ton

That's helpful, but imprecise. If a vehicle such as our Ford Lightning (Registration CCC-333) weighs exactly three ton, is it classified as Medium or Heavy according to the above definition? We talk to the business, and nail down the so-called "boundary" rules for ranges, resulting in the following specification:

Weight Code	Weight Desc'n	Range Start Specific'n	Range End Specific'n	Range Description
L	Light	>=0	<2	From zero to less than 2 ton
M	Medium	>=2	<3	From 2 ton to less than 3 ton
H	Heavy	>=3	<=5	From 3 ton to 5 ton inclusive
XH	Extra-Heavy	>5	999	Above 5 ton

Table 16: Vehicle Weight classification

If we look at the specifications, they are precise, but there seems to be some inconsistency. The Medium range is *up to but not including* three ton, and the Heavy range is *up to and including* five ton. We check with the business, and they confirm that's exactly what they want, so all is good.

Now we know what each classification means precisely. If we want to, we can add a Vehicle Weight Classification column to the Vehicle table and let those doing data entry record the results. There are two problems we might note here. The first is that those doing data entry may make mistakes. The second problem is that if the business changes its specification for the meaning behind the ranges, we will have to check and possibly update many vehicles whose weight is the same as before but that now falls into a different range. What a pain.

There's a better way. If we load the Vehicle Weight classification data into a table as reference data on steroids (many reference data sets only have things like codes, names and descriptions but not range specifications), then we can ask the technical people to derive the classifications dynamically. As we add new vehicles, their classification is automatically available, and if we update vehicle weights (for example, from 1.9 ton to 2.1 ton), if the weight falls into a new range, the vehicle is automatically reclassified. It's that easy!

We've already looked at the Vehicle Model reference data set and noted two models for the Ford Motor Company, namely the Ranger and the Lightning. But is the Lightning a base model of Ford, or is it merely a sub-model of the F-150 model? And does the Lightning have sub-models under it? And similar questions can be asked of the Ranger. With apologies to Ford if I have misunderstood this section of the Ford range of models, a subset of their models could look something like Table 17.

Make	Model, Sub-model ...		
Ford			
	F-150		
		Lightning	
			Lightning PRO
			Lightning XLT
			Lightning Lariat
	Ranger		
		Raptor	
		Wildtrak	

Table 17: Some Ford vehicle models

Table 17 is easy to read and understand, but if the nesting of sub-models goes deeper (e.g., sub-models of the Lightning PRO), a new column will need to be added. That's easy while it's a spreadsheet, but the consequences can be more significant if it's a table in some computer system.

An alternative structure appears in Table 18. Each line holds details of one model or sub-model, including the "parent" model. (Note that any entry at the top of the hierarchy does not have a "parent" as it is the ultimate root for its hierarchy.) The advantage of this structure is that you can nest sub-models as deep as you like and the structure doesn't change. The disadvantage is that it may be harder for a human being to read. This so-called "self-referencing" structure is represented in the data model pattern for Classification. It's moving closer to technical implementation and further from a simple business view, but it is just shared here to let your business people know this flexibility exists.

Model Code	Model Name	Parent Model Code
F150	Ford F-150 Truck	
F150L	Ford F-150 Lightning	F150
F150L-PRO	Ford F-150 Lightning PRO	F150L
F150L-XLT	Ford F-150 Lightning XLT	F150L
F150L-LRT	Ford F-150 Lightning Lariat	F150L
FRGR	Ford Ranger utility vehicle	
FRGR-RPT	Ford Ranger Raptor	FRGR
FRGR-WLD	Ford Ranger Wildtrak	FRGR

Table 18: Self-referencing vehicle Model

It is to be noted that the Body Type column could potentially also follow a similar structure, as shown in Table 19.

Body Type Code	Body Type Name	Parent Body Type Code
U	Utility	
TC	Twin-cab utility	U
SC	Single-cab utility	U
P	Passenger	
SED	Sedan	P
SW	Station wagon	P

Table 19: Vehicle Body Type

It's important for the business to be able to classify things of interest, but we've now introduced two ways the business can do this: taxonomies or reference data. Which way do we go?

I came across an interesting example while working with the "risk" people in a major bank. Many people would see Country as being a simple "Code and Description" data set. For this bank, it was an important core business concept, appearing as a subtype in the Location pattern. A surprising number of attributes were used to calculate the risk of lending money in a given country.

As always, inform the business of the options and their relative merits and reflect their preferences in the Data Town Plan. Remember that the technical folk may choose a different physical implementation, but that should be a conscious decision in light of the desires expressed by the business.

Looking more closely at the Classification pattern

The Classification pattern is not one of the nine "pillars," but is important. A view of its core pattern appears in Figure 69.

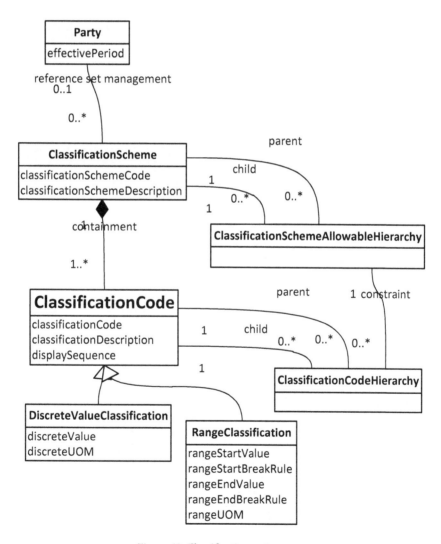

Figure 69: Classification pattern core

The previous section gave examples of simple reference data and hierarchies of reference data, such as Make within Model, Models within Models within Models, etc. Also displayed was the idea that certain reference data sets have numeric ranges, such as a Light vehicle being up to (but not including) two ton. The elegant model in Figure 69 handles all of these variations. (The Classification Scheme Allowable Hierarchy is basically used to define things such as Makes can have Models, but Models can't have Makes.)

If you're interested in the more technical details, please refer to the appropriate Appendix entries.

Associating Classifications with the other pillars

It's really common to associate reference data with all sorts of things. For example, a person might have attributes such as country of birth, first language, gender, hair color (if you're lucky enough to still have hair—an increasing challenge for some of us), and more. Similarly, a fire truck might have attributes of make, model, color (not all fire trucks are red) and so on. Where helpful, there may be dedicated, single purpose sets of reference data for Country, Make, Model, Color, etc. All that's pretty standard stuff.

The Classification pattern not only facilitates greater richness in defining reference data, it can "attach" this richness to any desired pattern. In the diagram below, we reintroduce Party and Resource, this time in association with the Classification pattern. (Note that these are just examples of using the Classification pattern, and the Party Classification and Resource Classification elements are not included in Appendix 2).

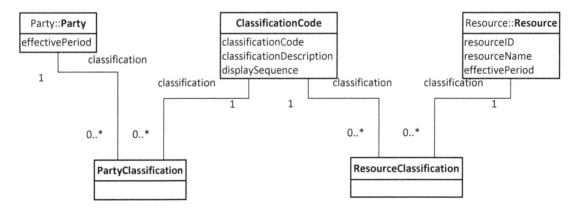

Figure 70: Examples of generic Classification

Now, here's an interesting consideration. When we looked at the Product pattern, we noted potential complexity related to pricing. A product might have a base price, but it can be increased if the customer takes up certain options. I bought a white car, but if I had chosen other colors, the price would have increased (and increased by varying amounts depending on the color I nominated). By combining features of the Classification pattern with the Product pattern, we can move towards more flexible pricing. Some of the pattern books published by authors such as David Hay and Len Silverston take product pricing much further. This book does not attempt to compete with their publications but rather suggests that the business be consulted as to their desire for product price flexibility, and, based on that, the works of Hay and Silverston can be leveraged to contribute to technical solutions for implementation.

Key points

- The idea of "classification" of things was introduced in the chapter on the Resource pattern. Two approaches to classification were described, namely:

  - Classification via a "taxonomy."
  - Classification via management of reference data.

- Taxonomies can be great for visual presentation to the business. They are simple to understand. But they are relatively static. Taxonomies are described in some detail in the chapter on the Resource pattern, but are _not_ elaborated in detail in this chapter.

- The basics of reference data mechanisms were introduced in the chapter on the Resource pattern. In contrast to the relatively static nature of a taxonomy, the use of reference data mechanisms are flexible; once physically implemented, they can be changed by simply entering new values in the reference data sets.

- Further flexibility for the management of reference data via the Classification pattern is described in this chapter.

- The Classification pattern:

o   Manages interrelationships between reference data sets (e.g., Make and Model for a vehicle), and for hierarchies within a data set (e.g., Models within Models).

o   Allows for specification of specific numeric values and for ranges of numeric values (optionally with units-of-measure).

o   Can enrich the specification of entries in other patterns, e.g., pricing options for the Product pattern.

Your turn: Representing reference data

Outline of requirement(s)

Let's assume that we use the Event pattern to capture details about individual sporting events and the Party pattern to capture details about players and their teams. We want to look at some aspects of classifying the events, players, and teams.

For these exercises, you can hand-write samples of reference data (or enter them into spreadsheets or tables in a word processing document). Please feel free to adapt examples from 'Understanding reference data' above.

Considerations for you

There are many types of sporting events, with football, tennis, and basketball being just a few. We are going to start by classifying sporting events in two different ways.

- First, add these three, plus a few more, as direct subtypes of Event. That is, create a more formal taxonomy with types and subtypes written up on a sheet of paper (or in a modeling tool).

- Second, we start again with the sheet of paper (or another model in a modeling tool). As an alternative subtyping of Event, subtype Event into (1) Sporting Event and (2) Occupational Health and Safety Event. Then, add a Sporting Event Type attribute to the Sporting Event subtype. Finally, create a sample data set of reference data for types of sporting events.

Consider these two approaches. Comment on how they both might respond to the addition of a large number of sporting event types.

Sports can be grouped into broad categories, such as Team or Individual sports. Set up a hierarchy of classification using the Team/Individual grouping, followed by another reference set of data listing perhaps a dozen or so sport types, clustered under this grouping. [Hint: Consider the Make/Model hierarchy above.]

Extend the above data set by identifying Sport Types within Sport Types. For example, perhaps have Football as one Sport Type but have some of its variations nested (including possibly having Rugby as a subtype but with further separation into Rugby League and Ruby Union). [Hint: Consider the Model within the Model hierarchy above.]

You will now have a Sport Type reference data set, with the Team/Individual grouping as a supertype. Add another supertype for Indoor and Outdoor sports.

Finally, comment on your observations and preferences for different approaches to classification.

PART 3

Let's Assemble a Data Town Plan!

I estimate that I have developed something like 20 enterprise-level models (Data Town Plans) over the years.

The good news is that this book seeks to consolidate the lessons of experience from those initiatives, hopefully equipping you to successfully do likewise.

The bad news is that, in reality, each of those 20 projects was different. While this book portrays common themes across them all, for each one, I needed to make sensitive adjustments to reflect the business requirements, corporate culture, personalities, availability, and more. Please consider the messages in this book as guidelines, and adapt them as you find prudent or necessary.

Gather your team, use this book as a checklist of possible actions, and launch out. Enjoy the journey, and take pride in delivering value to the business.

CHAPTER 14

Getting the Tooling in Place

Please note that the following is all about structuring and managing the Data Town Plan as a data model. I suggest that it is essential reading for those performing the modeling for the Data Town Plan. However, for business people, it may be of interest but is not essential reading.

Data modeling tools (and repositories versus diagrams)

Before we start the Data Town Plan build, I need to mention data modeling "tools." At its heart, a Data Town Plan *is* a data model, as much as non-technical folk might want to avoid that term. But the good news for the business people is that it is not the highly technical artifact that's used by IT developers to specify, for example, a database design. Juha Korpela, a highly respected voice in the industry, stated that, *"The single most important decision you have to make before you start working on a data model is this: … Are you modeling the business, or are you modeling a solution?"*[13] Thankfully for us, we are focusing on modeling the business, and that means we don't have to get tied in knots with the details that people modeling a "solution" need to consider.

So, if we don't need all of the technical bits of typical data modeling tools, what do we need?

While the Model-on-a-Page can easily be produced by some general-purpose tool for preparing slide presentation packs or for drawing pictures, we need more than that for the serious business of capturing and maintaining the full model that I refer to as a Data Town Plan.

---

[13] Korpela, J. (2024) https://www.linkedin.com/feed/update/urn:li:activity:7180462854427295745/

The completed model will likely have too many bits and pieces to fit usefully on one diagram. We can expect to need multiple bite-sized diagrams, each portraying easy-to-digest aspects of the single underlying model.

> [*A side note with a technical aspect: Many people talk of a diagram as if it is the model itself. For our purposes, I suggest that we want a single underlying repository representing the model, with that central repository supporting multiple diagrams. More on this shortly.*]

A major reason for having a serious tool relates to model maintenance. It's safer to assume that it's not a matter of *if* changes will be made, but rather *when*. The Data Town Plan must be dynamic and able to be easily and inexpensively changed. For example, if you change something you had initially called "Client" into what you now want to refer to as "Customer," you want that change applied directly to the underlying model in the repository, with the changes automatically and immediately apparent on all affected diagrams. Such features save a lot of time in manual, boring, and error-prone application of the same changes again and again on multiple diagrams.

We've just looked at the need to manage *entity* definitions centrally. Similarly, one *relationship* may be displayed on multiple diagrams. Perhaps over time, the description of the relationship, or its optionality and cardinality, may change. As for entities, the relationships must be managed in a single, shared repository, with selected details displayed as required on multiple diagrams. Any change at the repository level must immediately be visible on all diagrams that display the relationship.

Going one step further, it is reasonable to expect that if pre-existing entities are added to a diagram, and if those entities already have pre-existing relationships between them, the tool should prompt the modeler as to whether or not those relationships are to be displayed.

I would argue that you really do need a good modeling tool.

Perhaps you can get by without one as a student, or perhaps resort to good old-fashioned pencil and paper? But even then, I would suggest you think about getting a student copy of a modeling tool and play with it.

Some modeling tools require no installation—you just use them as a software-as-a-service in the cloud. Some are (relatively) cheap, costing a few hundred dollars for a powerful, professional tool that will do everything you want and more. For many organizations, that is petty cash. But other modeling tools cost a _lot_ more. They may have features that the organization values, and if they've already bought a tool that you can use—what a bonus!

This book does not endorse any given product. Instead, please just check that:

- It has a repository for the entities _and_ the definitions for the relationships between those entities. (I strongly suggest you avoid any tool that has a repository for entities but not for relationships.)

- It can support multiple diagrams across the underlying repository.

If it ticks those boxes, you probably won't go too far wrong (other than if you're the very well-known Aussie parliamentarian who didn't know the difference between a "repository" and a "suppository"—now that's dangerous!)

The tool must not only be chosen, but it must be installed and ready to use by the facilitator and the person nominated to carry ongoing responsibilities for management and maintenance of the Data Town Plan.

One final preparation aspect of the data modeling tool relates to the patterns. Ideally, these will be prepopulated in the tool. Some vendors might prepopulate their tool with patterns as a service for their customers. Otherwise, you might need to do this for yourself, but even so, it's worth thinking about doing before the workshop kicks off.

How many models do we have (Model-on-a-Page, Divergent, and Convergent)?

OK, so hopefully we are in agreement that we want a tool with one central repository that will facilitate the display of multiple diagrams, often with diagrams having overlapping content. But how many models do we need for the data Town Plan, and if we actually need multiple models, where do they fit into this tension between the model diagram versus the model repository?

Figure 71 is a copy of a figure shown earlier in this book. David Hay talks of one "conceptual model" that has three types of models within it, namely the Overview model, multiple Semantic model(s) and one Essential model. Some people would suggest that my Data Town Plan is really a broad-brush form of a conceptual model, so the names I am suggesting for a Data Town Plan are shown alongside David's names for elements within a conceptual model.

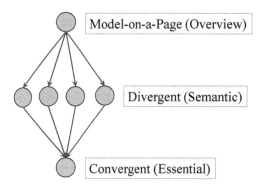

Figure 71: Drill-down for a Data Town Plan

We've already spoken quite a bit about the Model-on-a-Page that provides a single overview.

Then we have multiple Divergent perspectives, each reflecting the views of different parts of the overall enterprise. Perhaps they are subject area-centric (Customer, Product, etc.). Perhaps they come from nominated business units (Finance, Sales, Engineering, etc.). Perhaps they portray the data elements required to support specific business processes. Perhaps they focus on today's pain points or perceptions of tomorrow's needs. Or they might be a happy mix of all of these slices plus more! But importantly, is each diverse view just that—a view—or is it a distinct "model"?

> *[Now, here's a very important point that might be easy to miss. Earlier on, I cautioned on the topic of creating silos based on business units or business processes. Now I'm saying it's OK to slice the job of creating a Data Town Plan by these very same dimensions. Am I being inconsistent? No. The warning is about **starting** to create the enterprise view by analyzing one slice at a time. But once we've got that overarching framework in place, drilling down into specific slices is fine.]*

And then the last of David's three elements of a conceptual model is the Convergent view. We'll get to the details of this shortly, but first let's address the preceding Divergent slices.

To understand where divergent modeling fits in, let's simplify things and say, as an example, that we have only three "divergent" views. Do we have six models: one for the Model-on-a-Page, the four Divergent models, plus one Convergent model that tries desperately to pull the four Divergent views together?

I believe that my good friend, Rob Barnard, might argue that we should aim to see all of these six "models" as views of just one model. That would simplify life and make alignment between the models easier to manage. But how might that look? And is it even possible?

In Figure 72, I've shown just three Divergent "models" as an example for us to discuss. Let's start with the outer dotted-line box. It represents the repository holding definitions for entities and relationships. (A modern repository may also manage definitions for other enterprise architecture artifacts, but our focus here is on the entities and relationships.)

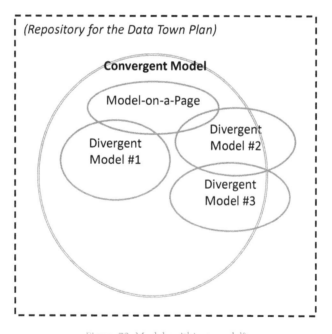

Figure 72: Models within a model?

The Model-on-a-Page

The Model-on-a-Page is relatively simple. It's a single diagram that presents a view of the core business concepts and how they interrelate. An earlier example is shown in Figure 73.

In this example, we have a few model elements. This includes entities such as Customer, Employee, and Work (and its subtypes of Install Meter and Read Meter). It also includes a few relationships, such as Employee performs Work. These appear in the single diagram but are, of course, also stored in the repository.

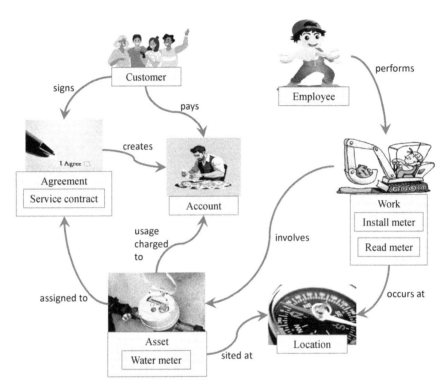

Figure 73: Model-on-a-Page Data Town Plan for a water utility

During the development of the Model-on-a-Page for the water utility, we can expect to also discover lots more entities and relationships. Subtypes of Asset may include not only Water Meters, but probably also Vehicles for company cars and repair trucks, Sewage Treatment Plants, and Laptop Computers. The business may decide that they don't need laptop computers displayed on the summary page, but they don't want to throw away the discovered details. Simple. They load the additional details (extra entities, their descriptions and attributes, and further relationships) into the repository, nominally as part of an emerging Convergent model, but we keep the Model-on-a-Page uncluttered.

The repository holds all this detail; the diagram selectively portrays just those elements that help in communication. Importantly, the extra details in the repository can be used later as we dig deeper into the Divergent models. These details also are vital for the progressive development of the Convergent model.

Ideally, the chosen data modeling tool can not only present "technical" diagrams but can also enhance the technical content with pretty, colored icons for the Model-on-a-Page. In reality, don't be surprised if you have to replicate the more technical display in your tool, but in a way that is aimed at presentation. Duplication? Unfortunately, yes, but the number of elements is small, and manual alignment should not be too onerous.

Divergent models (plural)

As described by David Hay, it is common to develop several Divergent models representing different views from across the enterprise. I often find that a whiteboard is a great modeling tool for initial thinking. In that sense, some understandably see the model on a whiteboard as a totally separate model, having nothing at all to do with the model(s) in the repository.

I actually challenge that thinking on two fronts.

First, the things we draw on the whiteboard will hopefully reflect elements from the Model-on-a-Page and its details, as appropriate. I say "as appropriate" because part of the fun of doing Divergent modeling is discovering things that don't align, disrupt earlier thinking, and show new and interesting ways of seeing old perspectives. It's a two-way interaction. The initial Model-on-a-Page thinking provides an enterprise-wide framework for evaluating new ideas, and we can sometimes use this framework to pin newly discovered details against what already exists. Conversely, the act of doing Divergent modeling typically challenges, refines, and extends the foundations laid during the initial Model-on-a-Page work, and we end up changing what we've previously modeled.

The second point refers to a model at a point in time. When the new Divergent model is only on a whiteboard, of course it is separate from our nice shiny tool and its underlying repository. But after the workshops and much debating, the Divergent model should be carefully aligned with the entries already in the central model, and entered into the tool. It is longer no living a separate life.

How might this work? Let's look again at 'Figure 72: Models within a model?.'

Divergent Model #1 is relatively simple. Some of the elements drawn on the whiteboard already exist in the repository, some of them are already in the scope of the Model-on-a-Page, and some nominally exist as part of a slowly forming Convergent model. For those elements that haven't yet been included in the repository, there was discussion about whether they really belonged to the enterprise view and, hence, the Convergent model. The decision was that they actually enriched the central model and did belong as part of the enterprise-wide view captured in the Data Town Plan. The new details are added to the repository. We can then simply use our modeling tool to re-draw the diagram(s) that were on the whiteboard. You now have a faithful, long-term, and easily maintained record of that first Divergent model. Importantly, its view of the world has been gently incorporated into the ever-growing Data Town Plan.

Divergent Model #2 is a little more challenging. Like the previous example, it had some bits that were already in the repository, and some bits that were deemed to be extensions worthy of being added. However, the consensus was that some other bits of this distinct view of the world were so specialized that they might never belong to the final Convergent model. Figure 72 shows parts of Divergent Model #2 outside of the emerging Convergent model. What this means is that these outliers are still captured in the repository. After all, perhaps one day they might "belong" centrally. But for now, we want to capture them, and include them in their own Divergent diagrams. If your modeling tool has only got one centrally shared repository (and that's what I am assuming), that's where these outliers go, but you might want to explicitly tag them as outliers (even though this fact *should* be derivable from the tool via the fact that these elements only appear in fringe diagrams). Conversely, if your modeling tool tends to store things in sub-containers (Folders, Packages, etc.) that are still within the overall repository but in a distinct area, then perhaps that's where they go. Nonetheless, they will be available for wider use if others want to embrace them later.

Finally, Divergent Model #3 is like its close cousin (#2) but with some sharing of elements between the two Divergent models. The repository only ever records one specification for any element, though it may appear on multiple diagrams.

We could have had separate folders/packages in separate repositories for each of the Divergent models, but that's what we're really trying to avoid. To go that way would require a mapping between them, with the resultant management overheads, where I would argue that if the same "thing" appears in different world-views, define it once and reuse it. After all, the goal is integration at the enterprise level. Let's not lose sight of this!

A single Convergent model

The Convergent model is the heart of the Data Town Plan. It is the end goal. And it most certainly is a single model.

It will have been partially populated during the development of the Model-on-a-Page, and further extended as each Divergent model is merged into the central repository, but all of these models are merely subsets of the final Convergent model.

In summary, the Convergent model is, as David Hay calls it, the "Essential" model. One repository supports several (logical) models, but here's the key message. These "models" are simply diagrams presenting a view over the top of the shared repository.

Structuring the storage of the diagrams

We've now spoken about there being at least one diagram for each "model" (one Model-on-a-Page, multiple Divergent models, and one Convergent model).

Now, we start to multiply the number of diagrams. For example, if one of the Divergent models has lots of content, we might find it unmanageable to represent all its elements in a single diagram. We might slice the "model" into several diagrams. And the "single" Convergent model is most certainly likely to have lots of slices so that the reader can view bite-sized chunks of the whole. These views are not representing independent, inconsistent silos. Instead, they are views of a consistent whole, but created so that each view can be "digested."

We shouldn't be surprised if we end up with dozens of diagrams. And we need to be able to navigate our way around them.

We are all probably familiar with Microsoft's Explorer and Apple's Finder, which allows you to file things in "folders." And, of course, the folders can contain folders that contain folders. That's a really clean structure that allows a hierarchy of containers that helps us manage where we put things.

If we only had a small number of diagrams sitting across the entire Data Town Plan repository, careful naming of each diagram may be sufficient for us to easily find whatever we want. In contrast, one Data Town Plan I developed had lots of Divergent models, and the total number of diagrams was more like 50. That might sound frighteningly large, but each represents a relatively simple slice that makes sense in its own context and is easily digestible.

But we still may need a way to manage filing and finding the diagrams by putting them into "folders," with as many subfolders as is helpful. Let's look at a sample hierarchy that can be simplified or extended to suit your needs.

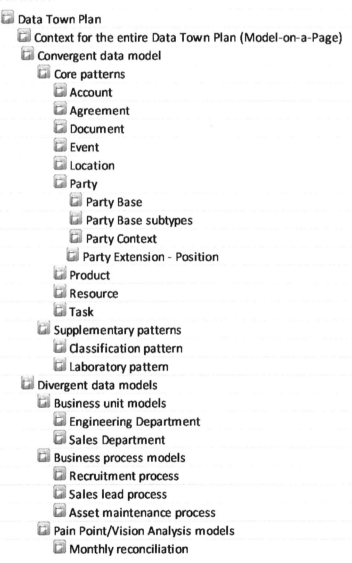

Table 20: Sample folder hierarchy

<u>Data Town Plan</u>: This folder is the overarching container for the entire Data Town Plan. It has many subfolders. Collectively they hold the diagrams and their supporting specifications of the underlying entities, attributes, and relationships. The major subfolders represent the Model-on-a-Page, the final Convergent model, and the multiple Divergent models that are assembled along the way. The Data Town Plan folder can be seen as the "master" folder.

<u>Context for the entire Data Town Plan (Model-on-a-Page)</u>: This folder typically holds just one diagram—the Model-on-a-Page. It presents a very high-level perspective of the entire Data Town Plan. A somewhat stylized example is 'Figure 1: Model-on-a-Page Data Town Plan for a water utility' and is duplicated earlier in this chapter for your convenience. The version you produce using a data modelling tool will probably be a little more technical and precise. For example, it may include optionality/cardinality specifications on the relationships. But it nonetheless should have the same content as the stylized version as exemplified in Figure 1.

<u>Convergent data model</u>: This folder is the largest. It holds all of the diagrams in the consolidated "Convergent" model. It is typically so large that it needs subfolders like these:

<u>Core patterns</u>: This is another large folder. It collectively groups together data subject areas based on common data model patterns (Account, Agreement, Document, Event, Location, Party and Party Role, Product, Resource, and Task), with each of these data subject areas having its own subfolder. Table 20 above shows all nine of these common patterns, with only one of them (the Party pattern) expanded to avoid unnecessary clutter in this book. The Party pattern was selected for expansion as it is often one of the more complex subject areas. The other eight of the "pillar" patterns have not been expanded but in practice would be.

<u>Party</u> (and Party Role): As is common for all the pattern-based "pillars", this folder often has sufficient complexity as to require subfolders such as those described below:

One folder for the "<u>Base</u>" pattern, reflecting the original pattern, modified as appropriate. Note that each of these patterns can be pre-populated with entities, attributes, and relationships, then refined/reduced/extended as needed to reflect *your* enterprise. One example is 'Figure 42: Party/Party Role core pattern.' This "Base" pattern is reasonably large in its own right, so it may be sliced into smaller diagrams, as portrayed in the preceding diagrams Figure 35 through to Figure 39.

One folder for a "Subtypes" diagram (or "Taxonomy" diagram if you prefer that term) takes the pattern's core entity (Party in this case), and displays subtypes as identified by your business people. (Note that if there are only a few subtypes, this diagram may be combined with the "Base" diagram.) For an example, see 'Figure 40: Health practitioner (and related) roles.'

One folder for specific data pattern "Context" diagram(s) that takes the pattern's core entity (Party in this case), and displays relationships to other core entities. For example, there may be a relationship between the Party (or perhaps a Party Role subtype such as Customer) and the Account entity, showing who is responsible for making payments on the Account. An example is shown in Figure 68: Account-to-Party. Another example, this time relating to Agreement, is shown in Figure 53: Agreement pattern—participating parties. Note that the context diagram to be created here would be an amalgamation of these two diagrams, plus more, all with Party (and Party Role) at the center. It is important to note that these relationships are expected to be replicated to reflect the two-way nature of (binary) relationships; just as the Party "Context" diagram will refer to the Account entity, the Account "Context" diagram will refer to the Party entity. It is the same relationship, just portrayed from a different starting point.

Optional additional "Extension" folders to capture special features relevant to your enterprise. For example, I have sometimes had extensions for the Party pattern to manage rules for contacting people ("Monday to Friday during office house, use the office landline; after hours during the work week, use the work Mobile; on weekends, etc."). Another example is to model a richer Position data set as presented in Figure 44: Enriched Position pattern.

Divergent: This folder is a collective grouping for possibly many Divergent models (each with its own subfolders). Some organizations will focus all of their Divergent models along just one dimension, e.g., Divergent Models for today's "Pain Points" and future "Vision," or Divergent models for separate Business Units or Business Processes. Others may do deep-dive modeling across several such dimensions. The following hierarchy portrays an example of multiple dimensions, drawn from several clients.

<u>Business unit models</u>: This folder groups Divergent models sliced according to departments/divisions/sections, or whatever, within the organization's structure. These are *not* models of the business units themselves, but of the data required to support each business unit. Examples of business units might include:

<u>Engineering Department</u>: A folder for possibly multiple diagrams portraying the data entities and relationships deemed important to support the "engineering" business unit.

<u>Sales Department</u>: Another example for a different business unit.

<u>Business process models</u>: This folder groups Divergent models sliced according to business processes. These are *not* models of the business processes themselves, but of the data required to support each business process. Examples of business processes might include:

<u>Recruitment process</u>: A folder for possibly multiple diagrams portraying the data entities and relationships deemed important to support the process of recruiting new employees.

<u>Sales lead process and Asset maintenance process</u>: More examples for different business processes.

<u>Pain Point/Vision Analysis models</u>: This folder groups Divergent models sliced according to deep-dive analysis of declared "pain points" and desired flexibility for the future. An example might be:

<u>Monthly reconciliation</u>: One client of mine had a whole team whose life was spent each month trying to reconcile contradictory end-of-month reports. Sometimes deep-dives into problem areas do reveal potential for "data" solutions, but other times it may require a change of business culture, or business process, or … The conclusion of the analysis is that there are certain data structures (some likely to be futuristic as well as current state) that need consideration. These Divergent models can capture the relevant entities and relationships.

Sound complicated? If we go back to the city's town plan analogy, each component can be understood in its own right, and can also be seen alongside other aspects. It's a bit like a street directory (remember those?). The whole model can appear daunting, but you can focus just on the bits you need.

Please remember that the structure shown above is just a suggestion. Adapt the bits that work for you, and put the rest aside. You can do it however you like as long as there is one central repository and multiple views over the top.

Key points

- A data modeling tool should:

  o Have a central repository for definitions of entities (and their attributes), and relationships between entities.

  o Allow multiple diagrams to view parts of the central repository, with any changes at the repository level automatically being reflected in the diagrammatic views.

- The Data Town Plan should be made up of multiple views against one central repository. Views to be included are:

  o A single model-on-a-page overview.

  o Multiple divergent views, each reflecting the perspective of a different slice through the organization.

  o The essential convergent model that unifies the divergent views.

- A fully developed Data Town Plan is likely to involve many diagrams. Managing them may be easier if arranged in folders (and nested subfolders).

- This book uses the Unified Modeling Language (UML) notation for Class diagrams to present data models; you are free to use any data modeling notation you choose.

CHAPTER 15

Preparing for the Data Town Plan Build

Iterating on the scope (for a little while)

So, where do we start on this venture? Clear candidates include:

- Defining the scope of the "enterprise." After all, it's a Data Town Plan for the enterprise, but you might be surprised at how controversial that scope turns out to be.

- Picking the team.

- Nailing down what "success" will look like. We don't want the Data Town Plan to become shelf-ware, gathering dust but delivering zero value.

I'll cut to the chase here. All of the above and more are interdependent, and as you progress on each one, you may need to go back and revisit the bits you have already described and scoped.

Be prepared to revisit, challenge, and change earlier positions.

Perhaps you might start by assuming that the "enterprise" matches the scope of the company as it appears in some government register, only to find that, when you pick the team, they want to expand the scope to include business partners or to shrink the scope to one country's concerns rather than an international perspective. You move on to defining "success," only to discover that the team membership includes people who have zero interest in the proposed focus, and what's worse, it's missing some vital visionaries. You get the team re-arranged, and then they challenge what's really important for "success," even though this is what was the catalyst for them being invited.

Please let me share a warning here. Beware iterating forever in a fruitless attempt to get a rock-solid scope definition. Yes, remain open to adjusting things, but make a start with imperfection. Toss things around a little, but then get going, having clearly defined the agreed position on "enterprise," team membership, and "success."

These scope-setting elements are important but adaptable, so let's look at each one.

Defining the enterprise (after all, it's all about enterprise integration)

Remember that we said earlier that there had been an historical shift over the decades from a "micro" focus on modeling for discrete, independent (and siloed) IT systems to an increasing demand for getting an understanding of the enterprise-wide "macro" picture of the corporation's data? In the same section, we also noted that if we're planning to support enterprise-level initiatives, perhaps it's a good idea to define the scope of our "enterprise"?

In my book, *The Elephant in the Fridge*, I noted a couple of examples. One was a church-based welfare organization that I questioned on the scope of their intended enterprise-wide model. Did it cover the "church" aspect as well as the "welfare" aspect? Did it address the local needs in my part of Australia, or all of Australia, or was an international perspective appropriate? And seeing the welfare arm has numerous beneficial associations with other similar church-based, private, and government agencies, were they in scope, too?

The other example was for emergency response to wildfires. The agency paying for me was a sliver within a massive government department. Did it include all of that department? (Thankfully, the answer was a resounding, "No.") Did it include other fire-related agencies? "Yes." All 17 of them! And did it include those responding to floods, earthquakes, disease outbreaks, and more, all under the general category of "emergency response"? Again, "Yes." But it was a state-based scope and did not include agencies in other Australian states.

Was that the "right" definition of scope? Going back to the point above on iteration, the initial scope was smaller, but over time was consciously and explicitly expanded.

Another example of wide scope that I've observed at arms' length is the USA's National Information Exchange Model (NIEM). OK, some would argue that it's less of an "enterprise" model, and more of an information exchange model—after all, that's what it is quite correctly named. But it is interesting to look at its scope. It spans multiple levels of government organizations, including, for example, justice, public safety, emergency/disaster management, intelligence, and homeland security, for the entire USA. That's a huge scope, and has taken years (decades) to shape it. But the main reason I wanted to reference the NIEM here is that, according to Wikipedia, the "… NIEM is designed to facilitate the creation of automated *enterprise-wide* information exchanges …" [emphasis mine]. Did they say "enterprise-wide"? How big is that "enterprise"?!

OK, hopefully your enterprise is a bit smaller and more manageable than that of the NIEM. But it may still need careful, considered nomination of scope. I finish with two more examples.

In Australia, we have what seems to me to be a sometimes awkward dance between government responsibilities and those of the private sector. Historically, public services such as water, power, phones, and public transport were run by the government. Then things shifted and these services were privatized. I observed from a distance the long-winded development of the Enterprise Data Model for one major telephone company. Some wanted a single model. Others wanted to recognize a separation between the "retail" and the "wholesale" operations, especially as the government mandated this separation. Their solution? A single model spanning both retail and wholesale, but kept at a highly generic level rather than diving into retail versus wholesale specialization.

Finally, I was responsible for driving a Data Town Plan for an organization that provided health insurance, health services such as dentistry and optometry, pet insurance, aged care facilities, and more. Without breaching confidentiality, considerations that could have been discussed included dimensions such as:

- Should separate product lines such as health insurance, dentistry and aged care villages be seen as separate "enterprises" in their own right?

- Should we model for the Australian operations, for the Asia Pacific conglomerate, or for a global perspective?

Sometimes there are no easy answers that will keep all players happy. Sometimes you get turf wars, or personality clashes, or the coexistence of competing consultancies. Sometimes compromises must be made, with the very real risk of also compromising the outcomes. At the end of the day, try to assemble a team of people who, while representing diverse backgrounds and interests, share a common goal for the common good. That leads us nicely into the topic of team formation.

Picking a team

One foundational member of the Data Town Planning team is the data modeler who will take ongoing responsibility for managing and extending the Data Town Plan. In some cases, that might be the facilitator. More commonly, someone from the world of data governance might be chosen. But whichever way you go, the nomination must be explicit, with management commitment to this ongoing role. Further, the facilitator and the Data Town Plan modeler roles must be filled by people competent in data modeling. And here's an important point. Some in the IT community talk as if the only forms of data modeling relate to data structures for analytics/reporting (e.g., dimensional modeling as introduced by Ralph Kimball, so-called "3NF" modeling for a Bill Inmon styled data warehouse, Data Vault as introduced by Dan Linstedt, "one big table", etc.). The modeler must be proficient in "normalized" modeling as required, for example, for operational/transactional systems.

One more bit on the facilitator. If he or she is from outside of the organization, as well may be the case, it is a courtesy for the facilitator to invest time upfront in gaining an understanding of the enterprise (with assistance from those in the organization). The facilitator and the lead data modeler are just one part of the team, albeit an important part.

The Data Town Plan is intended to represent the "town" (or in our case, the entire enterprise). It follows that we need representation from across the enterprise. That's often easier said than done.

If you work for an organization with thousands of people, you're not going to get them into one room and run a workshop that treats every participant equally, giving time for all of them. That's just not possible, and who would even try. But even if your organization is much smaller, I suggest you limit the numbers. I like a dozen or so people at a time, though a little larger group can be managed. I have run sessions with nearly 30, and it can be done, but it's hard work and you'll probably find that some participants are reluctant to participate, at which point I question if they are "participants."

On the other side of the coin, I find that having too few participants lessens the likelihood of rich, energetic debates that can be very enlightening.

So, who should we consider inviting? In a word, we want "thought leaders."

We would do well to get some top brass on board from the business side. Seniority/rank/title is actually of less importance. We're not after people with fancy business cards but people with a vision of the organization's strategic goals. Also from the business side, we want people who are at, or close to, the front line. These people have the scars from the real world. They are likely to have a vision, too, but in contrast to the strategic vision of senior management, they often have a vision of how things should be run, if only the management would listen to them!

Grounds for conflict or eye-opening exchange? There are some foundation stones for the participants:

- They have to welcome challenges to their position instead of being defensive.

- They have to be respectful in the way they challenge others.

From the IT side, ideally, we will have individuals who see the big picture (including dreams for the future) while having hands-on knowledge of the challenges of today's IT systems. They may have amazing technical skills, but you might be surprised when I say that this isn't the focus. They are not there to dazzle the business with their geeky knowledge. Yes, sometimes highly technical people can open the eyes of the business as to what may be possible. Still, it's not a case of proving how clever IT people are but demonstrating how they can listen to the business and contribute gently to the emerging vision of the Data Town Plan. IT is welcome at the table, especially when they can:

- Highlight their pain points (as compared to business pain points).

- Seed discussion with new possibilities that technology may offer (but with a caution that this project is not intended to focus on shiny new toys).

We want an interdisciplinary team of passionate people who will speak up boldly to share their vision while respectfully hearing and seeking to understand the views of others, and who are committed to articulating a shared 'town plan' vision for the benefit of all.

Finally, and for this one, take care, but perhaps you might want to invite the CEO or a similar high-ranking management team member. They probably won't have the time or interest to stick around for the whole show, but if they can kick off the first workshop by highlighting the importance of this project and share their perspectives and requirements, that can be a good thing. Also, as appropriate, you can include them as recipients of progress reporting. This can work brilliantly, and I've seen it work wonders. Nothing like the team seeing senior management's backing and interest! Conversely, with a culture that struggles to embrace open questioning and challenging across the layers, the CEO's presence can shut things down.

That may all sound somewhat idealistic. Might it not be true that conflict will emerge?

Variations on the ideal team

I really hesitate to even mention leveraging the knowledge of IT folk to represent the business, but you can get long-term stalwarts in the IT team who are more than capable of providing a business perspective. Some of these gems have breadth and depth of knowledge of the business way beyond that of many "business" people. I think of Jo and Michael from an insurance company, and Larry and Tony from a welfare organization.

My list goes on, but you get the idea. These "IT" individuals were so exceptionally talented that they did a stunning job representing the business. I go on record as thanking them for the delight of working with them. In all these cases, these individuals not only laid a solid foundation, they also worked with me to jump into focused sessions with the business to check, challenge, and round out the picture.

So yes, you can succeed with IT representing the business, but be very careful. By default, go to the business to get a business view, and please don't take my noting of exceptions as a free pass to avoid engaging with business folk.

I've touched briefly on IT folk who have the ability to represent the business. Before leaving the topic of multi-skilled individuals who have worked hard to get the big picture, I'd like to flip the discussion around and look at people apparently coming from the business side who can make contributions to the IT side.

I'll start with Damien. He was brought in on contract to deliver a government initiative to protect long-service leave entitlements. Even though an "outsider," he very quickly gained a greater knowledge of the business than almost anybody else, yet also had more IT skills than this modest man would probably be comfortable admitting to.

And then there was Andrew from Fire Management who was a very rare individual. I'll tell two stories about him.

First, while I was very new to the emergency response world, I had eventually got much-needed time in Andrew's diary to absorb his business knowledge. There were others there, but he was the man I really needed. I noticed that he carried a backpack into the meeting, but the significance didn't register with me. Partway through the meeting, his pager went off (if you don't know what a pager is, ask some old folks like me). He jumped up, grabbed his backpack, and literally ran out the door. I turned to another of his colleagues and asked where Andrew had gone. "To a fire" was the curt response. "So when will he be back?" I asked, naively, hoping to continue the interrupted meeting soon. "When the fire is out" was an even blunter answer, as if the speaker was thinking, "How stupid are you, John?" I tell this to communicate that Andrew was very much an active member of the fire response team. He didn't just talk about the business of firefighting; he was front-and-center, a hands-on bloke.

Ah, but he also had IT skills way ahead of most mere mortals. As just a trivial example, I introduced him to the basics of data modeling as we worked towards capturing a business-centered view of their data. At one point, he jumped up, grabbed the whiteboard marker out of my hand, exclaimed, "You're wrong," and, because of his business knowledge, made a correction to _my_ data model. Andrew is an absolute gentleman, so his grabbing the marker reflected his passion, not rudeness.

Some folk from the IT side are more than capable of representing the business, and some people from the business side excel in IT skills. So, my message is simple. While seeking representatives from the business side, don't overlook capable and available resources from the IT team. And the other way around—recognize business people who can contribute to IT discussions.

Seeking articulation as to what "success" might look like

I was called to help a project that was already spending lots of money on their Data Vault project. Any Data Vault project _must_ be business-centric.

I, and a few others around me, worked to support the project by focusing on the business needs. In spite of a few hurdles, we actually made some progress on developing a Data Town Plan for the business, but it was like swimming against the tide. Again and again, we seemed to be, at best, unsupported and, at worst, blocked, when we strove to nudge the Data Vault project in the direction of the business. I saw the project as shaping up to be a failure as it not only refused to embrace a business view, but some people actively opposed the inclusion of a business perspective. In my view, the project was technology-focused, failing abysmally to center the Data Vault design on the business concepts.

Imagine my shock when I was invited to a celebration to toast the "resounding success" of a milestone in the project. I declined to attend and was asked why I wasn't joining in. I simply stated that I would not participate in anything that purported to convey a message of success. Some senior IT folk were highly critical of my position, while a lot of the down-the-line IT team quietly cheered me on for making a stand. Politics and personalities aside, what on earth was happening?

It turned out that this was an IT-driven project, that the goal was to change the underpinning technologies (the old platform was no longer supported), and, as such, it was seen by some technical people as clearly successful. I am not being critical of that as a goal (though I did question the use or misuse of Data Vault as what I perceived as a questionable vehicle). What was a massive pity was that the goal of swapping platforms was not communicated succinctly and clearly to many of the implementation team, including myself, nor to some from the business units who were funding the project. I believe that many business people were under the illusion that the goal was to actually deliver business value to them.

So here's the message. It is arguable that any project, including the development of a Data Town Plan, should have a clear statement of "What does success look like?" expressed in terms understood by the business and signed off by the business. And communicated to IT. We need to know who wanted the Data Town Plan and make sure everyone understands how it is expected to be used to deliver value.

Two checkpoints to consider in drafting a statement of success:

• Think about today's "pain points" where managing data falls short.

- Think about the vision for the future and where the business would expect and like to see "data" in the foreseeable future.

Setting expectations that all participants are equal

Locking a bunch of high-energy, high-passion people into a room for a Data Town Plan workshop sounds risky. It doesn't have to be that way.

I'll start with a couple of stories about potential conflict scenarios, where things could have gone badly wrong but didn't. Both stories were set in the context of a consultancy in which I was privileged to work. I got the impression that the manager deliberately attracted people with real diversity, and the consultancy was much the richer as a result.

So the first story goes something like this. One consultant aligned with right-wing politics in a very certain way. He was actually an active member of one of our right-of-center parties. What's more, he actively served in Vietnam, fighting communism. Consultant number two was also active in a political party that was most definitely left of center and aligned with the communists of this world. He had not only opposed Australia's military efforts in Vietnam, but was willing to be punished by refusing to serve in our armed forces if conscripted.

For one consulting assignment, these two individuals who most definitely did not share common political views were seen as having complementary skills. In spite of their personal differences, they were able to work together constructively. That's impressive professionalism.

The second story really touched my heart. I understand that one employee of this consultancy had been raised as a Bosnian and the other as a Serb. The historical conflict across those two cultures runs deep. The two individuals were called into the boss's office and asked if they could work together on a particular assignment. One turned to the other and said, "It is possible that, at this very moment in time, some of my relatives are trying to murder some of your relatives, or that some of your relatives are trying to murder mine." With amazing graciousness, she reached out a hand of friendship to the other and said, "I came to Australia to start a new life. And yes, we can work together." With equal grace, the other person shook the hand as offered, and they formed a team. If the world had more people like those, it would be a better place.

Unfortunately, sometimes, we have to accept that certain combinations of people just aren't going to work. I could tell a number of stories where conflicts were judged to be unresolvable, but I don't want to focus on the negatives. Just be aware that you may have to be sensitive to possible tensions, and even showstoppers.

One consideration relates to cultures where junior people from within an organization might be reluctant to even consider offering a view that's different to the views of senior management. If they're invited to the same Data town Plan workshop, we may observe hesitancy to openly challenge. There is a true and tragic story about two pilots in another country. The captain made a mistake, and the less senior pilot hesitated to correct or challenge the more "senior" pilot. As a result, all on board died. In the aftermath, some Aussie pilots worked with this country to help them embrace a more egalitarian attitude. At times, rank must be seen as secondary to transparent, free communication. And airline safety and Data Town Plan workshops are two such settings.

Ah, but perhaps there are settings where respect for a position is important. A loveable but free-spirited member of my family was once in the presence of a king in the Middle East. The king asked a question of my relative, and she replied with her typical cheeky sense of humor. The blank face of the king made her wonder if her intended humor had backfired badly under the tests of cross-cultural appropriateness. Given that a king in such a setting has ultimate power, she was feeling a little uncertain about his response. In fact, he needed a bit of time to take on board what had just happened. The king did smile and actually gave her a gift so she could always remember the time she gave cheek to a king, adding that he loved Aussies for their sense of humor!

Now, I'll share another setting where the same individual exhibited her freedom, unencumbered by rank or protocol. This time, she was in the presence of the President of the United States. She had been invited to join a bunch of journalists seeking answers from Bill Clinton. She was used to Aussie journalists throwing unscripted, hard-hitting questions at our national leaders, and was perplexed at the way the American journalists seemed to be very gentle in their prodding for answers. She didn't realize that, at least in this particular setting, all questions had to be screened before being put to the President. In her typical, forthright, no-nonsense manner, she threw a very direct and confrontational question into the mix. And was immediately marched out of the room and grilled about her behavior. Oops.

Why do I tell those stories? To convey the message that not all settings will welcome the barriers of culture, rank, and title being put aside. However, for a Data Town Plan workshop involving participants from diverse backgrounds, it is good to communicate that, in such a setting, the goal is to see all as equal. Yes, respect the boss, but not because he or she is the boss. And expect the boss to respect the front-line workers. Set an expectation that we will have fun, be creative, and enjoy hearing and understanding the richness of varying perspectives as co-contributors.

Capabilities expected of the workshop facilitator

Facilitation skills

It should come as no surprise that any facilitator should be comfortable facilitating!

As noted above, they absolutely must be comfortable interacting with all levels of participants. They must also not be intimidated by the detailed knowledge of technology experts. After all, it is the knowledge of *all* participants that is needed.

> *The facilitator simply cannot be smarter than all those attending because if he/she were that knowledgeable, the other participants wouldn't be needed!*

A facilitator can most definitely be brought in from "outside." In fact, their independence can be a real bonus. What's more, some consultants have built up years, or decades, of perspective from a wide range of industries and can offer a freshness not always available from insider resources. Nonetheless, it is a common courtesy for the facilitator to do some homework and gain a broad understanding of the particular organization, the products, the market, the industry, and the roles and responsibilities (and personalities) of participants.

Bring a kitbag of techniques for handling difficult moments

Having done what you can to set the scene for a productive session, sometimes tensions may still arise. There can be all sorts of ways to facilitate keeping things running smoothly.

One issue is the domination of the conversations.

One prop that can help is to have two soft foam balls, a timer, and a bell. At the outset of each workshop session, the participants select one of their group to be the "umpire" to keep conversations flowing. The person holding one ball can talk for the agreed time limit. People can wave their hands to be given the second ball as the next speaker. And the umpire will ring a "time-out" bell when the current speaker has one more minute to wind up.

Another technique for keeping conversations flowing is to hand out two mini chocolate bars (or similar—remember, not everyone can eat chocolate) to each participant. Each time they talk for more than a few minutes, the group votes whether they can keep talking or have to eat one of their chocolates while others talk. After they've eaten their allotment of two, they have to ask permission from the group if they want to talk again for a lengthy time.

I often take such props and explain their use. In practice, I rarely use them as the message to give everyone a fair hearing is often carried just by the presence of the props. Judge your audience. Will they have fun with such toys, or actually feel offended as if the session is being trivialized. What's the answer? Ask them!

Another possible roadblock is the equivalent of writer's cramp. Instead of getting flooded with helpful creativity in problem-solving, everything goes quiet. You may have heard of "brainstorming"? It's a great way to generate creative ideas. Underpinning it is our foundation that all participants are equal contributors. I won't even try to teach brainstorming here—there are plenty of resources to assist you—but I encourage the facilitator to become familiar and comfortable with this technique. For those new to the idea, in short, the facilitator welcomes ideas and throws them onto a sheet of butcher's paper or on a spare whiteboard. All ideas are welcome. None are judged at the time. Some of the wilder ideas, while possibly being impractical, may generate even more ideas. Get them all down, fast. Later on, the better candidates can be put on a shortlist for further consideration.

Please note that the early Data Town Plan sessions are not intended to focus on problem-solving, but as people share data "pain points," sometimes a short, sharp conversation about how the pain might be tackled can be insightful. Capture the ideas now, as they may be hugely beneficial later.

One final tool I will mention here is the use of Edward de Bono's "6 thinking hats." As for brainstorming above, I encourage you to research the ideas and perhaps buy his book. My poor attempt to summarize de Bono's work is that people tend to have default ways of thinking. Some people are sunny and optimistic and exhibit yellow-hat thinking, some are negative and pessimistic, as represented by the black hat. Some respond from the head ("Just give me the facts") and are classified as white-hat thinkers, while others react from the heart—they're the red-hat thinkers. Then you've got the green-hat creative types looking for new ways to do things. Finally, the blue hat is for consciously managing how we're thinking—a great hat for the facilitator.

There are courses people can go on for use of de Bono's six thinking hats. For me, I carry a set of the six hats, explain briefly what each color represents, and then, at times, in a workshop, I will ask an individual to "wear" a certain hat. Sometimes, they, or a number in the group, tend to think a certain way, and the facilitator might prompt them to deliberately embrace a different perspective, as portrayed by a different color hat. Fun. Creative. And potentially, it can get things moving again if bogged down in one way of thinking.

Data modeling skills

Now, here's a recommendation that might surprise you. In addition to generic facilitation skills, I believe it is essential that the facilitator (or a joined-at-the-hip assistant) have deep knowledge of data modeling at the enterprise level and a solid understanding of data model patterns. If that sounds a bit frightening, please relax. By the time you finish this book, you should have gained the foundational working knowledge required. Sure, you *could* read the excellent publications by people such as David Hay and Len Silverston on data model patterns, but those authors alone have published over 2,000 pages on the topic. For those passionate about the topic of patterns, I encourage an investment in their books. For others, the lightweight data model patterns in this book may be sufficient.

Carving up the project into slices (if you must)

The ideal for developing a Data Town Plan is to start with the enterprise-wide perspective and then drill down into divergent models as appropriate. But what if you simply can't get the necessary people together for that enterprise-wide foundation? Do you have to sit on your hands and wait?

If you really have no other choice, perhaps you can still make progress by carving up the kick-off workshop into several sessions, each tackling one slice of the enterprise. But my first caveat relates to *how* you carve up the bits you model first if you're not going to start with a single, agreed Model-on-a-Page.

Earlier in this book I shared some red flag warnings. Basically, if you want to carve up the construction of the Data Town Plan into bite-sized chunks, I caution against certain approaches as they risk significant rework as new slivers are added. *Don't* start by carving up by <u>business process</u>. *Don't* start by carving up by <u>business unit</u>. *Don't* expect that the parts of the grand plan, as seen by progressive, siloed <u>projects,</u> will auto-magically assemble into a cohesive whole. Definitely *don't* use the data views of one current <u>IT system</u>, and then the next system, to try to create a unified vision of how the business sees and wants to see their data (in the Data Vault world, this is labeled as "source system Data Vault," and is soundly condemned).

OK, so what's left for us to use to divide and conquer? The one segmentation I recommend is by <u>data subject area</u>. I'll try to explain what I mean below, starting with "Customer" as a data subject area.

You've probably heard people talk about the desirability of acquiring a "Customer 360-degree" view? It's a bit like picking up one customer and seeing not only their immediate details, but also seeing what other things of interest that are connected to that customer.

To set the scene, let's look again at the water utility's Model-on-a-Page (the single, unified view we want but can't get in one all-in session).

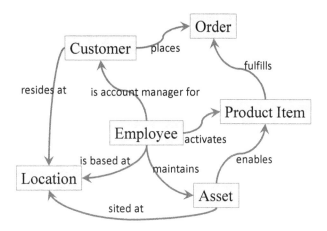

Figure 74: Water utility overview

For Sam, the water utility customer, we can start by drilling down into the detailed data customer record and look at attributes such as Sam's address, credit rating, current debt, and so on. But if we (metaphorically) pick up Sam's record and give it a little shake to see what other data is attached to it by pieces of string, we might discover an Employee acting in the role of Account Manager for Sam, what Orders are active, and the Location of Sam's address to get a map-based view and see where Sam lives. Using the same diagram as in Figure 74, but with an emphasis on Customer and its important neighbors, we get:

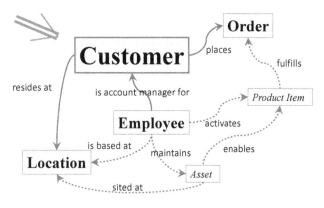

Figure 75: Customer 360 Degree

This view, selected from the overall enterprise view, can give us what was requested. It is a simplified portrayal of the much-discussed concept of Customer 360.

Without trying in any way to downplay the value of a single, consolidated view of customer data, some people want a different perspective. I remember talking to an engineer from a water utility, and his focus was on the billions of dollars invested in assets. While lots of people within his company did (thankfully) care about customers, he personally argued that assets were much more important than customers! He wanted an Asset 360-degree view.

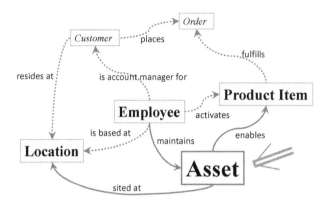

Figure 76: Asset 360 Degree

I could take the story further along a similar line. People from the Human Resources department could argue that Employees were the most important assets of the company (even if one particular engineer might disagree). In some companies, the Sales and Marketing folk might want to have Product at the center. Why not have Employee 360 Degree views, Asset 360 Degree views, Product 360 Degree views, and more?

So, where am I taking this conversation? In this simplified view of the water utility, each of those boxes could be seen as their own data subject area. We could pick any one of them to make a start on the Data Town Plan (Customer, Asset, Location, etc.).

Now, here's the bit I really want you to grasp. Let's say for the water utility, Asset was the first data subject area to be modeled. We could kick off the project by doing the following:

- Drill down into *detail* for that central data subject area, such as an Asset's identifier (for a water meter, it's the Meter Number physically stamped on the meter), make and model, purchase cost, written-down-value, replacement value, etc.).

- Include in the model all the touch points with *other* data subject areas, such as the fact that an Employee maintains an Asset, an Asset has a Location, and the Customer sees the Asset as enabling delivery of a Product Item. For each of these touch point data subject areas (Employee, Location, Product Item), only model just enough detail to be *sufficient* to represent that data subject area. Additional touch points and their details will be fleshed out when it's the turn of that subject area to be modeled in detail.

I'll say it again. Under reasonable circumstances, it only takes weeks to start with the single Model-on-a-Page view (and do some divergent drill down and then consolidation into the first-cut convergent model), and that's by far preferable. But if you have to divide the development of the Data Town Plan into progressive slices because you simply can't get backing for starting with all the key players at once, my recommendation is to divide and conquer by data subject area.

… and why did I recommend against dividing the project into slices based on business processes or business units, leveraging off other funded projects, or focusing on existing IT systems? Because in all of those cases, your modeling is likely to cut across multiple data subject areas, and each data subject area will probably have to be reworked as you move into the next slice. Rework? Technical debt? Who wants to go that way?!

A bit of administration

Perhaps the facilitator takes responsibility for chasing up the support tasks, or perhaps they gratefully accept the assistance of someone else. Either way, there are jobs to be done. They include:

- Communication of a request for workshop attendees to assemble material, including:

    o Background reading for the facilitator, especially material that can be read before the workshop.

    o Known IT and Business "pain points" as they relate to data. (Sure, there may be pain points relating to the quality of coffee in the canteen, but that's not a "data" pain point!)

    o Dreams for the IT/data future vision, prompted by the challenge, "If time, budget and technology had no limits, what would you like to see?" (This at least somewhat aligns with De Bono's Yellow hat thinking in Six Thinking Hats.)

- Preparing handouts for every participant in the form of:

- A hardcopy of the 9-pillar set of common patterns (cloned/clipped from Figure 23 and printed on a single piece of paper). This can be used to capture evolving subtypes.
- A hardcopy of the "pattern of patterns" that presents common relationships between the patterns (cloned/clipped from Figure 24 and printed on a single piece of paper). This can be used to prompt the participants with ideas on the relationships they may wish to capture.
- Hardcopy printouts of templates for defining entities, their attributes, and their inter-relationships (created by you, but possibly based on Table 2, Table 3, Table 4, and Table 5 from this book).

- Booking on-site facilities, including a main workshop facility with multiple whiteboards (at least one for every six team members, plus one for the facilitator), and a flip chart and easel for taking work-in-progress notes.

- Catering for the above as appropriate.

Key points

- Any enterprise-wide initiative, such as a Data Town Plan, needs clarity on the scope of the "enterprise" (and it may not be the obvious one).

- Don't assume everyone knows what a Data Town Plan is all about; explicitly communicate the goals.

- The core team ideally needs to be identified, with representation from:

  - The business *and* from IT.
  - Management *and* operations.
  - The facilitator.
  - A data modeler (possibly the facilitator themselves).

- The facilitator obviously needs facilitation skills but also needs data modeling abilities even if the team includes a dedicated data modeler.

- As much as possible, respectfully communicate that all members of the core team are equal. Rank and title can be left outside the door.

- Strenuously resist attempts to divide the *start* of your Data Town Plan (where you lay the foundation) into silos based on business units, business processes, IT projects, or IT systems. *If* the whole-of-enterprise Data Town Plan really must be sliced into subprojects, do it by data subject area. [And note that when you do Divergent modeling within the start-up foundations, it's *then* OK to consider analyzing things by business unit, business process, IT project, or IT system slices.]

- Don't forget the importance of the tedious administration that will help the Data Town Plan initiative run smoother!

CHAPTER 16

A look at a Nominal 4-week Data Town Plan Schedule

So, how long does it take to build a Data Town Plan (well, at least the first version)? True to form for a data modeler, my answer could be, "It depends."

I've seen some very detailed enterprise conceptual models that involve a whole team and take years. That's *not* what we want.

I shared the story earlier (in 'Bank: When we need to look at business processes, fast!') of delivering a Data Town Plan in hours. That was an exception, with many caveats, including that we came back later to clean things up over the following weeks.

In between the extremes of years versus hours, I have lots of examples of delivering the first cut of a Data Town plan in about one month. That can be realistic, but again, with a number of caveats. I didn't have to learn the core data model patterns before starting as I was already familiar with the patterns. The clients had already picked a modeling tool, installed it, and had people already trained and ready to go, or they were happy for me to use my tool (I've seen months of debate spent on tool evaluation, then more months on getting funding, then even more time on installation and training). And importantly, the business people wanted this deliverable and were willing to make themselves and appropriate staff available.

Please note that this "one-month" rule of thumb assumes all the preparation work has been done. An entire section above titled 'Preparing for the Data Town Plan Build' is dedicated to preparation. Don't underestimate the effort required to get ready.

Overview of one possible schedule

Once the preparation is completed, the following is an indicative checklist of steps involved in this nominal one month of work to build the Data Town Plan. Please don't put yourself under unnecessary pressure. If this is the first time you've done something like this, don't put yourself in a position of setting expectations that may not be met. Perhaps use the notes below as checklist items and a possible sequence of events, but you might choose to ignore the time estimates. Make a start, feel your way, and be transparent with your stakeholders that it might take a bit longer. Over-deliver rather than over-promise.

Week 1: Data Town Plan outline

The primary goal of the first week is to run a workshop with the people selected to represent diverse dimensions of the organization. A more detailed candidate schedule follows.

- Days 1 and 2: Familiarization. For the facilitator, this will include meeting the team and reviewing the material that the participants will have been asked to assemble.

- Day 3: A full-day workshop, possibly kicked off by the CEO. This is the single most important day of the whole month. If participants want to continue this day's discussions the following day, the workshop facilities, and participants, must be booked to allow that. This workshop is described in much more detail in the section titled 'Running the initial Workshop' later in this book.

- Day 4: Capturing the foundational Data Town Plan in the modeling tool.

- Day 5: Start with a short workshop to present the emerging model. For the balance of the last day, the entire team is to meet to discuss, prioritize, and select two topics for the next two week's deep-dive workshops. These deep-dive workshops may focus on:

  o Today's Data Pain Points and tomorrow's Vision, especially those that span multiple business units and/or business processes, and that seem intractable, or
  o Data Subject Areas that really need a unified vision, such as Customer or Product, or
  o Emerging new aspects of the organization, or

    ○   ...?

As a warning, it is suggested that caution be exercised in focusing too early on business units in the upcoming deep dives. After all, we aim for an enterprise-wide view, and early focus on separate business units can derail the Data Town Plan. I'm not saying that the Divergent models cannot drill down by business unit slices—they can—but just a warning that a premature focus on business units has risks.

Once the topics for the two deep-dive workshops are chosen, it is important to identify suitable participants. They are likely to include a subset of Week 1's pool; all are welcome, but not all may be needed to address the chosen focus. The participants will also likely include new subject matter experts who have not been identified until the deep-dive topics are nailed down. Sorry, this may mean some last-minute recruitment.

Week 2: Deep-dive (first nominated area)

This week's schedule is outlined below. Much more detail is provided in the 'Divergent Modeling (from Today's Pain to Tomorrow's Vision' section later in this book).

Day one starts with a mutual brainstorming exercise as participants toss around their views of the chosen deep-dive topic. Issues and candidate solutions can be shared, though, in the spirit of brainstorming, critique of what's presented is left aside initially.

Having generated ideas and gained a shared understanding, the facilitator helps the group sort through the material. Importantly, the facilitator, the data modeler colleague, and the rest of the group will generate candidate data structures (and supporting processes, technologies and work practices) to elaborate on the data issues being presented. As appropriate, certain follow-up research tasks may be assigned to individuals or mini-teams within the group (or recruited from further afield).

The rest of the week can be managed a little like an "Agile" project, with participants co-located (though not necessarily engaged full time, but available on demand), with each day kicking off with something like a stand-up to report what was done the previous day, what is planned for today, and roadblocks. Each day, the facilitator and his/her data modeling colleague will take much of the afternoon to refactor the Data Town Plan based on that morning's decisions.

The morning of the last day is for reflection and preparation of a presentation to the larger team. The afternoon will include the actual presentation, driven as much as is possible by the business people themselves (thus encouraging their ownership).

Week 3: Deep-dive (second nominated area)

(as for Week 2, but for the next nominated deep-dive topic.)

Week 4: Consolidation, direction-setting

This week is about tying up loose ends and getting things in place for the next strategic steps.

- Day 1: Remember we spoke of the Model-on-a-Page, multiple Divergent models, and finally, a single Convergent model? The first priority for this week is to close out this version of the Data Town Plan and its three model views. Part of the morning can be spent on presenting the consolidated model to the whole team, seeking feedback, and checking against the stated vision. The balance of the day is reserved for the refinement of the Data Town Plan based on that feedback.

- Day 2: We don't want the Data Town Plan to become shelf ware, gathering dust but not delivering value. In the morning, we want to assemble the whole team (participants across all weeks) and brainstorm candidate business and IT directions for the future.

  - We look to IT to seed the discussion with possibilities.
  - IT is also asked to provide order-of-magnitude indications of effort and cost for delivering identified solutions. Perhaps a look at Appendix 1 might generate some ideas.
  - The whole team can then suggest short-term and long-term priorities.

- Day 3: Based on the previous day's prioritization, it's time to assemble a roadmap for the next steps.

- Day 4: Make a presentation to the key stakeholders. Please note that, as much as possible, this involves business people presenting to business people. IT is important, and I never want to downplay their value, but if we are going to get the business to back initiatives, it is so much better for the ideas to be driven by their vision.

- Day 5: We've got a little bit of contingency here to mop up any remaining loose ends.

Some flexibility on the schedule

The outline above is a guideline for one month of effort. It may be run as a solid block of time. Alternatively, the total effort may be spread over a longer time period but still consume the full-time equivalent of 20 days.

A nominal week is set aside for each of the two deep dives. But will it take exactly one week to solve each issue? From my experience, the only thing common across multiple projects is that they are all different!

I've seen examples of seemingly intractable issues that have dragged on for months or years get resolved in hours. In one such case, I remember a colleague named Geoff coming in as a very experienced data modeler. He listened, tossed around some alternatives, and came up with a "simple," elegant solution. One of the client staff challenged Geoff as to why they were paying such a high hourly rate for someone to come up with something so obvious. Geoff is a delightful person with a sense of humor. He simply replied, "Well, it might have been obvious to me …" The message is that you might not need a full week to crack some of the tougher nuts.

Conversely, I am aware of two initiatives aimed at resolving the challenges to do with a Product catalog. In both cases, many weeks of careful and patient dialogue were required. Based on complexity (and personalities), it couldn't be rushed. The outcome was very well received, but it most certainly took more than one week.

The summary is that the schedule above can be used as a guideline. If appropriate, the deep dives can be time-boxed to deliver what is possible in one week, with follow-up sessions arranged as needed. But remember that you may wind down a given deep dive in less than one week or carry over into the next session.

Stay flexible. Adjust as needed. And as always, listen to the business.

Ongoing iterations

As noted in the introduction to this section, iterations are to be expected. As a guideline, they can follow the same approach as the "deep-dive" weeks described above. However, as we've warned, we need some flexibility on scheduling. Perhaps a pain point can be addressed in hours, or it may take weeks.

Importantly, these iterations typically respond to catalysts triggering action. You don't do another iteration just because you feel you should or you're bored! You do it to deliver value to the business.

Here's another observation on facilitating extensions to the Data Town Plan. While the initial version might have pulled together subject matter experts from across the organization, the resources can be more specialized for ongoing deep dives, focusing on the topic at hand. Having said that, I suggest you keep a core team of people who have the big picture. I sometimes call them the "keepers of the vision." And now a bit of human resource common sense: try to ensure that key people have others who can stand in for them (for illness, long service leave, or simply because people change jobs). The Data Town Plan is too important to put at risk in the hands of just one individual.

Key points

- Enterprise-level data models can take years to develop, but shouldn't. If prerequisites are in place, a Data Town Plan can take a few weeks for the initial version. In summary, the steps typically include:

    o   An initial collaborative workshop.
    o   Deep dives into multiple nominated topics to generate "divergent" models.
    o   Consolidation into a single "convergent" model.
    o   Consideration as to strategic "road-map" directions going forward.

- The initial Data Town Plan is often not the end point; ongoing refinements and extensions can be expected.

CHAPTER 17

Running the Initial Workshop

Earlier, I mentioned that my book, *The Elephant in the Fridge*, overlapped with this book. *The Elephant in the Fridge* went into depth in applying an enterprise data view (a Data Town Plan) to the design of a Data Vault but only touched relatively lightly on the actual development of that enterprise view. This book goes into a lot more detail on developing the enterprise view. The rest of this section on running the initial workshop contains new material, but also some selective extracts from *The Elephant in the Fridge*, woven in to reflect the focus of this book.

Why start here, with everyone involved?

We've very briefly mentioned the topic of "systems thinking" and Russell Ackoff. One of his humorous anecdotes suggested that getting the world's best car engine, the world's best gearbox, world's best car body, and more, and then bolting them together, we won't end up with the world's best car. For our purposes, yes, we want to get the "best" solution for numerous diverse challenges, but we want to start with the big picture, the whole-of-enterprise view.

I've seen all sorts of attempts at progressively assembling a whole-of-enterprise view by detailed studying of the parts, then stacking them side-by-side. I cynically call this "auto-magical integration." The proponents of this approach start by performing deep-dive analysis of silos, then they hope and pray that by some miracle, an integrated view will emerge. In the section titled "Modeling too small" I told the story of one department responsible for creating vehicle warranties and another for processing claims against those vehicle warranties. They both had a different view of what a warranty looked like. By adding the two views together, a unified picture was *not* created.

OK, so hopefully you agree that one dangerous extreme is to understand silos without understanding the entirety. But you might challenge me that there is another danger in working long and hard to get the big picture and never actually delivering value. I absolutely agree. Either extreme has dangers: a bottom-up approach that delivers silos and generally fails to see the big picture versus an inadequate top-down approach that's a bit like the children's film called The Never Ending Story.

So what's the solution? Simple really. Invest a relatively small amount of time in assembling the top-down big picture, then challenge and refine it, including with some bottom-up detail. But please, do start with the enterprise-wide, top-down, business-centric view. For the initial version of the Data Town Plan, we want to kick off by engaging with people representing a broad spectrum from across the organization.

Running the initial Model-on-a-Page workshop

Meet and greet

Like any workshop, there's always the kick-off housekeeping bits, such as pointing out the locations of kitchens, toilets, and fire exits. Importantly, it's now time for the participants to describe their roles and the particular perspective they bring to the table, including gripes about how things are today and dreams of how they hope tomorrow might shape up.

Gently introducing "modeling" and the pattern framework

I like to break the workshop participants into at least a few groups so that we can get some differing views. Please note that each group is ideally to be made up of some business people and some IT people. Too often there is an unhelpful divide between the business folk and the IT folk. Both views are important, and we all need to hear conversations from the other side.

Back in Figure 16, I mentioned that David Hay talks of three types of conceptual models. At the top of the stack is an Overview model (that I call a Model-on-a-Page) that facilitates conversation between business people and IT. An overview is where we start, using patterns to represent the important concepts in the enterprise.

Next, David has multiple Semantic models (or Divergent models), each representing the diverse views of different parts of the enterprise. That's why I suggest we break the workshop participants into groups to actually encourage the formation of different perspectives.

Finally, David has one Essential model (or Convergent model) that brings the divergent views together. That's where we will end, grappling with the consolidation of potentially conflicting views.

Everyone now gets a printed copy of the "Palette of patterns" for their own reference, plus an extra copy for each group to write on. You saw it earlier, but it is repeated in Figure 77 for your convenience.

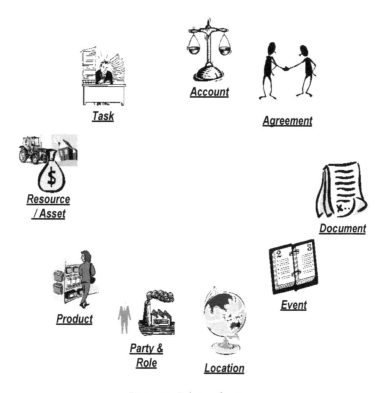

Figure 77: Palette of patterns

At this point, I suggest the facilitator do a quick run through the icons, explaining each in simple business terms. It might be helpful to take a moment and refer back to 'Table 6: Description of nine common patterns' to see how I describe each of the nine foundational patterns.

Kicking off with some initial patterns

What happens now is really straightforward. Perhaps half of the group doesn't have an IT background, and the idea of data models might sound frightening. And some of the other half (the IT professionals) might be comfortable with data models, but not have had much exposure to data model patterns. So I like to drill down into one pattern, usually starting with the Resource pattern as it is relatively simple to understand and can be used to introduce the idea of classification hierarchies ("taxonomies"). That gives an introduction to what a simple "pattern" looks like.

I then like to move onto the Party/Party Role pattern as described earlier. It's a bit richer than the Resource pattern. "Richer" is a less confronting description than saying it is more complicated, but I liken it to an extension of the address book they've got in their phone—people and organizations, their names, addresses, and contact details. Sure, the pattern offers some additional features, most notably the ability to record interrelationships, but that's not too hard to explain. I ask workshop participants to simply start writing about some of the important roles besides the Party icon.

For the wildfire scenario in my home state, we have a government organization where some of the full-time employees have what I call their "day job," but during the fire season, they are on call for fire duties. We've also got a community organization called the Country Fire Authority (CFA), with tens of thousands of highly respected volunteers. Then we have people on contracts, such as locals who drive bull-dozers and are recruited to join the team. Some of the employees and volunteers are assigned to front-line firefighting duties, others might fill roles in the incident control team. Reflecting those sorts of roles, we might end up with a first-cut taxonomy that looks something like this:

Party & Role

- Employee
- Volunteer
- Contractor
- Fire Fighter
- Incident Manager

Figure 78: Fire Party and Roles

If you look critically at the role classifications, you might be able to poke holes in them. Aren't the CFA volunteers also firefighters? Should the incident management role be broken down into its specializations (incident controller, logistics officer, planning officer, etc.)? Isn't the list incomplete? The answer is that it may not be a perfect list, but we've made a start and got the conversation going between the business and IT. Please don't underestimate the value of that.

It's worth noting the controversy on the Party/Party Role pattern. In the real world, it's not uncommon for some employees of an organization to also be customers. However, perhaps the business people don't want to have employees who are also customers explicitly joined at the hip. Or perhaps they do. This issue is not an IT technical question; it's a business question. Having identified the multiple roles a person can play, does the *business* want an individual playing multiple roles managed as one person with explicitly associated roles, or are the roles to be kept separate with no identification of the shared person? (And the same question applies to organizations, too. For example, does a supplier and a customer who are the same organization have the roles linked via a common organization entry?)

Documents and Agreements, and Relationships between patterns

Now we've got some comfort with the basics of data model patterns. Next, I typically drill down into a pair of related patterns, the Document pattern and the Agreement pattern. The description of these two patterns can be found in Documents and Agreements.

Both of these patterns are relatively straightforward, and just as importantly, the Agreement pattern ties to the Party/Party Role pattern, and the Document pattern ties to the Agreement pattern. We've not only got a couple of new patterns, but we are starting to look into the relationships between them. Let's look at the emergency response to fires scenario.

We have all sorts of types of Agreements. For example:

- In Australia, we often lease aircraft from the United States. The US is in the northern hemisphere, and we're in the southern hemisphere, so our fire seasons are generally six months offset. It works well for us to use their firefighting aircraft during our summer.

- While the government department responsible for fires on public land can redeploy some of its employees from their regular jobs, they also hire "seasonal firefighters" such as university students on summer vacation who want a bit of extra pocket money.

- Outside the peak fire season, we do "planned burns" to reduce vegetation in a safer way. Formal burn plans are prepared, documented, and signed off before they are acted on.

These examples are noted in the diagram in Figure 79. Importantly, not only do we have some interesting types of Agreements, but we also have relationships with the Parties that sign them. For example, an Agreement may be signed between some Aussie emergency response representatives and an American company that leases water-bombing aircraft.

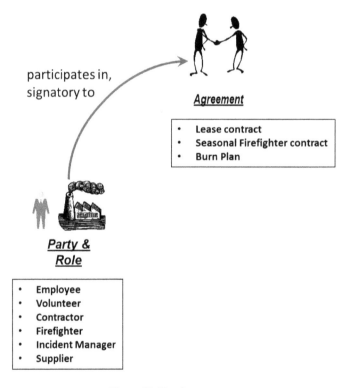

Figure 79: Fire Agreements

You might have spotted the additional role of "Supplier," added just under the earlier list of Party Roles. When we looked at types of agreements, we discovered that some parties played the role of supplier for the leased aircraft. Simple. In the actual workshop, it's all hand-written on the "Palette of patterns" sheet; we just change the working copy. The way I'm telling the story in this book, it sounds pretty straightforward. In reality, the changes can seem rather chaotic; as more and more patterns are introduced, there's more and more extension *and reworking* of what's come before. I call it "ordered chaos." Yes, the changes come thick and fast, but they are managed within the framework of proven patterns.

Not all agreements have related documents (or at least they may not have them available for central filing). Perhaps the lease contracts have commercial-in-confidence elements, and the seasonal firefighter contracts have personal privacy aspects, so they are held safely in paper files somewhere. However, the burn plans are of vital interest to a wider audience, and we want their contents easily viewable. They will be filed electronically.

Not all documents relate to agreements. Sure, the burn plan agreement and its associated document are a matched pair, but evidence collected about suspected arson activity causing the fire might come in the form of smartphone photos and videos from the public. We want that filed, but there most certainly wasn't a formal agreement for some ratbag to set the forest alight.

The evolving schematic (excluding Resources) now looks like:

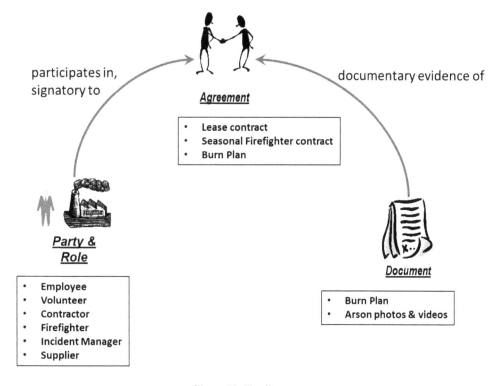

Figure 80: Fire Documents

We've now got some subtypes of a few patterns identified, and also relationships between them. We are actually progressing with the modeling of the Data Town Plan. We've done all this on whiteboards or hand-written extensions on participant copies of the nine base patterns. So, if we are doing data modeling (albeit in a way that's comfortable with the business folk), why not capture these details immediately in the chosen data modeling tool? My experience suggests that is typically *not* the way to go:

- We want multiple groups to be free to creatively represent their views without consideration (initially) of consolidation into the one "correct" model.

- The presentation using a formal modeling tool can be challenging for many participants.

- No matter how fast someone might be able to navigate around the multiple facets of a tool, they will probably slow things down relative to someone doodling on a whiteboard or a piece of paper.

Put simply, keep the workshop's modeling low-tech. By default, I suggest we leave the capture of workshop revelations in the modeling tool for later, especially as it may involve quite a bit of consideration (e.g., two groups using different names for essentially the same thing). Such resolution takes time, and the momentum of the workshop shouldn't be threatened by the forced introduction of the tool.

A checkpoint on patterns and their relationships

We've now drilled down into a few patterns and noted interrelationships. At this point, it can be good to revisit the larger palette and talk about common relationships between the patterns. This is when I hand out printed copies of the "Pattern of patterns" diagram. Again, you've seen it before, but another copy appears in Figure 81 for your convenience.

This diagram displays some of the more common interrelationships between the patterns. The reason for introducing it at this point in the workshop is to use it as a checklist to see if some of these relationships might apply as we progressively introduce more patterns.

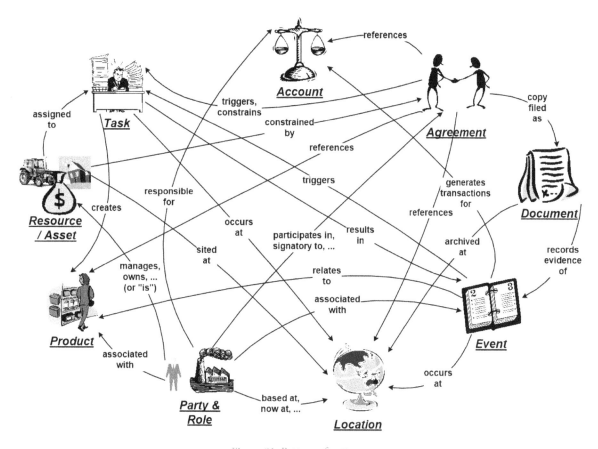

Figure 81: Pattern of patterns

Progressing with more patterns

Again, it's time to let each group have a go at adding the subtypes of importance to the business. As before, participants can simply write the subtypes on a whiteboard or the handout of the nine patterns. Also, as an optional extra, encourage them to write down discovered relationships as well, perhaps prompted by Figure 81.

Bit by bit, we introduce the remaining patterns and incorporate them into each group's diagram, adding (1) hand-written subtypes and (2) the interrelationships between the patterns. As we iterate to include each new pattern, each group presents their work-in-progress model. The other groups should feel free to take on board any ideas they like, but at this stage the workshop is still encouraging diversity of opinion. Consolidation will come shortly.

In this book, I will continue to use the fire scenario as a setting for understanding this process. Of course, in the real workshop, it will be the data of the specific enterprise that is captured. But for now, let's look again at "fires."

Next, we look at the Event pattern. For fires, types of events might include:

- Fire Detection, when a person in a fire tower or a member of the public notifies the central team that a new fire has been spotted.

- Fire Cause Allegation event, where an individual reports reasons that suggest the fire might have been deliberately lit by an arsonist, lightning, a campfire, or whatever.

- Fire Status event, when a fire has its official status changed, for example, from "Going" to "Contained" to "Out."

- Safety Incident, for example, when a firefighter is hurt while performing their duties.

- Communication event, for example, a public SMS message that is broadcast as a recommendation to evacuate.

As noted when the patterns were first introduced, there is a two-way relationship between Events and Tasks. For example, the Fire Detection event occurs, and Tasks are put in place to assemble and send a first-response team. The team arrives, and as one of their Tasks, they make a preliminary assessment of likely fire cause, and they suggest arson, hence creating an Event of type Fire Cause Allegation. This new Event then triggers tasks for forensic specialists to do a more detailed evaluation of the fire cause. Back and forth the Events and Tasks go. Within this context, the Tasks the workshop participants identify might include:

- First Response.

- Fire Cause Forensic Analysis.

- Fire Line Suppression.

These are some of the more obvious Tasks. But there are more, for example:

- Tasks such as Training and Fitness Assessment to prepare people for the upcoming season.

- For rostering purposes, not only is "work" on the front line treated as a type of Task, but "non-work" such as enforced Rest, Rostered Days Off, and Leave can be entered as types of "Tasks" in that they are entered into the calendar for consideration on availability.

Participants are again encouraged to use the fires examples and then consider their subtypes (and relationships).

The <u>Location</u> pattern is typically implemented as a Geographic Information System (GIS). The subtypes can be thought of as "layers" that could be turned on or off from display, including:

- Roads used to assist in finding the best route to the fire.

- Water points for collecting water.

- Airports for use by fire response aircraft.

- National and State Parks—these are important as, in my part of the world, fires in parks are primarily the responsibility of a government agency, but fires on private land are primarily the responsibility of a volunteer fire agency (though they help each other).

- Fire ignition points, fire line, and fire burn area.

- Conservation Zones within a park that have been set aside to study the ecology when it's not interrupted by man, including planned burns.

Two more of the nine common pattern pillars have not been mentioned. The first is Product. In my interaction with the fire people, "<u>Product</u>" was not seen as relevant. The one that might surprise you is that "<u>Account</u>" was also seen as being irrelevant! Sure, finances come into the larger picture, but the people I worked with to assemble the initial Enterprise Data Model simply did not see money as being that important. Saving people's lives was.

That's the nine pillars, but in the real-world fires scenario, workshop participants added another pattern, especially suited to the recording of the analysis performed by the forensic team. David Hay calls it the Laboratory pattern,[14] as it is commonly used for recording the analysis of diagnosis activities in laboratories. I recently worked in an organization performing forensics analysis, such as tests for alcohol or drugs in blood and saliva, and determining the DNA from skin samples. Their operational system used the Laboratory pattern.

The emergency response team also did analysis, for example, to determine the cause of a fire. The business wanted to call it the <u>Observation</u> pattern rather than the Laboratory pattern, and that raises an important point. It's a business-centric model, and they can assign names to the patterns that make sense to them. In a similar manner, some businesses like the word "Task," and others like "Activity." Let's be sensitive to their perspective.

The teams have been writing their subtypes on the "Palette of Patterns" sheet but have also added the interrelationships between the patterns. The final result has subtypes *and* relationships. A cleaned-up version of one team's hand-written schematic follows, showing relationships but suppressing the subtypes:

---

[14] Hay D. (1996) Data Model Patterns: Conventions of Thought.

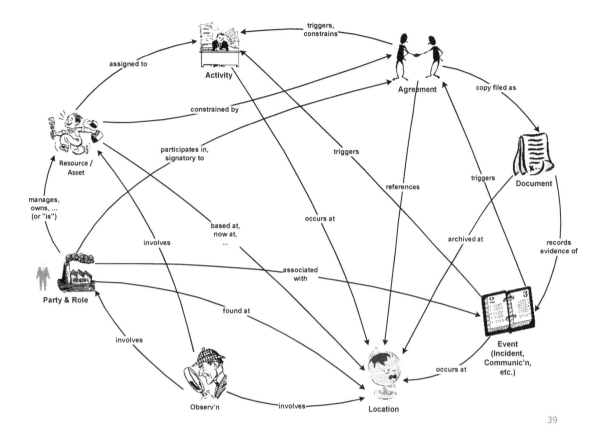

Figure 82: Schematic for the Fire emergency response scenario

That's the output from one team. The other team's models are likely to be a little bit different. Now, we want a single enterprise model that is somewhat aligned with David Hay's Essential model but still at the high level of his Overview model.

A consolidated enterprise model

We've deliberately encouraged diversity across the models produced by each group. That's one way to discover subtle but important differences. But now it's time for all participants to collectively work towards creating the one enterprise view.

If you've ever had to consolidate data from multiple sources, you will understand that merging models can be painful. I've already told the story of different views about fire trucks. In 'Figure 27: Making peace over Fire Truck naming,' and the accompanying text, I share how people with competing views can sometimes express quite a bit of passion about their perspective, yet gaps can nonetheless be respectfully closed. I have found that having people work with the common patterns creates an environment where differences are lessened and can often be relatively easily resolved. Often, different people contribute different subtypes of the same pattern and the subtypes can co-exist side-by-side. And if they actually represent the same thing, the participants can often agree on a name (perhaps Big Red Water-Squirting Vehicles), or simply use aliases. Too easy?

Unfortunately, there are times when the resolution can be a bit more challenging. It's time for another story.

We start with a fairly expectable snippet from the subtyping of Resource and Party.

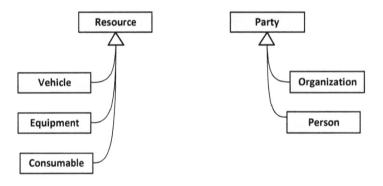

Figure 83: Common subtypes for Resource and Party

People have competencies (a license to drive a heavy vehicle, first aid training, ability to operate a chainsaw, etc.). Resources have capacities. A water tank can hold up to 1,500 liters, a crane can lift five tons, a fire truck has a driving range of 500 kilometers, and a chain saw can cut up to 500 mm/20 inches in depth in a single cut. We add a person's competencies and a resource's capacities to the model.

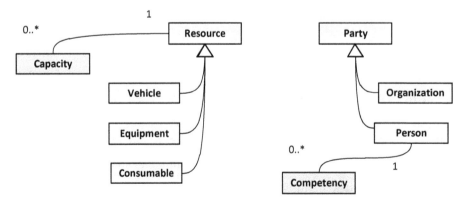

Figure 84: Capacity and Competency

Here's the twist. One of the groups suggested an alternative based on one of their member's perspectives as a Logistics Officer. To them, there's little difference between a person and a fire truck. We've mentioned this before, but simply restating that both need refueling (hamburgers in one case, diesel in another). Both need regular servicing (eight hours of sleep for one, a grease and oil change for the other). Both can be requested to be sent to the fire. Both can be deployed to front-line duties.

He saw the similarities going further. He suggested that we could say that competencies and capacities can be generalized and called "capabilities." His model for Resources was interesting.

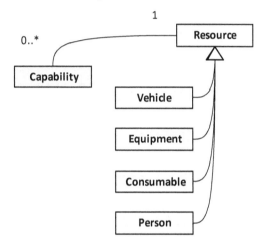

Figure 85: Person as a Resource

I called his model "interesting." The human resources (HR) people found it confronting. How dare someone liken a human being (a Person) to a fire truck (a Vehicle)?!

We reached some sort of a compromise.

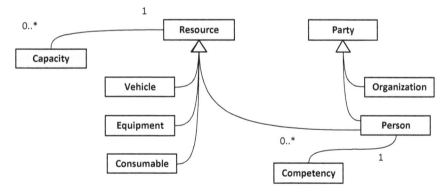

Figure 86: Person as a Resource and a Party

For those of you familiar with the UML, it's called multiple inheritance. A Person is a Resource, and a Person is also a Party. Would we directly implement something like this? Possibly not, especially as some object-oriented languages don't seem to be too comfortable with multiple inheritance.

But here's an important message. This is a model about business concepts, and at this level, some people see a person as a type of party, and others see them as a resource. The model captures both views and, if nothing else, will generate discussion when implementation has to be faced.

After a few twists and turns, we have a very high-level schematic resembling the group model in Figure 82.

Capturing the model

Earlier I encouraged the use of whiteboards during the workshops rather than capturing the emerging model directly into a data modeling tool. Now, it's time to flip things around. I suggest that, while whiteboards and butcher's paper are great for the workshops, the data model elements generated in the workshop need to be carefully and formally documented in a robust data modeling tool.

… and I will go further. This is not just a simple clerical act of transposing elements from the workshop notes into a tool to be performed by anyone who can type fast. Instead, I recommend that the data model experts in the team take responsibility for entry into the tool. Again and again, as I have done this myself, I am forced to consider and challenge ideas that were generated quickly during the workshop, but that might need to be thought about in more depth. As new perspectives emerge, get feedback from select members of the larger team, take a position, record it, and later share it more widely for sign-off.

Next steps

Assuming prior familiarity with the patterns and a good selection of creative participants, it is possible to assemble this framework in just days. It's helpful, it gives the business and the technical people a common vocabulary, it is pattern-based and hence likely to be able to be extended as new aspects are discovered. That's all good news.

But it is only a schematic, and for many purposes, we are going to need a bit more detail, though not so much that we drown in a never-ending search for the last attribute, so we want to target our drill-down efforts to where we will get the most value. Before I end the workshop, I seek feedback on where we might best focus our attention for deep-dive Divergent modeling. Sure, we could look at different business units or different business processes, or perhaps even think about doing further analysis on some of the data subject area patterns we've just discussed, and they may well be the choice of the assembled stakeholders, but by default, I do recommend instead that we focus on data problems that have caused pain in the past (and also consider options for the future). If we can contribute to solving some of these problems and delivering tangible value now and into the future, that's a win for all.

We've already encouraged participants (and their colleagues) to articulate pain points and vision. Now's a really good time to quickly review the list, see which ones are important, and seek some level of consensus on prioritization for deep-dive consideration, starting in the days immediately ahead of us when we perform Divergent modeling on what's important to the business.

Key points

- The goal is a unified, consistent view of core data across the enterprise.

  - Don't start by studying silos and hope for "automagical integration."
  - Do start by assembling a representative collection of people; Divergence into specialized views can (and should) come later.

- This "meeting-of-the-minds" workshop is focused on how the business sees their data.

  - Gently introduce data model patterns.
  - Ask the participants to identify pattern subtypes, and also identify major relationships.
  - While breaking the participants into groups during the workshop, aim to close the workshop by seeking a first-cut mutual view.

- Before the group breaks up, seek prioritization on drill-down topics for further analysis.

- After the workshop, the more technically minded data modelers can then consolidate workshop ideas and populate the first-cut Data Town Plan.

CHAPTER 18

Divergent Modeling (from Today's Pain to Tomorrow's Vision)

We've spoken about Divergent models. The setting for Divergent modeling happens when different groups of people see things in their own way, and *their* data model is articulated. Sometimes, one group is blissfully unaware that others see things differently. Other times, there is tension, where one group sees themselves as being "right," and they don't want to even consider cooperating with others.

I've already shared when I used the phrase, "Let's leverage off what is common and respect what is distinct." This isn't about seeing who can win. It's about developing a community understanding of the diverse perspectives. Perhaps it's a bit like politics, religion, or perhaps your favorite sports team? We may not always agree, but as some claim to be an expression from Voltaire, "I may not agree with what you say but I will defend to the death your right to say it." It is a precious thing to be able to freely express divergent views, but the rights to freedom of expression needs to be balanced with the responsibility of freedom; I suggest we do well when we are respectful of the views of others who see things differently.

Within the bounds of respectful communication, I think we can and should encourage open dialogue. But perhaps the next question is how we might slice up the enterprise to solicit divergent views? We've already touched on this topic, but we will briefly revisit it here as it is vital to understand.

Selecting the right slice through the enterprise

When we do the _initial_ Data Town Plan modeling, we deliberately try to create a foundational view based on a whole-of-enterprise perspective. We actively avoid trying to create a holistic view by studying parts and then trying to bang them together to see the whole. Instead, we want to start with a "systems thinking" view, as I have mentioned by referencing Russell Ackoff. We don't want to start by performing a deep analysis of business units, business processes, IT systems, or other such divisionary slices. Instead, we want to assemble a representative team from across the breadth of the enterprise to get a first-cut framework that represents the whole.

But when we get to performing _Divergent_ modeling, the ground shifts. We've already laid the foundation of a holistic view of data across the enterprise in the initial workshop. Now, we deliberately want to challenge and refine the emerging Data Town Plan by drilling into any slices that may help us. And yes, that can be by business unit, business process, pain point, future vision, data subject area, or whatever way the team prioritize.

Whatever the approach taken, let's remember that Divergent modeling provides detail within the context of the central overview model; these slices are not independent silos.

For the following notes, I have chosen just one pair, namely today's "pain points" and tomorrow's "vision." I often find that this is a beneficial default way to slice up the enterprise. After all, the business people have identified where it hurts and perceived limitations for tomorrow, and if we can deliver some relief, we will be appreciated and perhaps even funded!

Using today's pain points and tomorrow's vision to drive the drill-down

As a result of running the initial workshop and collating the results into the Data Town Plan on your chosen data modeling tool, the business and data folk now have an agreed framework for core data subject areas. They have a common language with a common understanding. The value of improved understanding and precision in communication should not be underestimated. Nonetheless, the larger goal is to turn this understanding into tangible delivery for the business.

The central message is that trying to flesh out the complete enterprise model can be like trying to boil the ocean. Instead, we only pay attention to areas most *likely to deliver welcome relief to the business. One approach is to perform multiple iterations, each time looking into a nominated "pain point" or dream for the future.*

These pain point/vision workshops are similar in nature to the initial workshops, but simply with a more focused audience and a tighter set of constraints.

So, we start with the current Data Town Plan, and develop a more detailed model. We take existing entities, relationships, and attributes, and challenge, extend and refine them. This new understanding can then be the foundation for high-level, generic discussions on possible solutions.

There's a warning here. I am the sort of person who loves to move from "problem" thinking to "solution" thinking. At times I need to remind myself to slow down and make sure I really understand what the business is saying before getting excited about solutions, especially if some solutions are somewhat technical.

Post-workshop clean-up

Just as we did for the initial workshop, we don't capture participant contributions into the data modeling tool during the workshop. But immediately following each pain point/vision workshop, I work with the data people to weave the new elements into the current version of the Data Town Plan. We never lose sight of the goal to have a unified, holistic Convergent Data model.

At every stage along the way, new revelations are carefully woven in. I like to allow time between workshops for this activity, but sometimes I have been pushed and will work another shift into the evening just so that I can start tomorrow with a new, clean baseline.

Bottom-up quality assurance?

The Data Town Plan has deliberately been developed in a top-down manner. That's arguably the best way to do town planning, be it for cities or to develop a business-centered view of the data of an enterprise. But there is also a role for bottom-up cross-checking.

For example, if your organization already has captured examples of data, why not use them to perform *quality assurance* on the Data Town Plan?

Or perhaps you can use extracts from existing IT systems, and perhaps employ a data profiling tool. However, there's a caution. Today's systems may have data structures that the business very explicitly wants to leave behind.

Presentation to participants

OK, so you've completed the documentation of the Divergent model, and performed a quality assurance to check it out. To finalize the exercise, it's time to present your work back to the stakeholders. This includes at least those who participated in the Divergent model deep dive, and possibly some also from the broader group.

Future iterations

The notes above address development of the first few deep-dive Divergent models. The Data Town Plan is best seen as a living artifact. Going forward, all sorts of things can happen. Companies can merge or split. Government regulations can force changes. Economic factors can trigger urgent reconsideration of the scope and direction of the entire organization. Or new IT ventures need some details to support their initiative.

Whatever the catalyst, the Data Town Plan can and should adapt. The approach for any review and extension can be based on the way the first Divergent models are developed as described above.

Key points

- The foundational unified view has been assembled; now it's time to consciously dive deeper into divergent views.

- One (of several) ways to slice up the deep dives is by analyzing "pain points" where data issues are really hurting the business today, and perceived visionary changes likely to occur in the future .

- As each separate topic is understood, the resultant insight is added to the Data Town Plan (but in a way where its unique perspective can still be seen separately).

- The Data Town Plan, by its very nature, is developed "top-down" i.e. starting with a big-picture perspective. At times, this helicopter-view should be challenged by more detailed (bottom-up) cross-checking.

- You could do analysis for divergent views forever ("analysis paralysis"). Don't do that. Instead, seek prioritization by the business, of the business, for the business!

CHAPTER 19

Did Someone say, "Convergent Modeling"?

I remember technical manuals from the 1970s and 1980s that had pages with the only words being "This page intentionally left blank." I never did understand such thinking. As a bit of a joke, I was tempted to say something about the chapter on Convergent modeling being *almost* left blank. The reality is that we've gone into quite a bit of detail for development of the initial Model-on-a-Page, and the subsequent Divergent models. But the goal is to assemble a single, unified, consistent Convergent model. So what's required?

Well, almost nothing!

I don't know whether I am going to disappoint you, or give you a feeling of elation, because if each divergent model is carefully woven into the whole, there is no more work to be done! The Convergent model is progressively created at each step.

… so we have an entire section of the book that's almost consisting of the words "… intentionally left blank"!

CHAPTER 20

The Principle of Iteration

Some initiatives are one-off projects. Developing a town plan for a new city commonly has an initial flurry of activity, with production of first cut documents, but then there will be refinements and extensions for probably the life of the city.

Similarly, a Data Town Plan often has an initial burst, with production of the baseline version. But then you can expect iterations from time to time, each one typically targeting a specific business catalyst. The Data Town Plan can be, and arguably should be, a living artifact. Not one that takes years to kick off, and not one that takes a large investment of time and money to maintain, but nonetheless an artifact that stays current and relevant.

Earlier we briefly introduced the idea of the "T-model" approach to fleshing out progressive details. The table is repeated in Table 21 for convenience.

Focus	Model type	Data subject area								
		Account	Agreement	Document	Event	Location	Party	Product	Resource	Task
Data Town Plan (Business)	Model-on-a-Page (Overview model)	x	x	x	x	x	x	x	x	x
	Divergent + Convergent models		x		x		x	x		
Technical design (Solution)	Logical data model		x				x	x		
	Physical data model						x			

Table 21: The T-model approach

We've spoken about forming the "model-on-a-page" view. It's a mile-wide, inch-deep perspective. It covers all the major elements of the entire Data Town Plan, but in very little detail. Table 21 shows *all* of the Model-on-a-page elements addressed.

Then we looked at developing multiple Divergent models. Each one will progressively provide more detail within the context of the overall Data Town Plan. Table 21 shows at least some detail created for Agreement, Event, Party, and Product.

That's as far as we go for the Data Town Plan, doing Divergent (and associated Convergent) modeling.

In the bigger scheme of things, the Data Town Plan will be used to drive implementation of technology solutions, and these may involve development of so-called "logical" data models and "physical" data models. Business people don't have to be concerned about what these are. It is enough to say that the drill-down we started does go further.

Going forward, sometimes the whole Data Town Plan might be revisited, but often it's just another one or two deep-dive Divergent additions, each one enriching the holistic Convergent model.

Too easy?! (I make light of the effort in maintaining the Data Town Plan, but we must recognize that there are likely to be several enterprise-wide data management initiatives that take significant effort, but these are best left to others in other books.)

PART 4

Reflections on Data Town Plans

It's time now to consolidate the learning. Before you launch out, it may be prudent to be warned of some of the myths that can devalue or derail a Data Town Plan initiative. You may benefit from understanding how the Data Town Plan can play happily with other initiatives, and how to communicate the message.

… and for those charged with the responsibility of turning the Data Town Plan into technology solutions, the appendix after this Part may generate discussion on options.

CHAPTER 21

Debunking Data Town Plan Myths

You might ask why we don't see Data Town Plans developed more often? At least part of the answer is that there are all sorts of concerns floating about, especially for the larger "conceptual" models. For example, people genuinely ask:

- Are "conceptual models" worth developing?
- Are they even feasible?
- Do we need to make a nuisance of ourselves and involve the business, or can IT do it on its own (after all, aren't they the "data" specialists)?
- It might work for others, but aren't we different?
- … and more.

Please, I am not trying to cynically attack responsible people who express genuine concerns. And let's face it, those concerns are often based on experience or observation of failures. Nonetheless, let's see if we can remove some of the roadblocks in an objective way, especially as the whole idea of a minimalistic Data Town Plan challenges assumptions often made about large and costly initiatives to develop conceptual models.

Myth: Data modeling is dead (or should be)

From time to time, I see conversations on platforms such as LinkedIn debating whether or not data modeling is dead.

To put my answer in context, let's look very briefly at a bit of (technical) history. In the early days, data models were almost exclusively aimed at physical implementation (with perhaps some logical modeling being performed while debates raged about alternative implementation platforms). In the 1980s, relational databases were dominating. Even back then, some developers argued that it was more efficient to just create tables directly without a model. Conversely, some would argue that there still was a model in such scenarios, but the model was in the developer's head, not on paper or in some tool. Whatever your opinion on that topic, I think we can agree that the focus was commonly on relational database design, for physical implementation, of operational systems.

Things keep changing. Data modeling for agile projects tends to be lightweight, if even done (formally) at all. Schema-on-Read means you don't need a physical data model up front. There are a variety of data models related to the data warehouse world. And the story goes on and on.

But here's the crunch. Most of the topics above lean toward design solutions for implementation. Sadly, many of our tertiary institutes, if they still teach data modeling at all, have buried their data modeling training inside some technology-focused curriculum. Even if they do include data modeling in more business-focused courses, I've heard cases where they continue to focus on technical aspects such as "first, second and third normal form." Unsurprisingly, the feedback tells me they succeed in convincing business-minded folk that they don't want to hear about data modeling again. Ever.

Ah, but perhaps the solution is to move our attention from physical (and logical) data modeling to "conceptual" data modeling? If the focus now shifts to business concepts and their inter-relationships, perhaps we're making progress, and that sounds more business-centric.

Before we go further with this line of thinking, I'd like to try and get clarity on a related matter. Some from the technical ranks define a conceptual model as nothing more than their solution-centric, technology-based data models, but with details such as attributes stripped out. If the attribute-free tables are a direct reflection of some implementation (especially a package that at best has an imperfect fit to the business), then I argue that's not a conceptual model. It's just a stripped back solution model.

Imagine the business concept of Project being presented as TABLE_0123! That's probably a bit unfair, as I might have taken a high-level view of a physical data model rather than a logical data model, but you get the point. Physical entities/tables, or even their logical equivalents, can be expected to typically focus on a solution view rather than necessarily on business concepts.

So I don't define a conceptual model as some high-level view (perhaps an attribute-free view) of a physical or logical *solution* model. Instead, I would like to define a conceptual model as something that focuses on business *concepts*. And I argue that the need for an enterprise-wide, business-centric view of data (a Data Town Plan) is more important than ever to support things like corporate data integration and sharing. Data modeling at this level is far from dead. (And I would argue that there is still a valuable role for logical and physical modeling, but that's another story.)

Myth: We can't expect business executives to get involved

I've already told a number of stories of client sites where a Data Town Plan was developed, but I now want to briefly focus on the involvement of senior management.

One such site was for a government agency that had been forced to embrace a merger of 83 other organizations, and they knew they needed help. They rolled their sleeves up and actively participated. That was great.

At a mid-tiered bank, again the senior team knew they had hit a road-block, and I was welcomed with open arms. Again, in a very short time, we collaboratively developed a Data Town Plan that got things going again.

Or take a church with a massive and well-respected social outreach arm. Three weeks of intensive cooperation between IT and management, and we collectively delivered tangible value.

In all those stories (and more), senior management were passionately involved with IT, and the outcome was well received by both groups. And in all those cases I was asked to come back and help them more.

Sometimes the involvement of the most senior management is less. For example, they may demonstrate their endorsement of the Data Town Plan development by kicking off workshops, then delegating to others. And that's fine. But sometimes they see a Data Town Plan as an IT thing, and simply won't make time. (As noted in 'Variations on the ideal team,' that can work if the IT folk have a deep understanding of the business, and are trusted by the business, but I suggest that should not be the default approach.)

Worse, there are times when management doesn't trust IT. Perhaps they have had their fingers burned too many times after investing good funds in failed initiatives. Perhaps some people who work in IT are the problem. Perhaps they look down on non-technical people and can't or won't build bridges.

So here's another bit of this book I don't really want to put into print, but feel I must. There are times when you may have to walk away. Absolutely keep the goal of business engagement front and center, but if your best efforts at building bridges and sharing your vision are resisted, perhaps put your energy into something else. Perhaps the words of one version of the Serenity Prayer are applicable here:

"God, grant me the serenity to accept the things I cannot change,

the courage to change the things I can,

and the wisdom to know the difference."

Myth: We don't have time, so let's take a shortcut

I enjoy the great outdoors, but some of my "shortcuts" have become infamous. There was a time when a group of us were at a beach, and our campsite was about one kilometer away in a direct line. There was a cleared track that wandered through the scrubby growth, but it was perhaps two kilometers long. I suggested that I and a few youngsters could make out own track through the undergrowth in a direct line, and start the billy boiling for a cuppa while the rest of the group went the longer route. Some Aussie bush is very dense. The "long route" took those who chose it about half an hour. The "short cut" took several hours!

Or there was the time we were driving to a beach on Cape York in north-eastern Australia. The long route was on an established track but a few hundred kilometers long. The short route was a mere 70 kilometers. The shortcut ended up so overgrown we had to clear small trees that had grown between the wheel ruts, forcing us to realize that nobody had used this track for years. And we discovered why: 70 kilometers took us two days of hard driving!

I say "driving," but much of that time was spent walking, trying to find the track that had petered out. We would turn off the engines, spread out in different directions, looking for wheel marks. When someone found signs of the track, they would return to the vehicles, toot the horn to call the rest back, and we'd drive for another few hundred meters and repeat the exercise. Again and again.

My shortcut was unpopular. And when we eventually got to the beach, it was infested with crocodiles. Unpopular again!

Shortcuts can end up being the long way!

It's true for IT as well. A friend of mine has a wall poster that questions, "How come we don't have the time or money to do things right the first time, but always have the time and money to fix things that went wrong?"

I've encountered good people who recognize the "right way" of basing certain solution designs on an enterprise-wide, business-centric view, and actually endorse this approach in theory, but in practice they seem to take short cuts. And one reason given is that they believe that the right way (of developing the Data Town Pan before spending time and money on building an IT solution) is simply unachievable.

One of the reasons I have heard for holding this view is that some of our best and brightest technical people are absolute gems at what they do, but they don't have the skills and/or interest to perform business-centric modeling. There is some truth behind that concern, but that doesn't mean you shouldn't look until you find people who *can* develop a Data Town Plan.

But the main reason for not even attempting to develop a Data Town Plan (or similar) is that many believe that it will take too long, so let's go for the shortcut ("just start coding"). Can these models take a long time? Sure. They _can_. But they don't have to.

I remember when "instant cakes, just add water" first came out. My mum emphatically announced you could have "good" (fresh eggs, fresh milk, fresh butter) _or_ "fast" (with a packet mix). This book encourages us to leverage off published data model patterns so that we can get "good" (the patterns are proven, implementable, extensible) _and_ "fast."

You've already read the earlier "Happy ending" stories, but how well is "good and fast" accepted? I worked with a team at one telecommunications company where one of the team left and joined another telecommunications company, and he asked me to "do the same thing" at his new company. One of his team subsequently left and joined Australia's organization that manages registration of medical practitioners, and he asked me to join him there and do for them what he'd seen me do at the telecommunications company. One of his team left there and joined a water utility, and asked me to repeat my fast and good there. One of his people left and joined yet another organization, and I was asked if I could help them … The moral of the story is that initial value can be delivered in weeks, and that value is clearly recognized by happy customers. Don't let unfounded fear of mammoth data modeling projects deter you.

Myth: Our reality is different and complex, so text-book solutions won't fit

"We're unique." How often have you heard that?

I've heard people express criticism of patterns as being too generic to be able to deliver value for the specific requirements of an organization. "We're different, so it's a waste of time trying to see if patterns that suit others can help us." That seems to be the thinking.

My first response is to look at how Len Silverston views the use of data model patterns. He suggests that you can walk into an organization and there's a good chance that something like 50% of their requirements can be represented with off-the-shelf patterns. After all, most organizations have employees, customers, products, and the like. Len goes further, suggesting that if you have some patterns more aligned to that organization's industry, you might get the fit to perhaps 75%. And he then suggests that the remaining 25% might be specific, for example, reflecting what gives that particular organization its competitive advantage. So there's a happy synergy between common aspects and uniqueness.

My next response relates to adjusting the generic patterns. I actually agree with those who caution against unthinking use of data model patterns. Sometimes the patterns offer more flexibility than is required; not all features may be helpful. Conversely, the patterns may be missing bits and pieces that truly are uncommon, but even in such cases, you may find the patterns offer a solid foundation for extending and refining.

I remember consulting to one organization with unusual requirements for their core IT system. A person was engaged to count the "function points" to get a feeling for the size of the development project. The project was discovered to be so large that this individual ran out of funding before completing counting the function points, but concluded that the project size for what had been counted would equate to $50 million Aussie dollars. I was part of a small, tight team of remarkable individuals that used some pretty challenging and highly technical data model patterns, and delivered the project for $6.2 million Aussie dollars. I had responsibility for the data model, and while I do think it contributed to this amazing outcome, I do have to concede the much larger factor was the caliber of the development team. But hey, the model certainly helped by providing the foundation!

Your organization might also be more unique than most, and if that's true, I applaud you for being willing to be different. Nonetheless, I do also encourage careful consideration as to what benefits proven data model patterns may bring to the table. As Len suggests, they may address many of your needs so that you can focus on the important stuff—what makes your business different.

Myth: There is only one "reality," and therefore can only be one correct model

Years ago some data practitioners expressed the idea that there is only one "real world" out there, and that a modeler's job is to articulate and map to that single reality. In the minds of some, it followed that if there could only ever be one "reality," there could only ever be one correct model. That would certainly simplify things if it was true, and if it was also true that the involved modelers could agree on that reality and how to model it.

In the 1990s, Graeme Simsion, a highly respected Australia data modeler, took a different view that suggested data modeling is a design activity rather than being a deterministic description of what exists. He published that view as a magazine article, and was surprised when he became recognized with the dubious distinction of having the most negative reaction of any article ever published in that magazine. The reaction came from a particular quarter, and Graeme dug deeper, going so far as to complete a PhD on the topic of design versus description, and subsequently publishing a matching book[15]. If people believe that there is only one reality and one correct model, there can be real tension between modelers. If my model is different to yours, one of us must be wrong. If, on the

---

[15] Simsion, G (2007) Data Modeling Theory and Practice.

other hand, modeling is seen as a creative design task, then alternative designs can be gracefully and respectfully considered for their relative merits.

If you hadn't guessed by now, I am convinced by the rigorous research performed by Graeme, concluding there is no single correct model. However, even recently I was surprised to encounter an individual who was from the old "one reality" school. Just be aware that such attitudes still exist, and that they can, in my opinion, cause unnecessary tension, with debates as to who has "the" correct model.

So my advice is pretty straightforward. Help the business articulate how *they* see their data. Work collaboratively to deliberately generate alternative perspectives. Seek some level of agreement on the relative merits of these alternatives. As a team, pick one model, but definitely document why you chose that design, and note the alternatives—who knows, as the future unfolds you may wish to reconsider designs that didn't make it the first time.

Myth: There is no role for "business keys"

Some of the more technical folk amongst us see an absolute need for "identifiers" when we implement most if not all IT solutions. For example, in the relational database world, there are candidate keys, primary keys, and foreign keys. And there may be "natural" keys and "surrogate" keys.

But we're trying to focus on the business perspective. Do we even care about identifiers for things? In some settings there is resistance to nomination of the "business keys" tied to business concepts, but I suggest that it is often helpful to open up the discussion on identifiers, and to record the results. Let have a bit of fun looking at some examples.

For some real-world objects, the identifiers are clear and unambiguous. Some of the things you and I might buy will have a globally unique serial number stamped on them (well, at least it's unique for that given manufacturer).

The cars you and I drive are a bit more interesting. They typically can be identified by the registration plates (for a given state or country), the Vehicle Identification Number (VIN) stamped on their body, or the engine number. Now things get interesting.

I don't know if it's' true, but I was told that one state in the USA uses the VIN as its primary identifier of a vehicle, which works well if the car gets re-registered. Then another adjacent state apparently uses the engine number, which again is stable if the vehicle is re-registered. But what on earth happens if two car enthusiasts retain their car bodies but do an engine swap, one from one state and one from the other?

Or here's one that might make you smile. A friend of mine worked with a system to help coordinate services for indigenous people in remote communities in Australia. He's a data professional, and wanted to know how to identify each person.

He spoke to one person, and asked their name. The answer was, "Do you want to know my current name, my previous name, or my next name?" As a child, this individual had been named after a tribal elder, but this elder had recently died, and out of respect for the deceased, his name could not be uttered, so the individual was given a temporary name until his mother decided which living elder would be the basis for his new name.

My friend asked if he knew the number of his driver's license. He didn't have one. He did drive, but for driving within the enormous area of his tribal land, a license presumably wasn't required.

Ah, perhaps he could use a birth certificate. He didn't have one. He didn't even have a birth date. He didn't even know the year he was born, just that he was born in the "wet" (that part of Australia has two seasons—wet and dry).

He didn't have a passport, and didn't even know what a passport was. Not an issue, as he had no intention of travelling overseas. Perhaps an electoral registration? He had never voted. A medical identifier? He'd never needed health care. And the list went on and on.

The message from this story is that it may be really important to talk to people about how they identify things rather than making assumptions (And yes, the Party pattern does make some assumptions about the details of people, and as stated before, patterns may need to be challenged.) Chat to the people, note what they use to identify things. That can be helpful later on. But don't fret if the best you can find are "soft," imprecise identifiers.

Key points

- Data modeling as a practice is still evolving, but also still continues to be important, increasingly for enterprise-level integration.

- Business people can be enthusiastically involved in defining their perspective of essential business data, especially if introduced to data modeling in a non-threatening, non-technical manner.

- Development of the enterprise-wide strategic view of core business concepts is valuable, and should not be avoided due to (false) perceptions that the model cannot be delivered in a timely manner.

- While it is true that every business has elements that are unique, there are also many common aspects; leverage of what is common and respect what is distinct.

- The Data Town Plan should not be limited to what some people think is a single "reality." Instead, have fun, be creative, and add value by dreaming of what could be.

- Unique identifiers for business objects can become a technical focus for IT folk. Relax, and let the business tell us what identifiers are important to them.

CHAPTER 22

Beware of Concept Definitions that are too Vague

In the earlier section titled 'Myth: Data modeling is dead (or should be),' I argued that a conceptual model should be all about concepts. I'd like to think that's a self-obvious statement, but in case there is still some debate about that, I would like to turn to the position taken by Juha Korpela, a fellow data modeler whom I highly respect (both as a professional, and as a truly delightful person). I quoted him earlier, but in summary, when he noted some debate on what a "conceptual" model was, he cut to the chase in a beautifully succinct manner, asking if the focus was on the *business* or on a *solution*, suggesting that solution-centric modeling was applicable to logical and physical models, and a business focus was applicable to conceptual models.

OK, so assuming we all agree that conceptual models (and hence Data Town Plans as a high-level variant of conceptual modeling) need to represent business concepts, we might still have a problem or two. It has already been noted that getting precise, unambiguous agreement on terms like "Customer" can be challenging, but I've seen an even more fundamental issue, namely some people resisting even trying to pin down precise definitions.

Some data modelers I have observed are happy to leave definitions vague. Perhaps they're just lazy, but I think the issue goes deeper. If they point-blank refuse to provide precise definitions, I suspect they feel safe because nobody can challenge them! That may be fine for their self-protection, but it's very unhelpful for creating a unified, agreed enterprise view.

Observations of vague definitions

I have painful recollections of being asked to review the conceptual model of another person who I will call Matt (not his real name). The model had named concepts represented by words in boxes on a diagram, and some unnamed lines between them, and little else. And I was instructed to provide a critical analysis of the model.

One of Matt's concepts was "Product." As I talked about earlier, each instance of Product *could* represent one entry in the company's product catalog (with attributes such as Product Description and Recommended Retail Price). Alternatively, each instance of Product *might* represent precisely one item as sold to a customer (with attributes such as Product Serial Number, Customer Number, Sale Price and Sale Date). For example, Apple might have a few dozen mobile phone products in their product catalog, and may have millions of items recorded as sales for each model.

Both concepts are distinctly different, and pattern authors portray each concept separately, with unique names. For example, David Hay refers to Product Type to represent product catalog items, and Product to represent individual stock items.

But here's the crunch. Matt had one Product concept, and he refused to add any attributes that might clarify which of the two concepts he was representing. OK, the inclusion of attributes in a conceptual model is controversial, so I can give a little ground there (though I still hold that a business-centric Data Town Plan can be enriched by inclusion of attributes that the business see as being important). But Matt also absolutely refused to add a description to any "concept." I repeatedly requested provision of descriptions, but Matt stubbornly refused, defending his position of non-cooperation with the argument that his model was "just conceptual."

I simply could not review a model where a concept could be interpreted as anything the reader wanted it to be, and Matt would not provide unambiguous definitions, so I saw no option other than to escalate the issue to the manager who was paying me to review Matt's model. The manager completely agreed with me, ordering Matt to add definitions. Matt went through the motions of obedience, but his definitions were half-hearted to say the least. I can still remember his definition for a concept he had titled "Asset Type"—Matt's full, complete, unabridged definition was "Type of asset."

That definition added absolutely nothing to help with communication, and given that one goal of a data model is to aid communication and remove ambiguity, I gave Matt's model a resounding "fail."

So what are my recommendations? Every concept should have a helpful definition, supplemented where reasonable with some examples (and perhaps examples of what real-world things do *not* fit into this concept). And yes, selective attributes, synonyms, and type/subtype classification hierarches where the business deems them to be helpful.

Bridging the conceptual/implementation divide

Going back to the town planning for a city, there are patterns for everything from hospitals and schools to industrial estates and essential infrastructure. The important thing is that the "concept" of a hospital is implementable. You can actually build these things.

Another of my issues with Matt's model was that he included concepts that, in my opinion, had not even the slightest possibility of being built. The concepts were not only too vague, they were also ungrounded in reality. I tried to ease the tension by suggesting that if a concept of perpetual motion had been portrayed, perhaps it should be removed on the grounds it simply could never be realized. He was unmoved. To him, concepts didn't have to have any semblance of reality; as long as things were "just conceptual," he seemed to hold the view that there should be no constraints on his creativity.

I unequivocally support Juha's separation between models that reflect the business, and models that reflect solutions, but I also like to have the comfort that business ideas portrayed in the conceptual model might have paths to implementation. However, I will express a caution here. Some technical people hear of a business problem, and jump too quickly to just one technical solution, sometimes before really showing the courtesy of trying to fully understand the problem. Please be aware of that danger, but don't reject technical people who may wish to at least table some solution options to enable and enrich further discussion.

So here's where I try to seek peace between the business and technical parties. If we use proven patterns that are (1) able to aid communication at the business concept level, and (2) also provide insight into solution options for implementation, why not leverage off the accumulated wisdom they contain? Len Silverston and Paul Agnew wrote an entire book with this as one of the book's central themes[16].

In conclusion, I prefer to use proven (and implementable) data model patterns to guide the shaping of the Data Town Plan, but where new concepts are identified that might not comfortably fit with these patterns, I still seek some assurance that the new elements in the Data Town Plan have a reasonable expectation that the world of business concepts can be bridged to get into the world of technical solutions.

Key points

- A given term such as "Customer" can be seen differently across the business. We need to articulate clear, unambiguous definitions, supplemented as appropriate with things like examples, synonyms and classification hierarchies.

- There is a potential tension between business concepts and IT implementation. Data model patterns can aid conceptual thinking *and* facilitate implementation.

---

[16] Silverston, L. and Agnew, P. (2008) The Data Model Resource Book, Volume 3: Universal Patterns for Data Modeling.

CHAPTER 23

Keeping Things in Balance

Top-down versus Bottom-up and As-is versus To-be

Let's take a scenario to try and open up discussion on when and where we might start our modeling top-down or bottom-up, and then also consider these choices against another dimension, namely an "as-is" versus a "to-be" perspective. For the sake of trying to make sure you and I are on the same page, I am proposing the following definitions:

- Top-Down: Whether for a city, a house, or a data model, I suggest that "top-down" involves starting with the big picture or, as some people like to phrase it, the "helicopter view." From there, we can drill down into details later.

- Bottom-Up: Unsurprisingly, "bottom-up" is the reverse. You start by looking at the details in various silos, and bit-by-bit seek to assemble the larger, overall perspective.

Many conversations stop there, but in order to assemble a Data Town Plan, we might also consider whether we are modeling the "As-is" (current state) view of the world or the "To-be" (future state).

Now we can have some fun, combing these two dimensions. First, let's look at someone who is thinking of building/renovating/selling a house.

Let's look at each of the quadrants in Table 22.

	Top-down (Start with the big picture "helicopter view", subsequently drill down into detail)	Bottom-up (Start with detail, subsequently develop the big picture)
To-be (Future state)	Quadrant A: I want a new house, so I sit down with an architect. I share broad requirements (3 bedrooms plus a work-from-home office, capture the views to the west …). The architect sketches concept drawings. The architect & I discuss the merits of those drawings. If something "feels" good, then we can drill down into detail so we can get a more detailed idea of costs and delivery schedules.	Quadrant B: I want a new house with a Trombe wall for heating, earth-tube for cooling, internal water containers for thermal mass, straw-bale external walls for insulation …). As long as those detailed features are delivered, I initially don't particularly care about the big picture. Options on a big picture can come later if my essential needs are met.
As-is (Current state)	Quadrant C: I want to sell my existing house, and I want an estate agent to profile my home against others on the market. I'm not asking for advice on how to renovate it for profit; I just want a big-picture view so we can value the house. If the results are disappointing, then I might drill down into detail to see what improvements I can make.	Quadrant D: I want to asses my current house to determine if I should invest in renovations or simply bulldoze the whole thing. To make a decision, I need some details on topics such as: - Thermal imaging to assess heat loss. - Blower tests to detect poor sealing. - Termite inspection. - Black mold detection. From those details, I will subsequently take a position on if the house is worth improving, and develop a big picture perspective of "how".

Table 22: Top-down versus Bottom-up (for As-is, To-be)

Quadrant A is a Top-down approach to designing a new (To-be) house. Because we're doing a top-down design, the conversation begins with big-picture requirements. Later we can drill into fun details. This is a very common combination (top-down with to-be) for articulating future vision, be it for a city or an Enterprise Data Model. Please read the text in that quadrant to reinforce the ideas here.

Let's jump to Quadrant D, where today's "as-is" current state is inspected in detail by looking at what currently exists. (Again, please read the text in the quadrant.) This is again a very common combination. In IT, what is sometimes referred to as "reverse engineering" is practiced to get a detailed, bottom-up view of existing systems. OK, it's common, but is it what we want to be doing for developing a Data Town Plan? The answer is we often will get real value from a detailed (bottom-up) analysis of current-state IT systems, but for a Data Town Plan, that's not where we want to *start*, especially if we are embracing an overall "top-down" approach. Let's now look at Quadrant C.

Quadrant C is interesting. It's top-down, and it is looking at the "as-is" current state. For a Data Town Plan, we not only want to hear of dreams for the future (quadrant A), but we also want to know the reality of today's pain. Both perspectives are important. To assemble this quadrant's view, we want to get people who are familiar with today's landscape (and who are able to express it in broad-brush terms—we don't want to get bogged down in details yet).

Quadrant B is included for completeness, but may be less common in *initial* development of a Data Town Plan. Later on, after the Data Town Plan foundations are laid, we will want to hear details about today's "pain points" (Quadrant D), and also details if applicable about vision for the future (Quadrant B). But we don't want to spend too much time in either of these detail quadrants at the outset. Please read on.

The devil's in the details, or the devil is the details?

In the above paragraphs, I emphasized what we do at the *start* of developing a Data Town Plan, but hinted that we might wish to go into more detail later. A few comments follow.

Cross-checking the Data Town Plan

Eventually, we hope that the Data Town Plan will influence the implementation of actual IT solutions. But before taking the Data Town Plan and selectively transferring its ideas into logical and physical models, we should cross-check and challenge it in detail. And this may require more detail than we welcomed in the formative stages of developing the Data Town Plan. Some ways of cross-checking are:

- We can engage with subject matter experts who live their day-to-day lives with sleeves rolled up in the mess and challenge of keeping things operating.

- We spoke earlier about data profiling tools and using sample data. The section on 'Bottom-up quality assurance?' suggests that if you have access to such material, now might be a good time to look at the detail to challenge (and perhaps refine) your Data Town Plan, but again checking to see if the views presented reflect today's views or tomorrow's.

Data quality

For a Data Town Plan, I may choose to start with a design that embraces flexibility. However, this very flexibility, if directly implemented in an IT solution, may permit data entry that is in breach of detailed business rules. For example, for something as simple as data entry into a screen, if you want an address, you want a valid address, and if you want a date-of-birth for a job applicant, you might want to make sure the applicant is older than a primary school child and younger than 100 (though you may want to be careful on the 100-year-old age limit—the way my "retirement" is going, I may end up working with you when my grey hairs are replaced by total baldness!)

So, we can start with a Data Town Plan that is used as an outline and has inherent flexibility, but as we move towards implementation using logical and physical models, we will need detail.

The feedback loop (concepts and implementation)

One of the goals behind having a future-based Data Town Plan is that we take the idealistic business concepts then turn that vision into working reality within some new IT solutions. Shouldn't that be the end, with everybody living happily ever after like happens in fairy tales?

Figure 87 seeks to convey the message that sometimes, when we delve into the inevitable details of solution delivery, we may discover holes in our conceptual thinking. And that's OK. We used the Data Town Plan's vision to create initial solution designs, discover implementation difficulties, challenge the originating conceptual thinking, and adapt the Data Town Plan to reflect new thinking.

The two perspectives have a lovely symbiotic relationship, enriching each other. The concepts drive implementation of solutions. We are grateful for improved solutions, but we discover that they are not perfect. That may drive a creative review of the Data Town Plan, that in turn drives improved (but imperfect) solutions that …

Concepts must be implementable

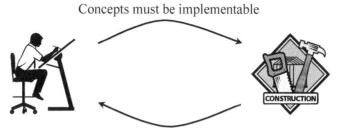

Implementation discoveries can be the catalyst
for creative review of business concepts.

Figure 87: Conceptual/implementation feedback loop

It's a value-adding cycle, where we welcome feedback. The last thing we want is people getting defensive about the Data Town Plan as if it cannot be challenged or changed.

CHAPTER 24

Communicating the Model

You may encounter comments that non-technical people can struggle to understand some technical data modeling notation. They are unlikely to immediately warm to things like optionality and cardinality (or multiplicity if you are presenting an Object-Oriented perspective).

They may more easily engage with a data model by looking at natural language expressions (such as "Each Project must be funded by one and only one Sponsor," or flipped the other way around, "Each Sponsor may fund zero, one or more Projects"). However, the sheer volume of natural language expressions required to describe a large model can be daunting.

So, here comes an alternative view.

There is a common phrase that "A picture is worth a thousand words." I like a version of this from a Russian writer, Ivan Turgenev, who said, "The drawing shows me at one glance what might be spread over ten pages in a book." For me, if I see a collection of natural language phrases about relationships between entities, I tend to grab some scrap paper and draw a diagram so I can see the larger picture. But that's just me and, as noted by the natural language enthusiasts, diagrams and notations are not liked by all. So who's right?

Years ago I met a person who had been graded as a Fellow in the Australian Computer Society. At the presentation of her award, she shared her background: she and her husband were both gifted mathematicians, but their young daughter was performing very poorly in even simple mathematics, sometimes getting scores of zero out of ten. When the problem was analyzed, it was discovered that the daughter was dyslexic, and was spending the test times trying to write down the problems, and not even getting to attempting the answers. To check this out, the teacher gave the daughter pre-written questions, and the daughter's grades went from zero to perfect scores!

The mother was inspired to see what other people struggled to learn due to some underlying issue, and she went on to complete a PhD on the topic.

She worked with one prison inmate who had been classified as having attention deficit issues. He wanted to learn to play a violin. She said she would arrange tuition *after* he'd built his own violin in the prison woodwork shop. So much for attention deficit—this inmate spent hours, days and weeks with absolutely focused attention on the task of building his violin! And this delightful lady was good to her word, and rewarded the inmate with the lessons he desired.

Another heart-warming story related to a school student who could not read or write but was gifted as an artist. This lady helped the youngster "write" a story using pictures in a comic-book style.

Her conclusion from many such examples is that different people learn and communicate differently. So for some people who want to engage with a data model, textual descriptions will work best, while others will be happier with diagrams. Let's carefully engage with people, and respect their preferences.

I'll finish this segment with a personal story on communication styles. The wool industry was historically the foundation of Australia's economy. A bright and visionary PhD student had ideas for radical and revolutionary reshaping of the wool industry, and wanted an IT solution to back up his ideas. The proposed data model was complex, but we needed the executive team to understand it, and to sign it off. Neither textual descriptions, nor traditional diagrams, were going to be sufficient to enable effective communication with the management team.

I worked with a subject matter expert to create a hypothetical end-to-end scenario, with realistic samples of farmers, bales of wool, overseas wool mills, and their orders. I wrote up sheets of paper with details on them. I had Farmer Jones in Western Australia on one sheet, and separate sheets for each lot of wool of a given specification (micron thickness, average length and strength of fiber, color etc.) grown by Jones. I also had similar lots of wool as requirements from the mills, also each on their own sheet of paper.

In preparation, I assembled a "data model" on the board-room wall. I had a label called Farmer (representing the data model concept/entity of Farmer), a label called Available Wool, (with a piece of string joining Farmer to Available Wool—a crude but effective way of portraying a data model relationship).

We assembled the executive team, and I talked through the scenario. I started by talking about Farmer Jones, and used adhesive to place his pre-written sheet under the Farmer concept. This roughly simulated "populating the database," but I didn't talk in such terms. Then I spoke about the wool he had available for sale, and "populated" the Available Wool concept. Part way through we spoke about the heavy-duty mathematics that sought optimal matching of supply and demand (along with optimal transport logistics). Finally, we got Available Wool delivered to mills in China and Europe.

The executives loved the "model," loved the solution, and signed off. And all without mentioning data models, entities, relationships, cardinality and optionality, or attributes and their data types.

Is that what I suggest as the only and best way to communicate a data model? No, it's just an example of adapting the message to suit the audience.

Key points

- When we articulate core business concepts:

  o We could focus on the current-state ("As-is") perspective or the future-state ("To-be") perspective. For a Data Town Plan, there is merit in embracing both time dimensions.
  o We could start with the big picture ("Top-down") perspective and then later drill into detail, or we could start with the detail ("Bottom-up") perspective and then later seek to develop the big picture. For a Data Town Plan, it is highly recommended that we *start* with the "Top-down" big picture as identified previously.

- While the Data Town Plan may start with the big picture, we may seek understanding through (selectively) digging into the details over time.

- Over time, as a consequence of implementing our business concepts in working software, we may get feedback that our initial models were less than perfect. Rather than defensively resisting feedback, we should welcome constructive criticism and iteratively improve our model.

- A data model (including a Data Town Plan), can be understood more easily by some as a set of diagrams and by others as textual descriptions. Understand your audience, and be respectful of their needs.

CHAPTER 25

Where to from here?

Sharing the message with students (and old-timers)

In at least some cases, our institutes of higher education only teach "data" subjects in computer science faculties (or the like), and the material sometimes reaches back decades and is aimed at physical database design for relational databases. For the technically minded, this may include normalization to "third normal form" (3NF) and little else. (From my own experience, even that education carries the implied message that 3NF is the same as "fully normalized," which it is not necessarily true, but that's a separate issue).

I'm not discounting the value of such technical topics, but I am saying we could be doing better. For example, I would suggest that we could teach computer science students some tips and techniques on how to interact with non-technical business folk. Hopefully these technical people can then reach out and build bridges to the business folk, helping the business people to then articulate how they want to see their data represented.

Computer science students are one audience that this book could reach, but there's another exciting opportunity: what if we caught the attention of students in business/commerce faculties by sharing the power of data, and then taught them how, as future business practitioners, they could then express their vision of data as they saw it, and in a way that could be communicated to the IT delivery teams? Far too often IT people struggle to communicate their ideas to non-technical managers. What if we turned this communication dilemma on its head, and taught business people how to communicate their vision to IT? It would then be the dog wagging the tail, rather than the tail wagging the dog. At the end of the day, IT is there to *serve* the business, not just to have fun (though I will be the last to condemn IT practitioners who have fun performing their roles—I am theoretically at an age where most people would retire, but that hasn't happened yet—I'm still having too much fun!)

Or perhaps even better, what about engaging with MBA students, especially those who already have work experience and could immediately apply the lessons at work?

Data is vital to any modern organization. The above expresses the desirability of graduates being armed to deliver value on the data front, but what about the vast army of people already in the workforce who haven't seen or heard of this "bridge-builder" approach? The contents of this book can reach out to them, too. It's "Never too late to learn."

And back to the topic of fun: I have so many times been a party to business folk and IT professionals actually enjoying the journey together.

Some other reading

This book provides some lightweight data model patterns. For many, that will be sufficient. However, I suggest that at least the more technical readers would do well to look at the works of David Hay and Len Silverston. David's early book, *Data Model Patterns: Conventions of Thought* is an oldie but goodie. He subsequently updated and expanded his patterns in *Enterprise Model Patterns: Describing the World*. Then there is the three-part *Data Model Resource Book* series by Len Silverston. I consider Len's series an invaluable reference resource for serious data modelers. My book, *The Nimble Elephant*, explains how to implement the patterns in an Agile way. For those interested in Data Vault, the sequel, *The Elephant in the Fridge*, applies these same data model patterns to the design of a Data Vault.

Some of you may want to dive deeper into the more technical aspects of data modeling in general. I recommend Graeme Simsion and Graham Witt's book, *Data Modeling Essentials*[17].

If you want to read a complementary publication to this book, Steve Hoberman, Donna Burbank, and Chris Bradley published *Data Modeling for the Business*.

---

[17] Simsion, G and Witt, G (2004) *Data Modeling Essentials*.

Finally, some technology to help apply the Data Town Plan

This book focuses on capturing how the business wants to shape their data. It has deliberately kept technical solutions somewhat at arm's length. But in addition to helping people communicate, Data Town Plans can constructively offer guidance to IT teams as they work to implement solutions that will deliver value to the business.

Appendix 1 provides some hints at how a Data Town Plan might contribute to IT delivery.

Key point

- The techniques presented in this book for developing business-centric, enterprise-wide Data Town Plans will be helpful to practitioners and students from both IT and business streams as they bridge the communication gap between business and IT and go on to deliver solutions the business will value.

How might IT actually use a Data Town Plan?

This book focuses on how to create a Data Town Plan. However, it is arguable that a Data Town Plan is of questionable value if it fails to bring positive change in some form or another.

Perhaps the benefit is simply improved human-to-human communication, with an associated appreciation between colleagues as to the interdependent roles played by all. In this scenario, there may be no tangible deliverables from the IT department that can point back to the investment in the Data Town Plan. But typically, traceable change is realized in technical implementation. This appendix looks mainly at how IT might use a Data Town Plan.

But before we dive into technical topics, let's discuss why this part of the book is presented as an Appendix.

Data Town Plans are (ideally) technology agnostic. It is my opinion that technology changes more often than the fundamentals of Data Town Planning. I want the bulk of the book to have greater stability than would be true if it depended on certain technologies. The primary reason I felt motivated to present suggestions on applying Data Town Plans to technology solutions was to provide examples and to generate discussion as to how you *might* benefit, given some of the technologies available at the time of writing this book. Business people may choose to ignore this appendix; technology people may enjoy reading this appendix, challenging it, and adapting it.

Understanding the solution spectrum, from Smoke and Mirrors through to At-Source data integration

As the number of IT systems in an organization grow, the challenges of data integration also grow.

As the number of tool vendors grow, passionate debates about achieving data integration also seem to grow.

I'll take two extremes to start the conversation.

The first is what I am here calling "smoke and mirrors" data integration. Before you read further and possibly start to push back, I am very comfortable that this *image* of seamless integration covering up underlying problems has merit, and may well be the best solution in quite a number of settings. But nonetheless, I do want to highlight that it is a false image of conformity. It can be a bit like the duck that seems to be gliding effortlessly, but underwater there's a heck of a lot of paddling going on! If your organization has embraced a "smoke and mirrors" data integration approach, that may well serve a very valuable purpose, but it must be recognized for what it is—a façade that may cover up serious problems when you lift the lid and peek underneath.

The second extreme says that an organization must only ever hold data for a given object in one place. There's an employee, Dan, and *all* of Dan's details are physically stored in one place. And all of the myriad of details about customer Alex are likewise only ever stored in one data store, with no duplicates permitted. Ever. And this argument can then be applied to assets, events, tasks, locations, or whatever. Again, before I get attacked, I did say it's an extreme!

I saw a statement from a tool vendor. I'm choosing not to identify the vendor nor provide a precise quotation, but the gist of the statement was that data integration involves amalgamating data from multiple *source* systems so as to assemble a single, consistent *view* that will facilitate analysis. That position assumes that integration at or close to the sources is not an option; that may well be true in many cases, but not all. So let's start with this "leave the nasty source systems alone" attitude and see how it might work, then challenge the assumption that integration can only occur outside the operational source systems.

Data warehousing

Several approaches to Data Warehouses have been popular over the years, including the dimensional/data mart/star schema approach and more centralized approaches of so-called "3NF" Data Warehousing, and Data Vault. Whether you need "dimensions" for a Data Mart or "hubs" for a Data Vault, they are intended to represent business concepts such as a customer, a product, an asset, and so on. The requirement to base the Data Warehouse on business concepts makes using a Data Town Plan a natural fit. Similarly, a business perspective on the relationships between the business concepts is helpful for some forms of Data Warehousing.

As a side note, if your interest is specifically in Data Vault, my book titled *The Elephant in the Fridge* goes into detail about the application of a Data Town Plan to shape a Data Vault design.

Data warehousing can be a solution for data integration. It's an approach used very widely, sometimes with great results, sometimes less so. But here's the crunch. At best, it provides a smoke-and-mirrors perception of unity and conformity, while behind the scenes, it is often a suite of ugly, inconsistent, aging source systems.

And how many source systems might be in this mess? I worked for one organization that had an IT system intended to keep track of its IT systems! They stopped funding this inventory of systems after they had analyzed the first 1,000 IT systems. Putting a data warehouse over the top of this chaos wasn't going to solve the more fundamental problems of data duplication and data redundancy.

Data warehousing is often the first technical solution considered for the integration of data across an enterprise. But here's a possibly confronting idea: would we even need a data warehouse if our operational systems were already integrated? The answer may still be, "Yes, we want a data warehouse." Still, perhaps constructing a data warehouse might be much easier if we sought to solve data integration earlier and closer (or even in) the source systems!

Enterprise service bus technology

Australia is probably not unique in having a history of railway lines with different rail "gauges" (the measurement between railway tracks). We are a single country, but different states (and even different parts of any given state) had their own gauge. The benefits of having a standard rail gauge are well-recognized. Herding the cats to achieve this is harder.

Different data standards can be discovered within organizations. There can be good reasons, or it can boil down to turf wars.

One approach moving towards integration is often referred to as the provision of an Enterprise Service Bus (ESB). Different applications retain their autonomy, but when they want to exchange data, there are data packages neatly wrapped inside object-oriented "services."

I was engaged in this approach to enterprise integration in the 1990s. OK, in the IT world, that dates it as belonging to an almost pre-historic era (though modern variations might still have merit—I will leave that debate to others better versed in platforms and technology architecture). The key message is that to facilitate the implementation of the ESB by this very large corporation, they needed a Common Information Model (CIM). It is important to note that, while the development of the CIM started with highly generalized patterns as we have seen used within Data Town Plans, the full model required lots more detail to drive implementation.

As a side note, we could ask how the project went. A quarter of a century after my involvement, I was speaking to one of the head office IT people involved. He reported that it ended up being a massive and trouble-plagued project. It apparently hit obstacle after obstacle due to turf wars. Each business unit had funding to run their own operations, but zero funding for initiatives involving the "common good." The problem apparently was not the Common Information Model nor the technology, but politics and siloed budgets.

Master Data Management (MDM) and Reference Data Management (RDM)

What on earth are Master Data Management (MDM) and Reference Data Management (RDM) systems all about? First, at the heart is managing data centered around a single data domain, such as customer or product. In *Data Modeling for the Business*[18], Steve Hoberman and his fellow authors have a helpful entry on MDM. He notes that it is similar to data warehousing in that it aggregates

---

[18] Hoberman S, Burbank D, and Bradley C. (2009) Data Modeling for the Business: A handbook for aligning the business with IT using high-level data models.

data on a single topic (such as customer). Let's note that the multiplicity of sources, with all their ugliness, still exist. For one of my clients I encountered relatively recently, they had more than 50 operational systems containing customer data! Like with data warehousing, under the duck there's still a lot of frantic paddling.

Another differentiation from data warehousing is that it is operational in nature and used throughout the day to run the business. This reality can actually make it harder, trying to enforce alignment across systems that don't want to cooperate. Steve draws an analogy to trying to change the wings on an airplane during flight—you're trying to fundamentally change operational systems while they are still in daily use!

Having said all that, if you can achieve effective deployment of MDM solutions, it simplifies day-to-day operations _and_ makes subsequent consolidation in the data warehouse simpler because a lot of the hard data integration work has already been done.

My next comment may already be obvious to you. If we're going to consolidate operational systems around a central, agreed, unambiguous business concept of (for example) "customer," then we'd better jolly well have a central, agreed, unambiguous definition for this business concept.

And that's not always easy. Earlier in this book, we've noted cases of divergent definitions for concepts such as "customer." One example cited was for a cemetery where a person who has pre-paid for a funeral plan is a customer, but after they've died, has the customer role shifted to someone representing the estate of the deceased? Or another example I touched on was for another client providing dental care, and they debated whether the customer is the young child in the dentist's chair or the parent who brought the child (or the grandparent paying for the policy). Resolving definitions is not always easy, but it's always important. Drum roll please, as we welcome the Data Town Plan onto the stage to assist.

Implementing data subject area (pattern-centric) modules

We've noted that a data warehouse presents a unified view of underlying chaos. Implementing Master Data Management solutions can be the same thing, albeit for bite-sized and more manageable modules. I want to go one step further towards solving integration at the source.

One of my clients initially had "asset" data in all sorts of systems, but they bit the bullet and implemented a single, central asset management system. Other systems that were required to read and maintain asset data delegated the responsibility for managing their asset data to this shared facility. The central asset system had published interfaces for handling queries for retrieving current data values and interfaces for creating, updating, and (logically) deleting asset records.

OK, some of the systems might have chosen to internally duplicate the records, but there was one master, and any copies were "managed copies."

The central asset management system did more than keep records. It handled depreciation. It handled the scheduling of maintenance. It kept records for analysis of reliability. It did lots of things. But from the perspective of other systems, it was the "go to" place for all things "asset." They did not have to take responsibility for the data records.

Likewise, this client had one shared geospatial information system and was moving to have one place to store all employee data. The goal, being progressively realized, was to have commercial-off-the-shelf (COTS) systems for assets, locations, employees, customers, agreements, and more, with each of these systems making real-time access available as required by other systems.

At one stage, they needed a new system to interact with the public through their corporate website. The development was totally unique to that organization, but the developers stitched together some code that used the existing foundations. It worked a treat, and this new application introduced absolutely zero data of its own.

I've seen this approach followed at other sites, sometimes with less rigor and discipline, but again heading towards a goal of keeping only one record for each fundamental business concept that needed to be shared.

… and you shouldn't be surprised if I tell you that a Data Town Plan can contribute to precise specification as to what the shared core business concepts should be!!!

Corporate database (really?!)

We've been moving along a spectrum, from smoke and mirrors integration towards at-source integration. I had declared that I wanted to take you on a journey along that spectrum and perhaps be a little controversial. Fasten your seatbelts!

Back in the 1980s, there was the dream of each enterprise creating its own "corporate database." It was to be the single database that held everything for an organization. By and large, these ventures were expensive failures. Here in Australia, the word on the street was that one such venture almost sent a very large organization into bankruptcy.

Have I ever seen this single application or single database actually work? Only once, and that's in more than four decades of consulting to a large number of organizations. And that organization was relatively small. If you take away the subcontractors, I estimate that the core workforce was a few hundred people. The IT department had some very bright, very loyal visionaries who made this corporate database work and work very well. I take my hat off to them, but I could not with a clear conscience recommend this approach as the default goal for other organizations.

… so that's been a quick journey touching on a few approaches I've seen in action along a spectrum from multiple systems hiding behind a single façade through to one operational system (that, if you were brave enough or silly enough to try it), would benefit from a Data Town Plan. Quite a journey?

Now, let's look at some other approaches that might benefit from a Data Town Plan.

A smorgasbord of other solutions

We've just looked at a spectrum of data integration solutions, from presenting a façade of integration via a data warehouse or an Enterprise Service Bus, through Master Data Management (and Reference Data Management), then operational integration around data subject areas such as Customer and Asset, and finally introduced the somewhat utopian dream of the whole of an enterprise running on a single IT system or data base.

Now we look at a few more implementation options that may benefit from the use of a Data Town Plan, recognizing that these are just examples that may prompt discussion, and that may well date quicker than the fundamentals of the Data Town Plan itself.

Also please note that while the earlier examples mentioned in the opening paragraph typically address enterprise-wide initiatives, one of the following applications of the Data Town Plan had a broader focus than one enterprise, and others had a narrower focus.

Common Information Models for exchanging data packages

Earlier in this book (see "Wildfires: When you and others need a shared view"), the idea of exchanging data between diverse organizations via agreed standards was introduced. One example given was the National Information Exchange Model (NIEM). While having its roots in the United States, it has become not just a national standard but is used internationally.

This topic is similar in many ways to the explanation of an Enterprise Service Bus discussed earlier in this appendix; the reason for further describing the data exchange approach is to look at such initiatives when they involve more than one enterprise.

The fundamentals sound pretty simple at first glance. If I represent one organization and you another, we can exchange data about people, places, events, and more in data packages using, for example, XML or JSON structures to facilitate the exchange.

Having technology such as XML or JSON is the (relatively) easy bit. Getting agreement on the standards looks a lot harder. It has taken more than two decades to get to the current NIEM standard. But sometimes, the effort involved in reaching common ground is worthwhile. Above I have spoken of data exchange in relation to wildfires. When a fire (or flood, earthquake, or similar emergency) suddenly appears, we need a shared language to facilitate communication. That applies to not just computer-to-computer communication, but also to human-to-human communication.

I was engaged to develop what was called a Common Information Model for the emergency response agencies. You will not be surprised to learn that I leveraged the same building block data model patterns as those we can use for a Data Town Plan. Sure, the scope of this model was more than that of a single enterprise (it actually had the potential to involve 17 organizations), but the Data Town Plan approach worked wonderfully well.

I recently had the privilege of meeting some inspiring people from the University of Western Australia. I cannot do justice to their mammoth efforts, but put simply, they are seeking international standards for data structures as they relate to, for example, the maintenance of assets as large as off-shore oil rigs. It is my understanding that aspects of their work may differ from mine in some ways (they know much more about "ontologies" than I ever will), but we nonetheless share the motivation to enable cross-industry sharing of data. If it can be challenging to get agreement within a single organization, it is even harder to get agreement across multiple organizations, especially if in some settings they are competitors, but the message is simple: the ideas behind a Data Town Plan for a single enterprise can potentially contribute to much larger multi-enterprise initiatives.

Data mesh

We've just looked at data integration (and data sharing) initiatives that embrace entire countries, such as the United States, down through single-enterprise initiatives, and now we scale back even further to initiatives involving data integration but within a much smaller part of the business.

You may come across terms such as Data Mesh, Data Products, Domain-Driven Design (DDD), and Data Fabric. I don't want to debate these technologies or their relative merits. But there is one key point I wish to make about Data Mesh. And that relates to its scope. While Data Fabric approaches things from a centralized (read "enterprise"?) perspective, Data Mesh may consciously decentralize things so that each "domain" (a business unit, a business process, etc.) has a level of autonomy.

There is the real danger of building silos. Within each of these silos, some of these approaches aim to drive implementation via a single, unifying "ubiquitous language" that provides commonality *within the domain* but does not strive to embrace a whole-of-enterprise model as might be represented by a Data Town Plan. There's the danger.

So what do we do? Do we outlaw Data Mesh because its focus is less than the entire enterprise and we might end up perpetuating silos? Not necessarily, but we do need to consciously consider its merits for a given setting.

One approach to lessen possible negative impacts of the silos is to use the Data Town Plan to contribute to the shaping of the "ubiquitous language" for every one of the domains.

Enterprise architecture

Some organizations wisely perform formal strategic planning before investing in the development of IT solutions. They want to avoid spending money and time in creating silos. Even if full-on strategic planning is not done, at least some less formal consideration is advisable. Sometimes, this planning falls within the broader practice of "Enterprise Architecture." Steve Hoberman, in his book *Data Modeling for the Business,*[19] states, "Enterprise Architecture (EA) is a broad initiative that attempts to create a high-level roadmap of an enterprise's technical infrastructure." I like Steve's term of a "roadmap" rather than the phrase "strategic planning." It is less formal and very descriptive. The purpose of a roadmap is to help us navigate from where we are to where we want to be.

For navigation, we need to know not just the target destination, but where we are right now! The target "To Be" data architecture can be informed by our Data Town Plan, but do we need a formal Data Town Plan to articulate our "As-Is" current state as well? Sometimes, "Yes," sometimes, "No." I have encountered cases where the business people (and the technical ones, too) know only too well the pain of where they are today.

Please note that Enterprise Architectures includes lots more than just data architecture aspects. As noted in *Data Modeling for the Business*, Enterprise Architecture (and hence also Strategic Planning) can include people, process, hardware, networks, and more. So, your strategic planning may involve a lot more than the future state Data Town Plan, but the it should be seen as a valuable contributor.

---

[19] Hoberman S, Burbank D, and Bradley C. (2009) "Data Modeling for the Business: A handbook for aligning the business with IT using high-level data models."

One parting comment on strategic planning. If the technology being considered is new to your organization, you may be well advised to do some proof-of-concept familiarization with the technology before finally committing serious coin to a project that seemed like a good idea at the time!

Corporate mergers

I've just mentioned the potential contribution of a Data Town Plan to enterprise architecture initiatives. If two organizations merge, the same requirements exist, but on steroids!

As a side-note, you might like to refer back to the good-news story of the merger of 83 organizations as described in a small segment of "Multiple clients: When we need day-to-day operational integration."

Delivering individual IT systems

Data Town Plans have an enterprise-wide perspective. But they can be used to provide tremendous value to IT initiatives on a micro scale. We're going to look at two distinct aspects.

The first is <u>benchmarking of an IT package solution</u>.

Earlier on, in 'Commercial-off-the-shelf IT solution delivery: When we need an objective, independent benchmark,' I shared a story about one of my clients, a delivery organization, that wanted to evaluate candidate commercial-off-the-shelf (COTS) IT solutions. They were concerned that, by looking in detail at proposed software solutions, they might be "talked into" believing the sales pitch. They wanted an independent benchmark that represented the organization, including its vision for the future. I was engaged to develop a "sufficient" Data Town Plan, and given one day to do it!

Then I spent one more day diving into the shortlisted candidate solution's data model. Most vendors are reluctant to expose the inner workings of their package, and understandably so, but if the requirement to see inside the package is communicated transparently from the outset, and backed up by a non-disclosure agreement if appropriate, they will often open up. On a number of occasions I have been able to take an under-the-covers peek on behalf of my client who wants a truly independent evaluation. And on some happy occasions, the package vendor has been delighted to receive constructive feedback on improvements to their product.

This particular vendor was less happy. I highlighted an apparent shortcoming in their solution that would be a total roadblock, a deal-breaker. The model they provided was a hard-copy printout of the physical model. It consisted of so many sheets of paper that I had to borrow the boardroom table to "navigate" my way around the model. I tracked down the limitation built into the database design, and concluded their package was not going to be acceptable. They weren't happy; my client was delighted to have saved an estimated few million dollars in purchasing the tool only to find it could never work.

A similar but happier benchmarking engagement was for a bank. I spent about a week articulating a more detailed benchmark model, then flew overseas to the head office of the software company offering a total banking solution as a package. The package was a good fit against the independent benchmark. I got a holiday in a part of the world I had not visited, and my client and the software company were happy.

The second aspect to look at is <u>designing your own in-house tailored system</u>.

I will never forget a challenging consulting assignment related to a proposed radical change to Australia's national wool industry. I touched on this scenario earlier.

A delightful and very clever youngster had come up with a game-changing idea with national implications. But not only was his idea revolutionary, the software required to support his proposal was unique.

Prior to my engagement, a team had already spent a lot of time, and a lot of money, working on development of the essential software. The IT manager, who knew me well, called me in to perform an independent review. I suggested we create a Data Town Plan as the benchmark, then use it to evaluate the details of the physical design. He agreed.

The development team already had 600 tables created, and many more needed to round out the solution. They had only eight months to go, and the IT manager, and the developers, all shared a concern it could not be delivered in time.

My conclusion? I agreed! They could not deliver in the remaining eight months.

My proposal? Put the entire project on hold. Spend the next four months doing a holistic design. Then start the entire development afresh with a hand-picked team of four (myself and three others), replacing the large team that had stalled.

We worked hard, often 16 hours a day, seven days a week. We had bookings at the local motel for the next four months because we rarely got home. My wife would come in occasionally and stay at the motel. I would quietly creep in near midnight, sleep for a few hours, get up, have breakfast with her, and then she'd head home again until she would drop by again for another flying visit.

My three colleagues were what I might call "super programmers." Each one of them could, on their own, outperform several regular programmers. That four months was tough, but we were a tight team, and we delivered.

And again, this quite remarkable story was founded on a Data Town Plan, based on patterns, plus a few elements that were significant extensions to patterns.

Chief Data Office (and the like)

What I might call head-office IT may see itself as having various responsibilities, including things like data governance. Some might argue (with merit) that some of the responsibilities should rest with "the business." I guess the reality is that it is helpful if IT and "the business" work together. And if the Data Town Plan was developed jointly as a cooperative effort, good foundations are laid, with both sides talking the same language. (Don't underestimate the value of shared terminology that may, for example, guide things like business glossaries.)

In *Data Modeling for the Business* there is a section on Data Governance[20]. One of the points made by the authors is that, "The most effective approach [to Data Governance] tends to be by subject area," which again is where the Data Town Plan comes into its own.

---

[20] Pages 110 to 112 in Hoberman S, Burbank D, and Bradley C. (2009) Data Modeling for the Business: A handbook for aligning the business with IT using high-level data models.

In closing

There are, of course, many other ways a Data Town Plan can contribute to IT implementations—I just wanted to provide you with some examples of how a Data Town Plan can play a crucial role.

Technology changes at a head-spinning pace, but some of the fundamentals of how a business wants to see its data managed are much more stable. I have just referred to *Data Modeling for the Business* by Steve Hoberman, Donna Burbank, and Chris Bradley. At the time of writing this, their book was already a decade-and-a-half old, but it still has much to say about today's use of high-level models that are business-centric. Likewise, while this appendix will undoubtably show signs of aging, I am hopeful that the main body of this book will prove to be resilient. Of course, things will change, and change must always be welcomed, but I believe that the importance of IT engaging with the business will never diminish!

Data Model Patterns with Accompanying Entity and Attribute Descriptions

Entire books, and series of books, have been published for data model patterns. The books from two authors alone exceed 2,000 pages in total. Some of these pattern books are referenced in 'Some other reading.'

Within this book, some light-weight patterns have been introduced. For many uses, they may be sufficient. Diagrams have been presented within the chapters on building blocks. This appendix provides most of the matching descriptions of entities and their attributes and relationships (but not all, as some entities are in diagrams for instruction purposes but are not part of the core light-weight patterns).

Entity index

Below is an alphabetic index of the entities in this appendix:

- Account
- Account Participation
- Account Payable (see entry under "Account")
- Account Receivable (see entry under "Account")
- Account Type
- Accounting Entry
- Accounting Transaction
- Accounting Transaction Item
- Accounting Transaction Type

- Actual Task (see entry under "Task/Specific Task")
- Address
- Address Service
- Address Service Type
- Address Usage Type
- Agreement
- Agreement Item
- Agreement Participation
- Agreement To Agreement Relationship
- Agreement To Agreement Relationship Type
- Agreement Type
- Calendar
- Classification Code
- Classification Code Hierarchy
- Classification Scheme
- Classification Scheme Allowable Hierarchy
- Communication Event (see entry under "Event")
- Customer (see entry under "Party Role")
- Discrete Value Classification (see entry under "Classification Code")
- Document
- Document Format
- Document To Document Relationship
- Document To Document Relationship Type
- Document Type
- Electronic Document (see entry under "Document")
- Email Address (see entry under "Address")
- Employee (see entry under "Party Role")
- Employer (see entry under "Party Role")
- Employment Contract (see entry under "Agreement")
- Event
- Event To Event Relationship
- Event To Event Relationship Type
- Event Type
- Geometry
- Geopolitical Zone (see entry under "Geospatial Object")
- Geospatial Explicit Proximity

- Geospatial Object
- Geospatial Object Type
- Goods Item
- Goods Type
- Line (see entry under "Geometry")
- National Park (see entry under "Geospatial Object")
- Object To Task Assignment
- Object Type To Task Assignment
- Observation Event (see entry under "Event")`
- Organization (see entry under "Party")
- Organization Name
- Party
- Party Identifier
- Party Role
- Party Role Type
- Party To Party Relationship
- Party To Party Relationship Type
- Party Type
- Person (see entry under "Party")
- Person Given Name
- Person Name
- Phone Number (see entry under "Address")
- Physical Address (see entry under "Address")
- Physical Document (see entry under "Document")
- Planned Task (see entry under "Task/Specific Task")
- Point (see entry under "Geometry")
- Polygon (see entry under "Geometry")
- Position
- Position Assignment
- Position Hierarchy
- Postal Address (see entry under "Address")
- Product Item
- Product Goods Component
- Product Services Component
- Product Subproduct Component
- Product Type

- Range Classification (see entry under "Classification Code")
- Resource
- Resource Type
- Safety Incident (see entry under "Event")
- Schedule Entry Recurrence Specification
- Services Item
- Services Type
- Specific Task (see entry under "Task")
- Structured Electronic Document (see entry under "Document/Electronic Document")
- Task
- Task Dependency
- Task Type
- Template Task (see entry under "Task")
- Unstructured Electronic Document (see entry under "Document/Electronic Document")

Entity descriptions

Account

Description

Each instance in this class represents an account within the company's financial ledgers (debtors, creditors, general, etc.).

The responsibilities for this class are expected to be physically realized in a commercial-off-the-shelf accounting package that may incorporate additional attributes. However, the concept of an "account," and its core attributes, are documented in this logical model as it is fundamental to business.

This class is subclassed to reflect some indicative primary types of accounts (e.g., a Debtor's account for a customer named John Smith).

Associations

Each Account must be classified by one Account Type.
Each Account may be the consolidation of one or more sub-Accounts.
Each Account may be a sub-account for one "parent" consolidation Account.

Each Account may involve one or more parties or party roles as Account Participations.

Each Account may have adjustments to its balance posted via one or more Accounting Entry(s).

<u>Attributes</u>

Attribute Name	Comments
Account Number	Ledger account number.
Account Name	Ledger account name.
Account Balance	Ledger account balance.

Account Payable (subclass of Account)

This class is a subclass of Account, provided merely as an example of specialized types of accounts. It represents money owed by a business to its suppliers.

<u>Attributes</u>

Attribute Name	Comments
(none yet identified)	

Account Receivable (subclass of Account)

This class is a subclass of Account, provided merely as an example of specialized types of accounts. It represents money owed to a business by its customers.

<u>Attributes</u>

Attribute Name	Comments
(none yet identified)	

Account Participation

<u>Description</u>

Each Account may have many participants e.g., an account may have a primary account holder, one or more secondary account holders, perhaps a guarantor, and so on. Conversely, each Party and/or Party Role may be a participant in one or more accounts e.g., a person who is responsible for the accounts related to several properties he/she owns, plus the account for another property where they are an owner/occupier.

Each instance in this class represents the participation relationship between one Account, and one Party or Party Role. This relationship may be further classified by a Participation Type e.g., to classify the Party (or Party Role) participating in the Account as fulfilling a contextual role such as "Primary," "Secondary," "Guarantor," etc.

[Note: In this model, participation of a Party is shown, but participation of a Party Role has not been included.]

Associations

Each Account Participation must be for one Account.
Each Account Participation must identify one Party (or Party Role) as a participant.

Attributes

Attribute Name	Comments
Participation Type	Classification of the type of participation e.g., "Secondary Account Holder."
Effective Period	Period during which the participation is active.

Account Type

Description

Each instance in this class defines one classification for Accounts. For example, types of accounts might include:

- Asset/Cash accounts.
- Asset/Accounts Receivable accounts.
- Liability/Accounts Payable accounts.
- Expense/Labor accounts.

This class has a self-referencing association that enables a hierarchy of types. The Account class that is "typed" by entries in this class is itself a superclass that is *also* typed by its subclasses. It is suggested that this class manage all type definitions, and that the inheritance mechanism be used as a supplementary specification where the static specialization of attributes and/or associations is required.

Associations

Each Account Type may be the classification for one or more Accounts.

Each Account Type may be the coarse-grained "parent" of one or more finer-grained "child" Account Types.

Each Account Type may be the fine-grained "child" of one coarse-grained "parent" Account Type.

<u>Attributes</u>

Attribute Name	Comments
Account Type Code	Code representing the classification e.g., perhaps "AR" might be the code representing the "Accounts Receivable" type of Account.
Account Type Name	Brief textual description for the classification e.g., "Accounts Receivable" might be the name of an account type used to classify monies owed to the organization by customers.
Account Type Description	Full textual description for the classification e.g., "Monies owed to the organization by its debtors."

Accounting Entry

<u>Description</u>

For each discrete Accounting Transaction (see the associated Accounting Transaction class), the total transaction amount may be allocated against several Accounts. Each instance in this class represents one account allocation of money, from an Accounting Transaction, to an Account.

Note that when using double-entry accounting, there must be at least two accounting entries, one for debits and one for credits, for each Accounting Transaction.

Note also that an entry may be cross-referenced against one or several other entries e.g., when a payment amount is matched against an invoice amount.

<u>Associations</u>

Each Accounting Entry must identify one Accounting Transaction whose whole or partial amount is to be allocated.

Each Accounting Entry must record the allocation of an amount against one Account.

Each Accounting Entry may be cross-referenced to one earlier Accounting Entry.

Each Accounting Entry may be cross-referenced by one or more subsequent Accounting Entry(s).

Attributes

Attribute Name	Comments
Allocation Amount	Amount of the total transaction amount allocated to the nominated Account.

Accounting Transaction

Description

Each instance in this class represents one accounting transaction, such as an invoice issued or a payment received.

Note that the single amount from this transaction may be broken down into one or a set of debit amounts and one or a set of credit amounts for posting to accounts—see the associated Accounting Entry class.

Associations

Each Account Transaction must be classified by one Account Transaction Type.

Each Accounting Transaction must (if using double entry accounting) have the allocation of its amount defined by two or more Accounting Entry(s).

Each Accounting Transaction may contain one or more Accounting Transaction Items.

Attributes

Attribute Name	Comments
Transaction Reference	Optional reference code e.g., an Invoice Number.
Transaction Effective Date	Date the transaction is deemed to be effective, not necessarily the date the transaction was recorded in a computer system.
Transaction Recorded Date	Date the transaction was entered into a computer system (compare with the Transaction Effective Date).
Transaction Comment	Textual notes for the transaction. (Optional)
Transaction Amount	The Transaction Amount records the total value of one transaction. Note that it may be broken into several smaller amounts and allocated to separate accounts via the Accounting Entry class.

Accounting Transaction Item

Description

Each Accounting Transaction may contain many "items." For example, an accounting transaction for a customer invoice may contain many invoice lines, each being an itemized charge as it relates to a discrete product purchase. Similarly, a payment might itemize the particulars of what is being paid. Each instance in this class represents one such item.

Associations

Each Accounting Transaction Item must be contained within one Accounting Transaction.

Attributes

Attribute Name	Comments
Sequence Number	A number to control the display ordering of the items within the containing Accounting Transaction.
Transaction Item Description	Textual description of the item.
Transaction Item Effective Period	Period to which this item applies.
Transaction Item Amount	The itemized amount.

Accounting Transaction Type

Description

Each instance in this class defines one classification for Accounting Transactions. An example might be an "Invoice" issued, a "Payment" received, or "Deprecation" against an asset.

Associations

Each Accounting Transaction Type may be the classification for one or more Accounting Transactions.

<u>Attributes</u>

Attribute Name	Comments
Accounting Transaction Type Code	Code representing the classification e.g., "DEP" for depreciation.
Accounting Transaction Type Name	Brief textual description for the classification e.g., "Depreciation."
Accounting Transaction Type Description	Full textual description for the classification e.g., "Depreciation of a corporate asset."

Address

<u>Description</u>

Each address records one point of contact for one or several parties. For example, one physical address (street number and name, town, postcode, etc.) may be nominated as the work address by several individuals.

Further, each address may be used in different ways to deliver different services. For example, it may be the work address for one (or several) staff, but may also be the postal address for the client company.

Types of addresses that may be recorded include physical addresses, postal addresses ("PO Box 123, etc."), phone numbers, and generic electronic addresses (e.g., e-mail addresses)—refer to the subclasses.

<u>Associations</u>

Each Address may record the contact point details for one or more Address Services.

<u>Attributes</u>

Attribute Name	Comments
Address Display String	This optional textual string for the address may hold an address display string constructed from multiple elements in the subclasses.
Effective Period	Record of the time period for which this is a valid address. For example, it may indicate that an address is no longer to be used, but may be retained as a record of the location to which past physical deliveries were made.

Email Address (subclass of Address)

Description

This class is a subclass of Address. It holds details of an e-mail address.

Attributes

Attribute Name	Comments
Email Address String	The string for an email address e.g., fred@acme.com.au.

Phone Number (subclass of Address)

Description

This class is a subclass of Address. It holds details of a phone number.

(Note that it may be used to contact a standard telephone handset, a fax machine, a pager, etc.—refer to the related Address Service Type class classifying the associated Address Service class.)

Attributes

Attribute Name	Comments
Country Prefix	Country code e.g., "+61" for Australia.
Area Prefix	Subscriber Trunk Dialing code e.g., "2" for a number in Sydney, Australia.
Local Number	Number dialed from within the same exchange area e.g., "98765432."

Physical Address (subclass of Address)

Description

This class is a subclass of Address. It holds details of a physical property e.g., "123 Main Street, Black Stump, VIC 9876, Australia."

(Note that it may be *used* as a residential address, a postal address, a business address, etc.—refer to the related Address Service class.)

Associations

Each Physical Address may record the address details for one or more Geospatial Objects.

Each Physical Address may define the location defined for one associated Physical Document.

Attributes

Attribute Name	Comments
Flat Identifier	(Optional) e.g., "Flat 2," "Unit 3," "Shop 4," etc.
Floor Identifier	(Optional) e.g., "Ground Floor," "Mezzanine Level," etc.
Property Name	(Optional) e.g., "Acme Towers"
Location Description	(Optional) e.g., "Rear of," "123 meters south of," etc.
Street Number	e.g., "123," "123A," "123 - 125," "Lot 123," etc.
Street Name	e.g., "Main Street," "Station Road," "High Street West," etc.
Town	e.g., "Black Stump."
State	e.g., "VIC" (Victoria), "NT" (Northern Territory), etc.
Postcode	e.g., "3456."
Country	e.g., "Australia."

Postal Address (subclass of Address)

Description

This class is a subclass of Address. It holds details of a postal property e.g., "PO Box 123, Black Stump, VIC 9876, Australia."

(Note that while physical addresses may be used to provide postal services, postal addresses cannot be used for (say) a residential address!)

Attributes

Attribute Name	Comments
Postal Delivery Description	e.g., "PO Box 123," "RSD" (roadside delivery), etc. (Optional—not required if using either the DPID of DX).
Town	e.g., "Black Stump."
State	e.g., "VIC" (Victoria), "NT" (Northern Territory), etc.
Postcode	e.g., "3456."
Country	e.g., "Australia."
DPID	DPID (Delivery Point Identifier)—a barcode for Australian postal delivery. An alternative to the traditional descriptive attributes above.
DX	DX (Document exchange) number. An alternative postal address mechanism (used in conjunction with a Town attribute).

Address Service

Description

Each party may have several addresses e.g., a person's physical home address, physical work address, perhaps a different postal address, and perhaps a couple of mobile phones.

Conversely, each address may be referenced by several parties e.g., one phone number may be nominated as the home phone for several people, and the business phone for a home business.

Each instance in this class records one party's association with one address for a given service type (refer to the Address Service Type class), and intended usage (refer to the Address Usage Type class) e.g., Fred Smith's use of phone number 1234-5678 as a facsimile service for business purposes.

Associations

Each Address Service must define address type and usage for one Party.
Each Address Service must be linked to its one Address that defines the contact details.
Each Address Service may be classified as to its usage by one Address Usage Type.

Attributes

Attribute Name	Comments
Effective Period	Period during which this record was effective.

Address Service Type

<u>Description</u>

Each instance of this class is used as a classification of the type of service offered by an address. These types have a strong correlation with the subclasses of the Address class. Examples include email address, physical address, and postal address. Also included are classifications for phone numbers (a subclass of Address), but with finer-grained classification according to whether the phone number relates to a fixed phone, a mobile phone, a pager, etc.

<u>Associations</u>

Each Address Service Type may classify the type of service mechanism applicable to one or more Address Usage Types.

<u>Attributes</u>

Attribute Name	Comments
Address Service Type Code	Brief code representing the classification e.g., "MOB" for a mobile phone.
Address Service Type Description	Full textual description for the classification e.g., "Mobile phone."

Address Usage Type

<u>Description</u>

Each instance in this class describes a classification for the intended usage of a service that is available at an address. For example:

- Where the Address Service Type is "Mobile Phone," its Usage may be classified as being home or business.
- Where the Address Service Type is "Physical Address," its Usage may be classified as being residential, work, or postal.

Note that the type of usage offered by an address of a given service type must be constrained by that address service type. For example, an email address cannot be used as a residential address, nor can a physical address be used for fax!

Associations

Each Address Usage Type may classify the type of usage for one or more Address Services.

Each Address Usage Type must be constrained to the type of service mechanism applicable via one Address Service Type.

Attributes

Attribute Name	Comments
Address Usage Type Code	Code representing the classification e.g., "POST" for postal usage.
Address Usage Type Description	Full textual description for the classification e.g., "Postal delivery service."

Agreement

Description

Each instance in this class represents one agreement between two or more parties. The agreements can be more formal agreements such as legally binding contracts, or less formal such as arrangements made for the time a company representative is to visit a client's premises.

The agreement class could have had several subclasses; only one is supplied, as an example of types of agreements. It must be noted that some agreements do not require any specialization and hence may be treated as a generic agreement (with an agreement type—see the associated class). Where agreements do not require any specialization but do require classification into various types of agreement, the Agreement Type class is expected to provide such a facility.

Associations

Each Agreement must be classified by one Agreement Type.

Each Agreement may have documentary evidence of the agreement recorded in one or more Documents.

Each Agreement may contain one or more Agreement Items.

Each Agreement may record parties and/or party roles as a participating in the agreement via one or more Agreement Participations.

Each Agreement may be the first of two participants in one or more Agreement To Agreement Relationships with other agreements.

Each Agreement may be the second of two participants in one or more Agreement To Agreement Relationships with other agreements.

Attributes

Attribute Name	Comments
Agreement Reference	Identifier for the agreement e.g., a contract number, or a quotation reference number.
Effective Period	Period during which this record was effective.

Employment Contract (subclass of Agreement)

Description

This class is a subclass of Agreement. This and other subclasses may be merely representative of types of agreements, to aid communication, and may not require specialized attributes or associations.

Each instance in this class records details for the engagement of an employee.

Attributes

Attribute Name	Comments
(none yet identified)	

Agreement Item

Description

Each instance in this class represents one item contained within the associated Agreement. For example, where the Agreement is a service agreement, this class may manage the individual products referenced in the service agreement. Similarly, where the Agreement is a work order, the Agreement Items may detail individual agreed tasks.

Note that this class may be subclassed where the varying types of agreement items require specialized attributes and/or associations.

Associations

Each Agreement Item must be contained within one Agreement.

Attributes

Attribute Name	Comments
Sequence Number	A number to control the display ordering of the items within the containing Agreement.

Agreement Participation

Description

Each Agreement may have many participants e.g., an employment contract may involve the new employee, plus a representative of the employer.

Conversely, each Party and/or Role may be a participant in one or more agreements e.g., a HR person who is the company's representative for several employment contracts.

Each instance in this class represents the participation relationship between one Agreement, and one Party or Party Role. This relationship may be further classified by a Contextual Role Type e.g., to classify the Party (or Party Role) participating in the Agreement as fulfilling a contextual role such as "Witness."

Associations

Each Agreement Participation must define the participation of either a party or party role in one Agreement. Each Agreement Participation must identify as a participant in an agreement *either* one Party *or* one Party Role.

Attributes

Attribute Name	Comments
Contextual Role Type	Classification of the type of participation e.g., "Witness."
Effective Period	Period during which the participation is active.

Agreement To Agreement Relationship

Each instance in this class represents one relationship between a pair of Agreements. For example, one agreement may be the replacement version of another, linked via a "succession" relationship, or one agreement may be the overarching agreement with the second agreement being "contained" within it.

Associations

Each Agreement To Agreement Relationship must be classified by one Agreement To Agreement Relationship Type.

Each Agreement To Agreement Relationship must nominate one Agreement as the first of two agreements participating in the relationship.

Each Agreement To Agreement Relationship must nominate one Agreement as the second of two agreements participating in the relationship.

Attributes

Attribute Name	Comments
Effective Period	Time period during which this instance is to be considered active.

Agreement To Agreement Relationship Type

Description

Each instance in this class describes a classification of agreement to agreement relationships. Examples might include:

- Containment
- Replacement
- Trigger (e.g., an Opportunity may trigger a Contract)

Associations

Each Agreement To Agreement Relationship Type may be the classification for one or more Agreement To Agreement Relationships.

Attributes

Attribute Name	Comments
Agreement to Agreement Relationship Type Code	Brief code representing the classification e.g., "REPL" for replacement.
Agreement to Agreement Relationship Type Description	Full textual description for the classification e.g., "Replacement."
Participant 1 Role	e.g., "Predecessor."
Participant 2 Role	e.g., "Successor."

Agreement Type

<u>Description</u>

Each instance in this class describes a classification of agreements. Fundamental classification of Agreement types is achieved by subclassing of the Agreement class. This class offers classification of generic agreements that may not require subclassing. It also offers further classification of Agreement subclass instances.

<u>Associations</u>

Each Agreement Type may be the classification for one or more Agreements.

Each Agreement Type may be the coarse-grained "parent" of one or more finer-grained "child" Agreement Types.

Each Agreement Type may be the fine-grained "child" of one coarse-grained "parent" Agreement Type.

<u>Attributes</u>

Attribute Name	Comments
Agreement Type Code	Brief code representing the classification e.g., "SA" for Service Agreement.
Agreement Type Description	Full textual description for the classification e.g., "Agreement between the company and a customer for provision of services."

Calendar

<u>Description</u>

In many cases, an organization uses a default calendar, and all tasks are assumed to be scheduled within that calendar. For example, their calendar may exclude work on weekends and national and state public holidays. It is not uncommon for this default calendar to be implied rather than explicitly declared within some contexts.

In other cases, certain projects may use their own specific calendars. In such cases, the details of the calendar must be identified. Details of a calendar structure are not included here as this class is primarily a placeholder for business appreciation of the role of a calendar. However, if a bespoke calendar facility is to be developed and implemented, its data structure may be inferred from similar functionality in desktop or smartphone applications.

<u>Associations</u>

Each Calendar may define scheduling possibilities for one or more Specific Tasks.

Attributes

Details of most attributes are not specified but could include:

- Calendar Name to identify a calendar instance.
- Standard daily start and finish times.
- Standard days of work.
- Recognized holidays.

Classification Code

Description

Many objects in the enterprise may need to be classified. For example, a party may be classified according to some standard industry code or internal market segmentation.

Each instance in this class defines one classification within one classification scheme (refer to the related Classification Scheme class). For example, there may be classification codes for "Ford" and "Toyota" within the "Make" classification scheme and classification codes for "LandCruiser" and "Corolla" within the "Model" classification scheme. (Note that the "LandCruiser" model may itself be linked to the "Toyota" make using the Classification Code Hierarchy class.)

While this class may be subclassed where measurements are associated with the classification, simple classifications require nothing more than entries managed by this (concrete) class.

Associations

Each Classification Code must be contained within the code set defined by one Classification Scheme.
Each Classification Code may be the "parent" code in one or more Classification Code Hierarchies involving other classification codes.
Each Classification Code may be the "child" code in one or more Classification Code Hierarchies involving other classification codes.

Attributes

Attribute Name	Comments
Classification Code	Brief code representing the classification e.g., "TOY" for Toyota.
Classification Description	Full textual description for the classification e.g., "Toyota."
Display Sequence	Control for display sequence of all members in a common classification scheme.

Discrete Value Classification (subclass of Classification Code)

Description

This class is a subclass of Classification Code, intended to be used when a simple classification code is required to be further defined with a discrete value. For example, in Australia we mighty define a "Standard" house door with a width of 820mm, a "Narrow" door with a width of 720mm, and a "Wide" door with a width of 920mm.

Each instance in this class defines the one numeric value associated with one code requiring the nomination of a discrete numeric value.

Attributes

Attribute Name	Comments
Discrete Value	Specific numeric value associated with a code set e.g., 820 for a door with a width of 820 millimeters.
Discrete UOM	Unit-of-Measure (e.g., "Millimeter") for the above metric. (Optional)

Range Classification (subclass of Classification Code)

Description

This class is a subclass of Classification Code, intended to be used when a classification is required to group a *range* of measures used elsewhere. For example, a classification of "Adjacent" classifying the availability of water utility services passing a property might be further qualified as relating to distances up to ten meters, while a separate instance described as "Nearby" might be further qualified as relating to distances greater than ten meters but up to 25 meters.

Each instance in this class defines the numeric values defining the range limits for a given classification code.

Attributes

Attribute Name	Comments
Range Start Value and Break Rule; Range End Value and Break Rule	A set of four attributes that can be combined to define number ranges. For example, a particular code may represent a range where values are "greater than" (the Range Start Break Rule) "100" (the Range Start Value) and "less than or equal to" (the Range End Break Rule) "500" (the Range End Value).
Range UOM	Unit-of-Measure (e.g., "Kilogram," "Meter," "Kilometers/Hour") for the above metrics. (Optional)

Classification Code Hierarchy

Description

Some classification codes are interdependent on each other. For example, a car's classification code of Mustang (as a Model) may be a sub-classification of Ford (as a Make). In this case, the instance in this class would link the Make of Ford as the "parent" scheme with the Model of Mustang as the "child" scheme.

Sometimes there can be a sub-classification hierarchy within one code set. For example, in Australia the car's Model classification scheme may have Commodore as a model, but sub-classify this into Commodore Executive, Commodore Vacationer, etc. In this case, an instance in this class would link Commodore (a Model) as the "parent" and Commodore Vacationer as the "child" (still within the Model scheme).

Each instance in this class defines the hierarchical relationship between a pair of Classification Code instances.

Associations

Each Classification Code Hierarchy must be constrained by the definition of an allowable type of hierarchy as provided by one Classification Scheme Allowable Hierarchy.

Each Classification Code Hierarchy must nominate one "parent" Classification Code as the first of two codes participating in the hierarchy.

Each Classification Code Hierarchy must nominate one "child" Classification Code as the second of two codes participating in the hierarchy.

<u>Attributes</u>

Attribute Name	Comments
(none yet identified)	

Classification Scheme

<u>Description</u>

Across the enterprise, many classification schemes may exist. Examples could possibly include:

- Classification of customers by industry code (retail, manufacturing, etc.)
- Classification of customers by sales area
- Classification of meters and valves on a factory floor by size, flow rate ranges,, etc.
- Classification of vehicles by make, model, etc.

In the above list, "Industry Code," "Sales Area," the factory equipment's "Size" and "Flow Rate," and the vehicle's "Make" and "Model" are examples of classification schemes. Each instance in this class represents one such scheme. Note that schemes may be sub-classified by yet other schemes. For example, a Make scheme may be sub-classified by Model. These allowable relationships between schemes are defined in the associated Classification Scheme Allowable Hierarchy class.

<u>Associations</u>

Each Classification Scheme must be the container for the code set enumerated by one or more Classification Codes.

Each Classification Scheme may be the "parent" scheme in one or more Classification Scheme Allowable Hierarchies involving other classification schemes.

Each Classification Scheme may be the "child" scheme in one or more Classification Scheme Allowable Hierarchies involving other classification schemes.

Each Classification Scheme may have its enumerations managed by one Party e.g., Country Codes managed by the United Nations.

<u>Attributes</u>

Attribute Name	Comments
Classification Scheme Code	Brief code representing the classification e.g., "IC" for "Industry Code."
Classification Scheme Description	Brief textual description for the classification e.g., "Australia and New Zealand Standard Industrial Classification."

Classification Scheme Allowable Hierarchy

Description

Some classification codes are interdependent on each other. For example, a classification code of Mustang (as a Model) may be a sub-classification of Ford (as a Make). In this case, the instance in this class would define the Classification Scheme of Make as an allowable "parent" to the "child" Classification Scheme of Model.

Sometimes there can be a sub-classification hierarchy within one code set. For example, in Australia the Model classification scheme may have Commodore as a model, but sub-classify this into Commodore Executive, Commodore Vacationer, etc. In this case, an instance in this class would define the Classification Scheme of Make as an allowable "parent" to the "child" Classification Scheme of Make (i.e. self-referencing relationship pointing back to the same scheme).

Each instance in this class defines one *allowable* hierarchical relationship between pairs of Classification instances.

Associations

Each Classification Scheme Allowable Hierarchy must nominate one "parent" Classification Scheme as the first of two schemes participating in the definition of an allowable hierarchy.

Each Classification Scheme Allowable Hierarchy must nominate one "child" Classification Scheme as the second of two schemes participating in the definition of an allowable hierarchy.

Each Classification Scheme Allowable Hierarchy may be the constraint defining an allowable type of hierarchy for one or more Classification Code Hierarchies.

Attributes

Attribute Name	Comments
(none yet defined)	

Document

Description

The enterprise may need to manage storage of electronic documents and paper documents. Each instance of this class represents one such item.

This class has several subclasses, handling different mediums of storage (electronic, physical).

<u>Associations</u>

Each Document must be classified by one Document Type.

Each Document must be classified by one Document Format.

Each Document may provide documentary evidence for one or more Agreements.

Each Document may be the first of two participants in one or more Document To Document Relationships with other documents.

Each Document may be the second of two participants in one or more Document To Document Relationships with other documents.

<u>Attributes</u>

Attribute Name	Comments
Document Reference	Optional identifier for the document.
Effective Period	Period during which this record was effective.

Electronic Document (subclass of Document)

<u>Description</u>

This class is a subclass of Document. Each instance represents one "document" (such as a spreadsheet, a word processing document, an image or digital photograph, a digitized voice recording, etc.) that is stored within a computer's digital storage.

<u>Attributes</u>

Attribute Name	Comments
Electronic Document Location	Reference to the electronic object's location (e.g., a URL, a drive and folder specification, etc.)
(*or*)	
Embedded Object	Copy of the original, available for viewing/processing.

Structured Electronic Document (subclass of Document/Electronic Document)

Description

This class is a subclass of Electronic Document. Each instance represents one "document" such as a spreadsheet, a text file in XML format, or a character-delimited file that has "structured" contents i.e. that are relatively simple for direct machine-interpretation.

Attributes

Attribute Name	Comments
(none yet identified)	

Unstructured Electronic Document (subclass of Document/Electronic Document)

Description

This class is a subclass of Electronic Document. Each instance represents one "document" such as a word processing document, an image or photograph, or a digitized voice recording that has no capability for simple automatic machine interpretation of its contents (though there are increasing facilities for interpretation of free-form text, interpretation of images, etc.).

Attributes

Attribute Name	Comments
(none yet identified)	

Physical Document (subclass of Document)

Description

This class is a subclass of Document. Each instance represents one "document" such as a hard-copy report, a physical fax set of pages, or a physical photograph.

Associations

Each Physical Document may have its location defined via an association with one Physical Address.

Attributes

Attribute Name	Comments
Physical Document Location	Description of the storage location of a physical document (library reference card, compactus unit/shelf, etc.) (Note that this may be a derivable attribute, with values determined via the associated Physical Address class.)

Document Format

Description

Each instance in this class identifies the storage format as an aid to accessing and interpreting the stored information. Examples of formats for electronic objects might include typical file extensions ("doc," "jpg," "xls," "PDF," "CSV," etc.). Further specification may be required e.g., a schema for a document that holds data as an XML document.

Note that this classification is not to be confused with the Document Type classification (Employment Contract, Service Agreement, etc.).

Associations

Each Document Format may be the classification for one or more Documents.

Attributes

Attribute Name	Comments
Document Format Code	Brief code representing the classification e.g., "CSV" for a comma-separated values file.
Document Format Description	Full textual description for the classification e.g., "Comma-Separated Values file."

Document To Document Relationship

Description

Each document may relate to one or many other documents. Examples of types of relationships may include:

- Composition. For example, one word processing document may contain associated spreadsheets.
- Replacement. For example, one version of a document may be the replacement for another document or even for several documents if it is a consolidation.
- Cross-reference. For example, there may be a textual document describing a suspicious wildfire, and there may also be an associated photograph of the point-of-ignition that supplements the textual description.

Each instance of this class represents one relationship between a pair of documents of a type as classified by the associated Document To Document Relationship Type class.

Associations

Each Document To Document Relationship must nominate one Document as the first of two documents participating in the relationship.

Each Document To Document Relationship must nominate one Document as the second of two documents participating in the relationship.

Each Document To Document Relationship must be classified by one Document To Document Relationship Type.

Attributes

Attribute Name	Comments
Effective Period	Time period during which this relationship is to be considered active.

Document To Document Relationship Type

Description

Each instance in this class describes a classification of document-to-document relationships e.g., "Composition," "Succession" (one Document is the replacement for another), or "Cross-reference."

Associations

Each Document To Document Relationship Type may be the classification for one or more Document To Document Relationships.

Attributes

Attribute Name	Comments
Document to Document Relationship Type Code	Brief code representing the classification e.g., "COMP" for composition.
Document to Document Relationship Type Description	Full textual description for the classification e.g., "Composition of one component document within another aggregate document."
Participant 1 Role	E.g., "container."
Participant 2 Role	E.g., "component."

Document Type

Description

Each instance in this class describes a classification of documents. For example, one document may be classified as an "Employment Contract," and another as a "Service Agreement."

Note also that this classification is not to be confused with Document Format that classifies the storage format (XML, CSV, MS Excel, MS Word, PDF, JPG, etc.).

Associations

Each Document Type may be the classification for one or more Document Types.
Each Document Type may be the coarse-grained "parent" of one or more finer-grained "child" Document Types.
Each Document Type may be the fine-grained "child" of one coarse-grained "parent" Document Type.

Attributes

Attribute Name	Comments
Document Type Code	Brief code representing the classification e.g., "SA" for Service Agreement.
Document Type Description	Full textual description for the classification "Service Agreement with and a customer."

Event

Description

There may be many types of events. For example, there are contact events such as a customer ringing and requesting information about available services, or making a complaint about an invoice.

Sometimes the event may trigger requests for action (refer to the associated Specific Task class).

Sometimes events are linked. For example, a series of customer complaints may be linked to another event such as a product defect event. Such associations can be managed via the associated Event To Event Relationship class.

The event class has several subclasses. Some subclasses are supplied as examples of types of events, while others have been defined to allow for capture of their requirements for specific attributes, operations and/or associations. Where events do not require any specialization but do require classification into various types of events, the Event Type class is expected to provide such a facility.

An event is fundamentally something that happened that someone deemed to be noteworthy!

Associations

Each Event must be classified by one Event Type.
Each Event may be the first of two participants in one or more Event To Event Relationships with other events.
Each Event may be the second of two participants in one or more Event To Event Relationships with other events.
Each Event may act as a trigger for initiation of work as defined by one or more Specific Tasks.
Each Event may be created as a record of the commencement or completion of one Specific Task, where the task commencement or completion is to be treated as a noteworthy event.

Attributes

Attribute Name	Comments
Event ID	Identifier for the event.
Event Description	Textual description of the event. (optional)
Status	Classification of the status of the event. (Optional). Note that the allowable status values are constrained by the event type. For example, a Customer Complaint event may pass through different status states than an Occupational Health and Safety event.
Effective Period	Period over which the event occurred.

Communication Event (subclass of Event)

Description

This class is a subclass of Event, and is only included as an example of types of events.

Each instance of this class represents one recorded communication event (a fax sent or received, a phone call made or received, etc.).

Attributes

Attribute Name	Comments
(none yet supplied)	

Observation Event (subclass of Event)

Description

This class is a subclass of Event, and is only included as an example of types of events. Each instance of this class represents one recorded observation (e.g., an automated weather station reading, or a forensic officer's field observations at the point of ignition of a suspicious fire).

Attributes

Attribute Name	Comments
(none yet supplied)	

Safety Incident (subclass of Event)

Description

This class is a subclass of Event, and is only included as an example of types of events.

Each instance of this class represents one recorded safety incident (e.g., a work-related accident).

Attributes

Attribute Name	Comments
(none yet supplied)	

Event To Event Relationship

Description

Each event may relate to one or many other events. For example, a series of similar complaint events may be linked to another event related a product fault event. Similarly, a marketing campaign event may be linked (hopefully) to a series of contact events requesting product details from prospective clients. Each instance of this class represents one relationship between a pair of events, of a type as classified by the associated Event To Event Relationship Type class.

Associations

Each Event To Event Relationship must be classified by one Event To Event Relationship Type.
Each Event To Event Relationship must nominate one Event as the first of two events participating in the relationship.
Each Event To Event Relationship must nominate one Event as the second of two events participating in the relationship.

Attributes

Attribute Name	Comments
Effective Period	Time period during which this relationship is to be considered active.

Event To Event Relationship Type

Description

Each instance in this class describes a classification of event-to-event relationships e.g., a marketing campaign event may be "cross-referenced" to a related product request event.

<u>Associations</u>

Each Event To Event Relationship Type may be the classification for one or more Event To Event Relationships.

<u>Attributes</u>

Attribute Name	Comments
Event to Event Relationship Type Code	Brief code representing the classification e.g., "XREF" for cross-reference.
Event to Event Relationship Type Description	Full textual description for the classification e.g., "One event cross-references another, related event."
Participant 1 Role	E.g., "Primary event." (Optional)
Participant 2 Role	E.g., "Associated event." (Optional)

Event Type

<u>Description</u>

Each instance in this class defines one classification for Events. For example, types of events may include:

- Communication events (call center phone calls, portal usage, etc.).
- Incidents (wildfire outbreak detection, an occupational health and safety accident, etc.).
- The raising of an "issue."

This class has a self-referencing association that enables a hierarchy of types. The Event class that is "typed" by entries in this class is a superclass that is also typed by its subclasses. It is suggested that this class manage all type definitions, and that the inheritance mechanism be used as a supplementary specification where static specialization of attributes and/or associations is required.

<u>Associations</u>

Each Event Type may be the classification for one or more Events.
Each Event Type may be the coarse-grained "parent" of one or more finer-grained "child" Event Types.
Each Event Type may be the fine-grained "child" of one coarse-grained "parent" Event Type.

<u>Attributes</u>

Attribute Name	Comments
Event Type Code	Code representing the classification e.g., "CCC."
Event Type Description	Full textual description for the classification e.g., "Incoming or outgoing phone call (a "Contact") involving the Call Center."

Geometry

<u>Description</u>

A Geographic Information System (GIS) typically manages information for objects that have a position relative to the surface of the earth e.g.:

- Polygons such as the area covered by the base of a building or defined by a land title.
- Lines such as the definition of the position of a road or a river.
- Points such as the position where an event occurred.

The Open GIS Consortium (OGC) makes a separation between the geospatial "shape" itself (the geometry) and the facts belonging to the spatially related object. For example, a Shire Council may have a geometry defining its boundary, and displayable on a map. It also might have quite a rich collection of data, including the name of the Council, a list of all contacts within the Council, statements on intended zoning changes, and so on. These "facts" are managed by the associated Geospatial Object class and its associated classes (Party, Agreement, etc.), while this Geometry class and its associated classes are responsible for the mapping aspects.

Associations

Each Geometry may delegate the responsibility for managing its structured data to one Geospatial Object (and the associated classes).

Attributes

Attribute Name	Comments
Effective Period	Time period during which this map shape is to be considered active.

Operations

Operation Name	Comments
Get Implicit Proximity	This operation is noted to highlight the fact that a geometry within a Geographic Information System (GIS) will have functions to determine one geospatial object's proximity in relation to other geospatial objects e.g., what it is contained within it, what it contains, what it shares a partial boundary with, what it partially overlaps, etc. [See also how explicit locational relationships are recorded via the Geospatial Explicit Proximity class.]

Line (subclass of Geometry)

Description

This class is a subclass of the Geometry class. Each instance in this class represents one line, typically as represented within a GIS.

Attributes

Attribute Name	Comments
(none specified here)	(The details of this class are expected to be the responsibility of an implementation of a GIS.)

Point (subclass of Geometry)

Description

This class is a subclass of the Geometry class. Each instance in this class represents one point, typically as represented within a GIS.

Attributes

Attribute Name	Comments
(none specified here)	(The details of this class are expected to be the responsibility of an implementation of a GIS.)

Polygon (subclass of Geometry)

Description

This class is a subclass of the Geometry class. Each instance in this class represents one polygon, typically as represented within a GIS.

Attributes

Attribute Name	Comments
(none specified here)	(The details of this class are expected to be the responsibility of an implementation of a GIS.)

Geospatial Explicit Proximity

Description

Each instance in this class records a relationship between a pair of Geospatial Objects, typically based on descriptive text that may not necessary be as precise as geospatial coordinates. A simple example might be that the driveway entrance to a farm property is "about one Kilometer north of the intersection of Eastern Highway and Black Stump Track."

Objects in the associated Geospatial Object class may have no associated definitions in the Geometry class. For example, at a point in time, the geospatial objects may contain an instance for Alex's sales region, and other objects for the real properties where Alex's clients live within the sales region. However, it may be that their precise locations have not been recorded as Geometry objects. If the relationship for relative location between geospatial objects is to be explicitly recorded, this Geospatial Explicit Geometry class can be used to note those objects that (for example) fall within another object's domain, or border it, partially overlap it, or have a certain distance between them. Conversely, if the example of Alex's sales region and Alex's clients is taken in the situation where their precise locations are recorded as Geometries, and their implied relative positions can be determined by the "proximity" operations of the Geometry class, entries in this Explicit Proximity class may not be required.

Associations

Each Geospatial Explicit Geometry must nominate one Geospatial Object as the first of two location objects participating in the relationship.

Each Geospatial Explicit Geometry must nominate one Geospatial Object as the second of two location objects participating in the relationship.

Attributes

Attribute Name	Comments
Proximity Type	Examples might include: • Complete containment of the first object within the second. • Partial overlap between the objects. • Sharing of a partial boundary between the objects. • "Closeness" (see attribute below).
Proximity Description	An optional measurement or description further defining proximity. For example: • Where the proximity type states that the two objects are "close," this may record a linear measurement such as "123 meters" to further define the closeness. • Sometimes the proximity description may give directions such as "Proceed from the first object in a northerly direction until you encounter the black stump, then turn left for another 50 meters."

Geospatial Object

Description

Each instance in this Geospatial Object class manages the information related to objects that:

- have a geospatial representation (typically on the Earth's surface), as managed by the Geometry class, but also

- have the need to manage rich sets of structured information.

For example, a Shire Council may have a geometry i.e. a position which we can locate on a map. It also might have quite a rich collection of data, including the name of the Council, a list of all contacts within the Council, statements on intended zoning changes, and so on. These "facts" are managed by this Geospatial Object class and its associated classes (Party, Agreement, etc.).

[Note that an associated "technical" Geometry class is not necessarily relevant in a conceptual modeling context. It is responsible for the mapping aspects of a Geospatial Object.]

The *types* of objects in this class have some similarities to the "layers" encountered in a geospatial information system (GIS). For example, a GIS might have a layer depicting customer sites, another layer for sales regions, and perhaps even layers depicting geopolitical areas such as states and council wards.

This Geospatial Object class has several subclasses. Some subclasses are supplied as examples of types of geospatial object, while others have been defined to capture their requirements for specific attributes, operations and/or associations. It must be noted that some geospatial objects do not require any specialization and hence may be treated as generic geospatial objects. Where geospatial objects do not require any specialization but do require classification into various types of geospatial object, the Geospatial Object provides this classification.

Associations

Each Geospatial Object must be classified by one Geospatial Object Type.
Each Geospatial Object may have been delegated the responsibility for managing structured data about its spatially located object, as located via one or more Geometries.
Each Geospatial Object may have its physical address details recorded in one Physical Address.
Each Geospatial Object may be the first of two participants in one or more Geospatial Explicit Proximities linked to other geospatial objects.
Each Geospatial Object may be the second of two participants in one or more Geospatial Explicit Proximities linked to other geospatial objects.

Attributes

Attribute Name	Comments
Location ID	Identifier for the geospatial object.
Location Description	Textual description of the geospatial object. (Optional)

Geopolitical Zone (subclass of Geospatial Object)

Description

This class is a subclass of Geospatial Object, and is provided as an example. Each instance in this class represents one geopolitical zone (a county, state, shire council, etc.).

Attributes

Attribute Name	Comments
(none yet identified)	

National Park (subclass of Geospatial Object)

Description

This class is a subclass of Geospatial Object, and is provided as an example. Each instance in this class represents one conservation area of national significance.

Attributes

Attribute Name	Comments
(none yet identified)	

Geospatial Object Type

Description

Instances of an object on a map can be classified by the type of real-world object they represent e.g., the shape of a council ward, the shape of a parcel of real estate, the shape of roads, rivers, etc. In a Geographic Information System (GIS), these shape classifications are often referred to as "layers." For example, a user can start with a base map, then overlay a council ward layer, then a roads layer, and so on to build up the view they wish to visualize.

While the GIS may use these classifications for its management, it may also reflect the subclass structure of the associated Geospatial Object class.

Each instance in this class represents one classification defining one type of layer.

Associations

Each Geospatial Object Type may be the classification for one or more Geospatial Objects.

Attributes

Attribute Name	Comments
Geospatial Object Type Code	Brief code representing the classification e.g., "PARCEL" for real property parcel.
Geospatial Object Type Description	Full textual description for the classification e.g., "Real property parcel as defined by the land titles register."

Goods Item

Description

Each instance in this class represents one item of tangible goods as it relates to one customer e.g., a battery charger supplied as a component of the Acme "U-Beaut" model mobile phone bought by Alex.

Associations

Each Goods Item may be contained within one Product Item.

Attributes

Attribute Name	Comments
(none specified yet)	

Goods Type

Description

Each instance in this class represents one type of tangible goods that may be included in one or more product types. For example, a particular type of battery charger may be included in one or more product types, with the relationship between this goods type, and the product types that contain it, recorded via the Product Goods Component class.

Associations

Each Goods Type may act as a component in product types, as defined by one or more Product Goods Components.

Attributes

Attribute Name	Comments
Goods Type Code	Mnemonic to uniquely identify an instance of Goods Type e.g., "BC" for a Battery Charger.
Goods Type Description	Full description of the Goods Type e.g., "Battery charger for a mobile phone."

Object To Task Assignment

Description

A task may have the need for many "things" to be assigned to it. For example, tomorrow's specific task for fighting the fire front for wildfire 123 may require some specific physical resources (the fire truck with registration number ABC-213, the dozer with roof number 123, and two specific radios, identified by their asset number). The same task may require some specific parties ("We want Alex, Brook, Chis, Dan, Ed and Fran"). It may also require some parties identified by specific party roles e.g., a person "Sam" who is explicitly registered in the party role class as a dozer driver.

Conversely, any given "thing" (a physical resource, party or a party role) may be required to be assigned to many tasks. Perhaps the dozer has been assigned to two firefighting tasks. If the tasks occur at different times (today and tomorrow), perhaps that's OK. Or perhaps it's assigned to two concurrent tasks, but with an assignment percentage of 50% allocation to each, and they are in close proximity, so that's OK, too. Or there might be a clash of demand, and a logistics officer is going to have to resolve the conflict.

Each instance in this class defines the assignment of one specific physical resource or one party or one party role, to one task.

It is to be noted that the tasks to which a physical resource, or party, or party role is assigned are subtyped. They can be specific tasks (further subtyped as either actual tasks or planned tasks), or template tasks. It is probably more likely that template tasks are assigned *types* of resources or parties or party roles rather than specific resources or parties or party roles (refer to the Object *Type* To Task Assignment class), but it is possible for a template task to have a nominated instance assigned ("Whenever we have dangerous hill-country fire breaks to be cut, use this template task, but always assign Sam as the dozer driver").

[Note that the model has this one class to link a task to one specific physical resource or one party or one party role. An alternative model would be to split this one class into three classes, one for assignment of tasks to physical resource, another for assignment of tasks to parties, and yet another for assignment of tasks to party roles. These three classes could then be split again two ways by explicit assignment classes for template tasks versus specific tasks. For the sake of being more concise, this class models a single generalized assignment approach.]

Associations

Each Object To Task Assignment must define the assignment of some "thing" (either a party or party role or resource) to one Task.

Each Object To Task Assignment must identify as a "thing" assigned to a task *either* one Party *or* one Party Role *or* one Resource.

Attributes

Attribute Name	Comments
Assignment Percentage	Percentage of the task's duration that the nominated resource is expected to be required e.g., "Chris will only be required for 25% of his/her time."
Effective Period	Period during which the assignment is active.

Object Type To Task Assignment

Description

A task may have the need for many *types* of "things" to be assigned to it. For example, a template task for fighting a fire front may require some physical resource types (a fire truck, a D9 dozer, and two radios). The same template task may require party types (e.g., one organization typed as a "fire crew"). It may also require some types of party roles (e.g., a dozer driver).

Conversely, any given type of "thing" (a resource type, party type or a party role type) may be required to be assigned to many tasks. For example, the D9 dozer type of resource may be assigned to several template tasks.

Each instance in this class defines the assignment of one *type* of physical resource or one *type* of party or one *type* of party role, to one task.

It is to be noted that the examples above picture types of objects (resource types, party types or a party role types) being assigned to template tasks. Of course, types of things can also be assigned to specific tasks e.g., "for tomorrow's specific task for fighting the fire front I want a diesel generator. I don't care which one you give me, but I am logging the fact that I want one."

[Note that the model has this one class to link a task to one resource type or one party type or one party role type. An alternative model would be to split this one class into three classes, one for assignment of tasks to resource types, another for assignment of tasks to party types, and yet another for assignment of tasks to party role types. These three classes could then be split again two ways by explicit assignment classes for template tasks versus specific tasks. For the sake of being more concise, this class models a single generalized assignment approach.]

Associations

Each Object Type To Task Assignment must define the assignment of some "thing type" (either a party type or party role type or resource type) to one Task.

Each Object Type To Task Assignment must identify as a "thing type" assigned to a task *either* one Party Type *or* one Party Role Type *or* one Resource Type.

Attributes

Attribute Name	Comments
Quantity	Number of resources of the nominated type that are required. (Default = 1)
Assignment Percentage	Percentage of the task's duration that the nominated resource is expected to be required e.g., "A D9 dozer will only be required for 25% of its time."
Effective Period	Period during which the assignment is active.

Organization Name

Description

An organization may have one or several names. For example, at one point in time, it may have a registered name and a trading name. Over time, it may have name changes.

Each instance holds one allowable name for an organization.

Associations

Each Organization Name must be contained within one Organization.

Attributes

Attribute Name	Comments
Org Name Type	For example, "trading" or "registered."
Org Name	Textual display string describing one name for an organization.
Effective Period	Period during which the name is active.

Party

Description

Each instance of this class holds details for one "party of interest," being a Person or an Organization (see these subclasses).

A "party" is a collective term for individual people and organizations. A party can be likened to an entry in an address book in a smartphone or a laptop computer.

Associated with each party will be information on names, addresses, contact details and relationships. It would be commonly considered that this class "holds" name and address details. It is to be noted that many such details are to be held in separate but closely associated classes. For example, names are held separately to facilitate the recording of more than one name at one point in time, plus name changes over time.

The parties may fulfill a variety of roles such as customers, suppliers, third-party contractors, etc.—refer to the associated Party Role class. Where appropriate, information will also be held on recognized roles that a party may play.

This class has the following sub-classes:

- Person.
- Organization.

Classification of the party's type is usually applied to organizations e.g., an organization might be typed as being a limited liability company, a partnership, a trust, a subsidiary, a department, a section, etc. Persons (a subclass of this Party class) are not expected to have extensive classification—they are just people!

Associations

Each Party may be classified by one Party Type.

Each Party may be identified via the details recorded in one or more Party Identifiers.

Each Party may fulfil one or more declared Party Role(s).

Each Party may nominate its addresses and their usage via one or more Address Services.

Each Party may be the first of two participants in one or more Party To Party Relationships with other parties.

Each Party may be the second of two participants in one or more Party To Party Relationships with other parties.

Each Party may be identified as a participant in an agreement via one or more Agreement Participations.

Each Party may be nominated as the participant in an account via one or more Account Participations.

Each Party may be assigned to a task via one or more Object To Task Assignments.

Each Party may be responsible for managing the enumerations of one or more Classification Schemes.

Attributes

Attribute Name	Comments
Effective Period	For a person, this attribute could record dates of birth through to date of death. For an organization, it could record dates from incorporation/creation through to deregistration/dissolution.

Organization (subclass of Party)

Description

This class is a subclass of Party. Each instance records one organization, such as a formal organization (e.g., a limited liability company), or an informal organization (e.g., a business unit or a team within a formal organization)

Most of the attributes of this class are held in associated classes such as Organization Name, and Address.

Associations

Each Organization must contain one or more Organization Names.

Each Organization may contain one or more Positions.

Attributes

Attribute Name	Comments
(none yet identified)	

Person (subclass of Party)

Description

This class is a subclass of Party. Each instance records one person of interest e.g., a person who plays the role of nominated contact at a customer's site.

Most of the attributes of this class are held in associated classes such as Person Name, and Address.

Associations

Each Organization must contain one or more Person Names.
Each Person may be assigned to as an incumbent for a position via one or more Position Assignments.

Attributes

Attribute Name	Comments
Gender	Most commonly "Male" or "Female" (but may have other values, including "Unknown").

Party Identifier

Description

Each party may have one or several identifiers. Each instance in this class records one identifier for one party. Examples of party identifiers could include:

- For Australian organizations, an Australian Company Number (ACN).
- A Tax File Number for an organization or a person.
- A person's Driver's License or Passport number.
- In some countries (but not Australia), a unique Social Security Number assigned to citizens.

Sometimes role-based identifiers may be used (e.g., customer numbers or employee numbers), but an alternative modeling choice is to record these as attributes of the relevant subtypes of the Party Role class.

These identifiers will be unique within a given domain, but are not necessarily unique globally. For example, if driver's licenses are recorded as identifiers for people, they may not be unique across all states in Australia. It follows that the identifier value may have to be a composite attribute that includes the code for the data domain.

Associations

Each Party Identifier must record details required to identify one Party.

Attributes

Attribute Name	Comments
Effective Period	Period during which the party identifier is active.
Party Identifier Type	For example, "Driver's License Number," "Passport Number" or "Australian Company Number."
Party Identifier Value	Textual display string describing one identifier for a party e.g., Driver's License Number "ABC-12345."

Party Role

Description

Each party may potentially play one or more roles. For example, a person may be both a customer and an employee.

As noted earlier in this document, there are "declarative" roles (e.g., a party named Dan is declared to be an employee) and there are "contextual" roles (e.g., within the context of a certain phone call informing the switchboard of an incident, you observe that a Dan seems to be playing a "notifier" role—but this isn't Dan's full-time job).

This class is responsible for managing declarative roles.

The Party Role class has several subclasses. Some subclasses are supplied as examples of types of roles. It must be noted that some roles do not require any specialization of their attributes and/or associations and hence may be treated as generic roles, with a party role type—see the associated Party Role Type class).

Associations

Each Party Role must be classified by one Party Role Type.

Each Party Role must be the fulfilment of a declared role for one Party.

Each Party Role may be identified as a participant in an agreement via one or more Agreement Participations.

Each Party Role may be nominated as a participant in an Account via one or more Account Participations.

Each Party Role may be assigned to a task via one or more Object To Task Assignments.

Attributes

Attribute Name	Comments
Party Role ID	Identifier for a party in the declared role. For example, while a person may have their Party identifiers such as Passport Number and Driver's License Number, in the role of Employee, their party role identifier is expected to be an Employee Number. Note: This is a generic placeholder for role-specific identifiers. An alternative is to model the identifiers within subclasses e.g., Employee Number in the Employee subclass, and Customer Number within the Customer subclass.
Status	Optional classification of the role's status. For example, an employee's status values might include Applicant, Active and Terminated.
Effective Period	Period during which the party role is active e.g., the period of employment for an employee.

Customer (subclass of Party Role)

Description

This class is a subclass of Party Role. Each instance manages details for a party in the role of customer i.e. a party that is a purchaser of the company's products and services.

Attributes

Attribute Name	Comments
(none defined yet)	

Employee (subclass of Party Role)

Description

This class is a subclass of Party Role. Each instance manages details for a party in the role of an employee.

Attributes

Attribute Name	Comments
Salary	Annual salary. [This attribute is included simply as an example of the specialized attributes that can be included in Party Role subtypes.]

Employer (subclass of Party Role)

Description

This class is a subclass of Party Role. Each instance manages details for a party in the role of employer.

Attributes

Attribute Name	Comments
(none defined yet)	

Party Role Type

Description

Each instance in this class describes a classification of roles. One level of classification is achieved via the subclassing of the Party Role class. This class provides for further classification, either of roles that have no need for subclassing (e.g., they have no specialized attributes), or as a finer-grained classification of a subclass (e.g., a classification of a Supplier into a role type of Manufacturer or Importer).

Len Silverston makes an important distinction between "declarative" and "contextual" role types. Declarative roles can be exemplified by considering that someone may declare Acme Incorporated to be a supplier, and declaring John Smith to be an employee. Declarative roles are typically relatively stable. In contrast, contextual roles tend to identify a more temporal role played by a party within the context of an event to a transaction.

For example, it may be noted against a customer complaint event that John Smith was the complainant, but it is (hopefully) not John Smith's long-term (declarative) role to lodge complaints!

This model focuses on classification for declarative types of roles, but this class can be equally used for classification of contextual roles.

Associations

Each Party Role Type may be the classification for one or more Party Roles.
Each Party Role Type may be assigned to a task via one or more Object Type To Task Assignments.
Each Party Role Type may be the coarse-grained "parent" of one or more finer-grained "child" Party Role Types.
Each Party Role Type may be the fine-grained "child" of one coarse-grained "parent" Party Role Type.

Attributes

Attribute Name	Comments
Party Role Type Code	Brief code representing the classification e.g., "CUST" for Customer.
Party Role Type Description	Full textual description for the classification e.g., "Customer."

Party To Party Relationship

Description

Each party may relate to one or many other parties. Examples of types of relationships may include:

- Organizational structures. For example, one holding company may be the parent for several subsidiaries. Similarly, each subsidiary may be made up of departments, sections, etc.
- Employment. For example, one organization may have several employees which we wish to note as contact personnel.
- Marriage. For example, two people are in a marriage relationship.

Each instance of this class represents one relationship between a pair of parties, of a relationship type as classified by the associated Party To Party Relationship Type class.

Associations

Each Party To Party Relationship must be classified by one Party To Party Relationship Type.

Each Party To Party Relationship must nominate one Party as the first of two parties participating in the relationship.

Each Party To Party Relationship must nominate one Party as the second of two parties participating in the relationship.

Attributes

Attribute Name	Comments
Effective Period	Period of the relationship. For an employment relationship, this would be the period of employment.

Party To Party Relationship Type

Description

Each instance in this class describes a classification of party to party relationships ("organizational structure," "employment," "marriage," etc.)

Associations

Each Party To Party Relationship Type may be the classification for one or more Party To Party Relationships.

Attributes

Attribute Name	Comments
Party to Party Relationship Type Code	Brief code representing the classification e.g., "EMP" for employment.
Party to Party Relationship Type Description	Full textual description for the classification e.g., "Employment."
Participant 1 Role	E.g., "Employer."
Participant 2 Role	E.g., "Employee."

Party Type

Description

Each instance in this class defines one classification for Parties. The Party class has Person and Organization as subclasses, but it is expected that the classification of Parties will primarily (exclusively?) apply to Organizations, potentially with a rich hierarchy of types that might include:

- Companies (limited liability, partnerships, etc.).
- Internal units (divisions, sections, etc.) of companies.
- Less formal groups of parties e.g., "Crews" formed to respond to an emergency, and "Households."

This class has a self-referencing association that enables a hierarchy of types. The Organization class that is "typed" by entries in this class is itself a superclass that is also typed by its subclasses. It is suggested that this Party Type class manage all type definitions, and that the inheritance mechanism be used as a supplementary specification where static specialization of attributes and/or associations is required.

Associations

Each Party Type may be the classification for one or more Parties.
Each Party Type may be assigned to a task via one or more Object Type To Task Assignments.
Each Party Type may be the coarse-grained "parent" of one or more finer-grained "child" Party Types.
Each Party Type may be the fine-grained "child" of one coarse-grained "parent" Party Type.

Attributes

Attribute Name	Comments
Party Type Code	Code representing the classification e.g., "LLC" for Limited Liability Corporation.
Party Type Description	Full textual description for the classification e.g., "Limited Liability Corporation."

Person Given Name

Description

This class is a component of the Person Name class, and exists for a somewhat technical reason to facilitate management of multiple given names (first given name, second given name, and possibly more). Each instance holds one given name for a person.

Associations

Each Person Given Name must be contained within one Person Name.

<u>Attributes</u>

Attribute Name	Comments
Given Name	Text string of the given name e.g., "Alex."
Sequence Number	Value to record the sequence within a set of multiple given names (e.g., my first given name is Alex, my second is Chris, etc.).

Person Name

<u>Description</u>

A person may have one or several names. For example, at one point in time they may have a formal name and a preferred name. Over time, they may have name changes (e.g., from a birth name to a married name, then back again to their birth name, then to another married name, etc.).

Each instance holds one allowable name for a person.

<u>Associations</u>

Each Person Name must be contained within one Person.

Each Person Name may contain one or more Person Given Names.

<u>Attributes</u>

Attribute Name	Comments
Person Name Type	Classification of the person's name type e.g., "Birth," "Married," "Alias," "Preferred," or even "Stage" name.
Salutation	(Optional) Examples may include "Mr," "Ms," "Sir." Can include concatenation of multiples e.g., "Prof. Sir."
Family Name	Also known as surname or last name. For example, "Smith."
Post Nominal	(Optional) e.g., "MP" (Member of Parliament), "FRACS" (Fellow of the Royal Australian College of Surgeons). Can include concatenation of multiple values.
Effective Period	Period during which the name is active.

Position

<u>Description</u>

An organization typically creates many positions for its staff and contractors.

It is a common practice to relate people via their positions. While in conversation, we may say that "Alex works for Brook," it is arguably more correct to say that the position filled by Alex reports to the position filled by Brook. Recording the management hierarchy via positions typically provides greater stability. The incumbents of a position may change relatively frequently, but it might be reasonable to expect that the position relationships are relatively stable. These position interrelationships are maintained in the associated Position Hierarchy class.

Other organizations, and their positions within those organizations, can be more dynamic. For example, in an emergency incident a Crew (a type of Organization) may be formed along with its positions, and then those positions can be filled even if only for a relatively short period of time.

Each instance of this class represents one position within an organization.

Associations

Each Position must be contained within one Organization.
Each Position may be the "senior" position in one or more Position Hierarchies involving other positions.
Each Position may be the "subordinate" position in one or more Position Hierarchies involving other positions.
Each Position may be filled by a person as an incumbent via one or more Position Assignments.

Attributes

Attribute Name	Comments
Position Title	Classification of the position's type e.g., "CIO."
Effective Period	Period during which the position is active.

Position Assignment

Description

Each Position will typically be filled by one (or perhaps several) incumbents.

Conversely, each Person may be the incumbent in one or several Positions.

Each instance in this class identifies one Person who is assigned as the incumbent for one Position.

Associations

Each Position Assignment must define a person as an incumbent in one Position.

Each Position Assignment must identify a position with an incumbent as one Person.

Attributes

Attribute Name	Comments
Incumbency Type	Classification of the incumbency type e.g., "Acting in role."
Percent Allocation	If the allocation of a resource to a position reflects a commitment of other than 100%, this attribute records the expected level. For example, two incumbents in a time-sharing arrangement might record a commitment of 50% each.
Effective Period	Period during which the incumbency is active.

Position Hierarchy

Description

Each position may have zero, one, or several subordinate positions reporting to it.

Conversely, each position may the subordinate position to zero, one or several senior positions.

Each instance in this class represents the relationship between one senior position and one subordinate position.

It is a common practice to relate people via their positions. While in conversation we may say that "Alex works for Brook," it is arguably more correct to say that the position filled by Alex reports to the position filled by Brook. Recording the management hierarchy via its positions typically provides greater stability. The incumbents of a position may change relatively frequently, but it might be reasonable to expect that the position relationships are relatively stable. This class manages the data for these position interrelationships.

Associations

Each Position Hierarchy must nominate one "senior" Position as the first of two positions participating in the hierarchy.

Each Position Hierarchy must nominate one "subordinate" Position as the second of two positions participating in the hierarchy.

Attributes

Attribute Name	Comments
Effective Period	Period during which the hierarchical relationship is active.

Product Item

Description

Each instance in this class represents one product instance, for example as it relates to one customer (Alex's Acme "U-Beaut" model mobile phone with the serial number 1111). Brook's Acme "U-Beaut" model mobile phone with the serial number 2222 is a different product item, even though both product *items* share exactly the same product *type* (see the associated Product Type class) i.e. they both are the same make (Acme) and model (U-Beaut).

A product item can be made up from one or more tangible goods items and/or one or more intangible services items and/or one or more other product items. For example, an Acme "U-Beaut" mobile phone product item as owned by Alex may contain the mobile handset itself as one goods item, plus a battery charger as another. It may also contain a missed-call answering facility as one services item, plus 12 months international roaming as another. Further, this product item may additionally contain a carrying case which is itself another product that *could* have been bought separately but which was bought as a bundle.

Associations

Each Product Item must be classified by one Product Type.
Each Product Item may contain one or more Goods Items.
Each Product Item may contain one or more Services Items.
Each Product Item may contain one or more other Product Items e.g., an Acme "U-Beaut" product item may contain a "Carrying Case" product item.

- Each Product Item may be contained within one other Product Item e.g., an Acme "U-Beaut" product item may be contained within a "New Home Owner Starter Pack" product item.

Attributes

Attribute Name	Comments
Product ID	Unique identifier for the product item e.g., its serial number. (Optional)

Product Goods Component

Description

Each product type may contain zero, one, or several goods types. For example, the Acme "U-Beaut" mobile phone product type may contain the mobile handset itself as one goods type, plus a battery charger as another.

Conversely, each goods type may be contained in zero, one, or several product types. For example, a particular type of battery charger (a goods type) may be contained in the Acme "U-Beaut" mobile phone product type, plus the Acme "Eco" mobile phone product type.

Each instance in this class records the containment of one goods type in one product type.

Associations

Each Product Goods Component must reference the Product Type that contains the goods type nominated by the other association for this class.
Each Product Goods Component must reference the Goods Type that is contained within the product type nominated by the other association for this class.

Attributes

Attribute Name	Comments
Quantity	The number of goods types contained in the product type. For example, a particular type of mobile phone may have two spare batteries included. [Default = 1]

Product Services Component

Description

Each product type may contain zero, one, or several services types. For example, the Acme "U-Beaut" mobile phone product type may contain a missed-call answering facility as one services type, plus 12 months international roaming as another.

Conversely, each services type may be contained in zero, one, or several product types. For example, a particular type of 12 months international roaming (a services type) may be contained in the Acme "U-Beaut" mobile phone product type, plus the Acme "Eco" mobile phone product type.

Each instance in this class records the containment of one services type in one product type.

Associations

Each Product Services Component must reference the Product Type that contains the services type nominated by the other association for this class.

Each Product Services Component must reference the Services Type that is contained within the product type nominated by the other association for this class.

Attributes

Attribute Name	Comments
Quantity	The number of services types contained in the product type. For example, a particular type of mobile phone may have a double pack of 12-month international roaming services included. [Default = 1]

Product Subproduct Component

Description

Each product type may contain zero, one, or several additional product types as sub-product types. For example, the Acme "U-Beaut" mobile phone product type may contain a carrying case which is itself another product type that *could* have appeared separately as well as appearing as part of this product type's bundle. It may also contain a T-shirt with Acme's logo.

Conversely, each product type may be contained in zero, one, or several "bundled" product types. For example, a particular type of carrying case (a product type) may be contained in the Acme "U-Beaut" mobile phone product type plus the Acme "Eco" mobile phone product type.

Each instance in this class records the containment of one (sub-)product type in one (bundle) product type.

Associations

Each Product Subproduct Component must reference the bundled Product Type that contains the component product type nominated in the other association for this class.

Each Product Subproduct Component must reference the component Product Type that is contained within the bundled product type nominated in the other association for this class.

Attributes

Attribute Name	Comments
Quantity	The number of sub-product types contained in the bundle product type. For example, a particular type of Acme T-shirt may have two of these included in the bundle product type. [Default = 1]

Product Type

Description

Each instance in this class represents one of the company's product types, as clients might expect to find in the company's product catalog. For example, one product type entry may be for the Acme "U-Beaut" model mobile phone. It is to be noted that individual purchases of this type of product by individual customers are recorded in the Product Item class.

A product type can be made up from one or more tangible goods types and/or one or more intangible services types and/or one or more other product types. For example:

- The Acme "U-Beaut" mobile phone product type may contain the mobile handset itself as one goods type, plus a battery charger as another. It may also contain a missed-call answering facility as one services type, plus 12 months international roaming as another. Further, this product type may additionally contain a carrying case which is itself another product type that *could* appear separately as well as appearing as part of this product type's bundle.
- The Acme "Basic Home Entertainment Pack," comprised of one set-top-box (a goods type), and access to a library of golden-oldies movies (a services type).
- The Acme "New Home Starters Pack," comprised of two Mobile Phone XYZ product types plus one Basic Home Entertainment Pack product type.

The first two product types are each made up from multiple goods types and services types. The third product type is a package made up of other product types.

Associations

Each Product Type may classify one or more Product Items.
Each Product Type may contain one or more Product Goods Components (which in turn reference their Goods Type).

366 • THE DATA ELEPHANT IN THE BOARD ROOM

Each Product Type may contain one or more Product Services Components (which in turn reference their Services Type).

Each Product Type may act as the bundled product type, containing one or more Product Subproduct Components (which in turn reference their own Product Types which, in this context, are component sub-product types).

Each Product Type may act as a component sub-product type, contained within one or more Product Subproduct Components (which in turn reference their own Product Types which, in this context, are bundled product types).

Attributes

Attribute Name	Comments
Product Code	Reference code used to identify a type of product in the product catalog.
Product Description	Textual name of the product type e.g., "Acme U-Beaut mobile phone."
Recommended Retail Price	Standard catalog price.
Effective Period	Period during which this type of product is available for sale.

Resource

Description

Each instance in this class represents a physical resource such as a vehicle (a car, truck, trailer, etc.), a piece of plant or equipment (a computer, an office desk, etc.), a consumable (fuel, stationery, etc.), and so on.

The class model diagram presented in this documentation is based on a wildfire emergency response scenario, with several subclasses portrayed (though the sample subclasses are not documented here as they are only provided as examples). Typically, the Resource class is subclassed when there is a requirement for specific attributes, associations, and/or operations. It must be noted that some resources do not require any specialization and, hence may be treated using the generic resource class (with a resource type—see the associated Resource Type class).

Associations

Each Resource must be classified by one Resource Type.
Each Resource may be assigned to a task via one or more Object To Task Assignments.

<u>Attributes</u>

Attribute Name	Comments
Resource ID	Optional unique identifier (e.g., a serial number) for the resource.
Resource Name	Optional brief textual description for the resource.
Effective Period	Period during which the resource is active.

Resource Type

<u>Description</u>

Each instance in this class defines one classification for Resources. For example, types of resources may include:

- Vehicle, itself sub-classified as Truck, Car, Trailer and so on (with any of these sub-classifications themselves being further sub-classified).
- Plant and equipment e.g., generators, computers, and pumps.
- Consumables e.g., fuel, stationery.

This class has a self-referencing association that enables a hierarchy of types. The Resource class that is "typed" by entries in this class is also a superclass that can be typed by its subclasses. It is suggested that this Resource Type class manage all type definitions and that the inheritance mechanism against the Resource class be used as a supplementary specification where static specialization of attributes and/or associations is required.

<u>Associations</u>

Each Resource Type may be the classification for one or more Resources.
Each Resource Type may be the coarse-grained "parent" of one or more finer-grained "child" Resource Types.
Each Resource Type may be the fine-grained "child" of one coarse-grained "parent" Resource Type.
Each Resource Type may be assigned to a task via one or more Object Type To Task Assignments.

<u>Attributes</u>

Attribute Name	Comments
Resource Type Code	Mnemonic to uniquely identify an instance of Resource Type e.g., "VEH" for a Vehicle.
Resource Type Description	Full description of the Resource Type e.g., "Vehicle: A mobile resource used to transport people and/or goods."

Schedule Entry Recurrence Specification

Description

This class is used to define recurring tasks entries, for example a task that occurs on the "First Tuesday of each month, starting next January, and going until June."

Full details of this structure are not included here, but may be inferred from similar functionality in desktop or smartphone applications.

Associations

Each Schedule Entry Recurrence Specification must define the rules for repeated execution of one Task.

Attributes

(Although the class data structure is not fully analyzed, some indicative candidate attributes are defined below.)

Attribute Name	Comments
Repeat Frequency	The frequency of repeating the task (daily, weekly, etc.).
Effective Period	The start and end dates for the period of repeats.

Services Item

Description

Each instance in this class represents one item of intangible services as it relates to one customer e.g., a missed-call answering facility supplied as a component of the Acme "U-Beaut" model mobile phone bought by Alex.

Associations

Each Services Item may be contained within one Product Item.

Attributes

Attribute Name	Comments
(none specified yet)	

Services Type

Description

Each instance in this class represents one type of intangible services that may be included in one or more product types. For example, a particular type of missed-call answering facility may be included in one or more product types, with the relationship between this services type, and the product types that contain it, recorded via the Product Services Component class.

Associations

Each Services Type may act as a component in product types, as defined by one or more Product Services Components.

Attributes

Attribute Name	Comments
Services Type Code	Mnemonic to uniquely identify an instance of Services Type e.g., "MCAF" for a Missed-Call Answering Facility.
Services Type Description	Full description of the Services Type e.g., "Missed-Call Answering Facility ."

Task

Description

A task represents a job to be performed. A task can represent a small unit of work e.g., a simple checklist item ("make sure that someone rings the client back to notify them of a delay," "perform a credit check on the prospect", etc.). A task can also represent a large and complex unit of work e.g., a major project or even an entire program of work. Each instance of this class defines some work that is required to be done and/or has been actually performed.

The task class has two subclasses, namely the Specific Task class and the Template Task class.

- Template tasks define an overall profile of tasks that occur frequently. For example, it would be reasonable to expect that a template would be defined that describes a profile for day-to-day responsibilities such as responding to a product inquiry. Templates have a profile, but are not related to any calendar dates/times, and may describe generic deployment of *types* of resources, but will not typically nominate *specific* resources.

- Specific tasks are instances of tasks that have been "attached" to a calendar. Whereas there might be a generic template for responding to a product inquiry, each planned &/or actual product inquiry resolution would be one specific task ("At 9:17 am today, we commenced processing a product inquiry initiated by Dan Daniels").

As part of a business process, a Template Task can be identified as being applicable and then cloned to create a Specific Task.

Tasks can be arranged in CPM (Critical Path Method), or PERT (Program Evaluation and Review Technique) dependency networks—refer to the Task Dependency class for details.

Associations

Each Task must be classified by one Task Type.

Each Task may have rules for repeated execution defined in one or more Schedule Entry Recurrence Specifications.

Each Task may be the predecessor task in one or more Tasks Dependencies that in turn, identify successor tasks.

Each Task may be the successor task in one or more Tasks Dependencies that in turn, identify predecessor tasks.

Each Task may have defined for its use one or more Object To Task Assignments (which in turn identify some assigned specific "thing," namely either a party or party role or resource).

Each Task may have defined for its use one or more Object Type To Task Assignments (which in turn identify some assigned "thing type," namely either a party type or party role type or resource type).

Attributes

Attribute Name	Comments
Task ID	Unique reference assigned to a task.
Task Name	Optional brief textual description of the task.
Task Description	Optional full textual description of the work task.
Task Comment	Optional additional comments relating to the task.
Duration UOM	Code defining the unit-of-measure for durations e.g., "Hours."

Specific Task (subclass of Task)

<u>Description</u>

This class is a subclass of Task. Each instance of this class represents a task that is linked to a specific calendar date and time (in contrast to a Template Task that defines the "shape" for a task profile but does not relate to any specific date and time). An example of a specific task might be a credit check performed for a customer named Jones, with the tasks commencing at 9:17 am today.

Note that Specific Tasks can be created directly, or they can be created as part of a business process where a Template Task can be identified as being applicable and then cloned to create a Specific Task - see the Template Task class for further details.

Tasks may contain other tasks. For example, the task to create a new customer might:

- Contain several tasks such as performing a credit check and assigning an account manager.
- Be itself contained in a larger task such as running a marketing campaign which resulted in the creation of this new customer.

These containment relationships are represented on the class diagram as a "composition" association.

Specific tasks may represent planned activities and/or actual activities—refer to the subclasses of this class.

<u>Associations</u>

Each Specific Task may have its scheduling possibilities defined by one Calendar.
Each Specific Task may be composed of one or more component Specific Tasks.
Each Specific Task may be a component within one composite Specific Task.
Each Specific Task may be cloned from one Template Task.
Each Specific Task may have its initiation for work triggered by one Event.
The commencement or completion of each Specific Task may be treated as a noteworthy event and hence result in the creation of one or more Events to record that noteworthy Event.

<u>Attributes</u>

Attribute Name	Comments
(none yet identified)	(Refer to the subclasses.)

Actual Task (subclass of Task/ Specific Task)

<u>Description</u>

This class is a subclass of Specific Task. Each instance of this class represents an actual task that has at least commenced, if not completed.

Note that an actual task may have no association with planned tasks (it just got done), or it may be the fulfilment of one or many planned tasks.

<u>Associations</u>

Each Actual Task may be the fulfilment of one or more Planned Tasks.

<u>Attributes</u>

Attribute Name	Comments
Actual Start Date and Time	Date and time marking the actual start of the task.
Actual Finish Date and Time	Date and time marking the actual end of the task. (Null if not yet completed.)

Planned Task (subclass of Task/ Specific Task)

<u>Description</u>

This class is a subclass of Specific Task. Each instance of this class represents one planned (or "intended") task.

Note that a planned task may have no association with actual tasks (it has been planned but no-one has started actual work), or it may be the trigger for the initiation of one or many actual tasks.

<u>Associations</u>

Each Planned Task may be fulfilled by the performance of one or more Actual Tasks.

<u>Attributes</u>

Attribute Name	Comments
Planned Duration Metric	Expected duration measurement (e.g., "5"), expressed in the duration unit of measure inherited from the Task class (e.g., "Days").
Planned Early Start Date and Time	The earliest expected start date and time of the task.
Planned Early Finish Date and Time	The earliest expected end date and time of the task. [Derivable from early start + duration]
Planned Late Start Date and Time	The latest expected start date and time of the task.
Planned Late Finish Date and Time	The latest expected end date and time of the task. [Derivable from late start + duration]

Template Task (subclass of Task)

<u>Description</u>

This class is a subclass of Task. Each instance of this class defines the "shape" for a task profile but does not relate to any specific date and time (in contrast to a Specific Task that is linked to a specific calendar date and time).

A template task may contain templates of many smaller tasks. For example, the "Create a customer" template task may contain the templates for certain jobs, such as performing a credit check and assigning an account manager. Conversely, template tasks can be assembled to create larger units. The credit check template task may appear as a subtask in many customer-related tasks. These possible relationships are defined via a many-to-many "composition" association relationship.

<u>Associations</u>

Each Template Task may be composed of one or more component Template Tasks.
Each Template Task may be a component within one or more composite Template Tasks.
Each Template Task may be cloned to create one or more Specific Tasks.

Attributes

Attribute Name	Comments
Planned Duration	Estimated duration of the task, expressed in the unit-of-measure defined in the Task superclass.

Task Dependency

Description

Tasks may be linked in a Program Evaluation Review Technique (PERT), or Critical Path Method (CPM), network. For example, some tasks cannot start until others finish.

Each task may have one or several predecessors.

Conversely, each task may have one or several successors.

Each instance of this class represents one such dependency between a predecessor and its successor.

Associations

Each Task Dependency must nominate one Task as the predecessor task participating in a dependency with one other successor task.
Each Task Dependency must nominate one Task as the successor task participating in a dependency with one other predecessor task.

Attributes

Attribute Name	Comments
Dependency Type	Typically "FS" (finish-to-start), but may be "FF" (finish-to-finish), "SF" (start-to-finish), or "SS" (start-to-start).
Lag	Gap between two activities with a dependency e.g., Task 2 is to start when Task 1 finishes, but with a delay of four days. (Note that the lag can be negative e.g., Task 2 is to start two days before the expected finish of Task 1.)
Guard Condition	Boolean condition on the commencement of the successor task.

Task Type

<u>Description</u>

Each instance in this class defines one classification for tasks. For example, types of tasks may include:

- Marketing campaign.
- Case management for activating a new customer or managing a customer complaint.
- Customer credit check.
- Training activities (e.g., running a course or employee induction session).

This class has a self-referencing association that enables a hierarchy of types. The Task class that is "typed" by entries in this class is itself a superclass that is also typed by its subclasses. It is suggested that this class manage all type definitions and that the inheritance mechanism be used as a supplementary specification where static specialization of attributes and/or associations is required.

<u>Associations</u>

Each Task Type may be the classification for one or more Tasks.
Each Task Type may be the coarse-grained "parent" of one or more finer-grained "child" Task Types.
Each Task Type may be the fine-grained "child" of one coarse-grained "parent" Task Type.

<u>Attributes</u>

Attribute Name	Comments
Task Type Code	Code representing the classification e.g., "CCHK" for Credit Check.
Task Type Description	Full textual description for the classification e.g., "Credit Check."

Index

www.ingramcontent.com/pod-product-compliance
Lightning Source LLC
Chambersburg PA
CBHW080608060326
40690CB00021B/4623